Business and Politics

Also by Wyn Grant

The CBI (with David Marsh)
Independent Local Politics in England and Wales
The Political Economy of Industrial Policy
The Politics of Economic Policymaking (with Shiv Nath)
The Political Economy of Corporatism (editor)

Business and Politics in Britain

Wyn Grant

with Jane Sargent

**MACMILLAN
EDUCATION**

First published 1987

Published by
MACMILLAN EDUCATION LTD
Houndmills, Basingstoke, Hampshire RG21 2XS
and London
Companies and representatives
throughout the world

Printed in Hong Kong

ISBN 0–333–39174–8 (hardcover)
ISBN 0–333–39175–6 (paperbark)

For Sophia, Rosalind and Amelia

Contents

Contents

Preface

This book draws on fifteen, admittedly intermittent, years' work on the relationship between business and politics in Britain. I have acquired so many intellectual debts over this period that it would be impossible to acknowledge them all. I have made use of a considerable number of interviews with business persons, business association officials, civil servants, politicians and others. I am grateful to all of them for giving up their time to answer what must often have seemed to be irrelevant questions.

The proximate stimulus for writing this book was my participation in a nine-country comparative international project on the organisation of business interests co-ordinated by Wolfgang Streeck from the International Institute of Management in West Berlin and Philippe Schmitter at the European University Institute in Florence. They were outstanding intellectual and organisational co-ordinators of a highly complex international project. I also benefited greatly from my discussions with other project members, particularly Professor William Coleman of McMaster University, Hamilton, Ontario, who has commented on drafts of this book.

Although, in some respects, the book represents one of the 'country studies' to emerge from the project, it has a broader scope than the particular concerns of the IIM study, encompassing such issues as the relationship between business interests and political parties, and the political role of the financial sector. Steve Kennedy, Macmillan's commissioning editor, played a crucial role in ensuring that I focused on the broad canvas rather than its intricate details.

The international co-ordination of the IIM project was funded by the Volkswagen Foundation, which also provided funds for the pharmaceutical case study reported in this book by Jane Sargent. However, the main funding for the British study was provided by the Nuffield Foundation. I have also drawn on work on employers' associations and training policy which was funded by the Econ-

omic and Social Research Council. I have made some use of
material gathered in a comparative Anglo–German study of
government–industry relations in the chemical industry, also
funded by the ESRC. The main results of this project (carried out
with William Paterson and Colin Whitston) will be reported in a
later volume.

Jane Sargent was a highly efficient research assistant on the IIM
project and I am grateful to her for finding time from her duties as
a business association official to contribute the chapter on the EC,
and also part of the chapter on the public policy functions of
business associations. Helen Rainbird worked with me on the
project on employers' associations and training policy and we have
continued to collaborate on the question of the delegation of
public policy functions to employers. I am grateful to her for
insights on a number of matters.

The University of Warwick provided a congenial intellectual
environment for work concerned with industry and allowed me to
take a period of sabbatical leave to assess the results of the IIM
project. I benefited from using the archives of employers' association material held by the University's Modern Records Centre. In
particular, I was able to read the written and verbal evidence given
to the Devlin Commission on industrial representation, although it
is not available for quotation at this time. I am also grateful to the
London Business School for inviting me to give a course on The Politics of British Business at a crucial point in the writing of this book.

The following individuals have provided helpful comments on
drafts of parts of the book: Cyril Coffin CBE; the Rt Hon. Sir Ian
Gilmour Bt, MP; Michael Moran; Professor Richard Rose; Martin
Trowbridge; Tim Stocker. Like any other person mentioned, they
bear no responsibility for the book's contents.

As with earlier books I have written, Dr Peter Burnell of the
Department of Politics at Warwick read through chapter drafts
from the perspective of someone whose main academic interests
lie elsewhere; as always, I found his comments a considerable aid
to clearer and more logical explanation. Last but not least, my
thanks are due to my wife, Maggie, for her support, and to our
children for their forbearance.

WYN GRANT
Leamington Spa

1 Introduction

In an economy in which privately owned firms remain responsible for the greater proportion of output and employment, and in which nationalised industries have some operational autonomy, government needs an effective working relationship with individual enterprises in order to achieve its economic policy objectives. Electorates judge the success of modern governments to a considerable extent in economic terms, and such success can in practice only be achieved through the co-operation of enterprises. However, despite its importance, all the available evidence suggests that the relationship between business and government in Britain is not a satisfactory one, whatever political perspective one takes. There is considerable mistrust between government and industry, the system of business interest associations leaves much to be desired, government finds it difficult to implement its policy objectives through autonomous firms, whilst business often considers that government misunderstands its problems and priorities. One solution to these problems would be to abolish private enterprise and bring all economic activity under state control. However, the cure would be worse than the disease: the record of state-controlled economies suggests that the problems that beset them are more intractable than those that face the western economies.

Even if one believes that markets are the best way of responding to the preferences of the individual consumer, and that reliance on the market mechanism promotes economic growth and avoids distorting and costly subsidies and interventions, some government intervention in the economy is going to be unavoidable for four principal reasons. First, there are areas of economic activity in which markets fail or where the short run benefits of competition are outweighed by longer run costs. Although many so-called natural monopolies may be artificial creations of legislative measures, and although regulated private companies or franchising

1

offer alternatives to outright state ownership, there are areas where public ownership may be the lesser evil, or where governments may need to intervene in an attempt to secure the smooth running of particular markets where it is difficult to attain a stable equilibrium between supply and demand (as in agricultural markets).

Secondly, government has to intervene to create a legal framework within which markets can operate smoothly. Such framework needs to go beyond the facilitation of the processes of exchange to include provisions that prevent actions that discredit markets: deception of all kinds and the shameless exploitation of ill-informed consumers. There is a case for the state intervening to ensure 'fair trading' in the general sense of that term, for without fair trading there cannot be genuine competition. There is also a *prima facie* case for government intervening to prevent or break up monopoly, although the precise way in which that should be done raises many complex issues which are beyond the scope of this study.

Thirdly, government needs to intervene to deal with the harmful social consequences that would result from unrestrained actions in a free market. Two of the most important areas of such intervention are actions to protect the environment and the health and safety of employees, and measures to prevent gross inequities in the distribution of income and wealth. Other examples are interventions to prevent discrimination against women and ethnic minority groups. Such interventions are necessary for two reasons: because they ought to be made if we want to live in a tolerably civilised society and because if capitalist societies tolerate spoilation of the environment and stark contrasts between wealth and poverty, support will accrue to movements seeking to replace capitalist free enterprise by other systems of production and social order.

Fourthly, government becomes involved in close relationships with business because it is a major, indeed the principal, customer of some firms and industries. Quite how that relationship should be discharged can be highly controversial. Some would argue that government has a particular responsibility to evolve a positive industrial strategy in relation to the defence industries and that it should use its position as their major customer to influence their development. Others would see the commercial freedom of companies to make their own decisions as overriding any conception of the national interest that might be held by government. What is clear is that there is a potential tension between government's role as the sponsor of an industry, where it has an interest in promoting its long run viability, and its role as a major customer, where it has an interest in securing value for money.

Questions of definition

A business is a company, public corporation, partnership or individual which sells goods and/or services with the intention of generating a surplus from its trading activities for its owners. The definition provided covers nationalised industries, because even if some of them lose money, or have to be compensated by government for providing services which are deemed to be necessary for social reasons, they seek to make a profit on the commercial part of their operations.

This book is concerned with businesses of all kinds: manufacturing, distributive and commercial. It excludes non-profit-making organisations of various kinds which simply seek to cover their (long run) costs so that they can provide and develop a particular activity (e.g. a museum) and charities which intend to make a surplus on their fund-raising activities, but apply that surplus to a designated group of beneficiaries who do not 'own' the charity. Clearly, there are marginal cases. For example, consider a privately owned steam railway which devotes most of its income to the task of preservation, but pays a deliberately restricted dividend to its shareholders. Unlike a preserved railway which ploughed all its surplus back into the activity, the former case would be counted as a business. However, these marginal cases represent a very small portion of the total universe of analysis. The main focus here is on the large privately owned companies and state enterprises which dominate the highly concentrated British economy, although attention is also paid to smaller businesses and the particular problems they encounter in securing political representation.

This book's concern with business and politics is not focused on the internal politics of businesses, although some references to decision-making processes within firms are necessary. Rather, the focus is on the interaction between business (as an aggregate of businesses) and political institutions: ministers and civil servants; Parliament; the European Community; and, to a lesser extent, local government. When the term 'government' is used in this book (with a lower case 'g' and without any reference to a particular administration), it means ministers of the crown and the civil servants who advise them and execute their policies. The term 'state' has gained popularity in recent years, particularly on the left, where it is often used in a pejorative sense to encompass the military, the police and the judiciary, as well as ministers and civil servants. I have tried to avoid the term as much as possible, not out of revanchist ideological prejudice, but because it is often used to depict the apparatus of government as more monolithic than it actually is. I have tried to avoid using 'state' as a synonym for 'government'. Where I have used the term 'state', it is intended to refer to purposive, strategic actions by governments; those instances when government pursues, or appears to be pursuing, an *Ordnungspolitik* (a 'politics of social order').

Reference will be made at a number of points in the book to various types of business interest association that seek to defend the interests of business enterprises. The nomenclature of such associations often gives rise to confusion. A 'trade association' seeks to defend and promote what may be termed the common commercial interests of business enterprises operating in a particular sector of the economy. An 'employers' organisation' is an association of business enterprises that is concerned with collective bargaining and related industrial relations questions, but not with commercial questions. This historical dividing line is difficult to maintain, and in many sectors merged associations perform both functions; they may then be referred to as 'employers' associations'. However, this term also encompasses the business interest associations which are not confined to a particular industrial sector or group of products. These occur in two main forms: the 'peak' or 'umbrella' associations such as the CBI which claim to speak for business as a whole at the national level, and the chambers of commerce and of trade which seek to represent all business enterprises in a defined territory.

The comparative context

This book is about business–government relations in Britain, but an attempt is made to place the findings within an internationally comparative context, a theme that is returned to in the conclusion. It is important to ask whether there is anything that is distinctive about business–government relations in Britain from the patterns to be found in other advanced western countries.

Relations between business and government do not occur within a vacuum: they occur within the context of a set of shared (or different) values, mutual understandings (or misunderstandings), and uncodified, but nevertheless significant 'rules of the game'. Mutual but unstated understandings between, for example, civil servants and business association officials about how relations should be conducted are generally of greater importance than formally stated rules in the British case. In particular, specific legal provisions play a relatively unimportant part in shaping business-government relations in Britain compared, for example, with countries such as France and West Germany where chambers of commerce enjoy public law status. In the United States, where adversarial legal proceedings play an important role in defining and enforcing the conditions under which business operates, regulation through the courts is much more important than in the United Kingdom. The British emphasis is on the mutual search for pragmatic, 'common sense' compromises, a search aided by the existence of a common language code shared by civil servants, business association officials, and even some business persons, particularly those 'industrial politicians' who regularly interact with government. This language code is characteristically one of understatement. Where there are conflicts of interest or value, they are hidden in the thickets of long sentences, hedged round with qualifying clauses.

Nevertheless, it is important to be cautious about cultural explanations. They can seem to explain everything, and yet explain nothing. It is too easy to assume shared values where they do not exist, or to accumulate evidence which appears to sustain a particular interpretation, without looking at conflicting evidence or alternative interpretations of the evidence used (see Grant, 1982a). Used improperly, culture can easily become a garbage can variable, to which everything that cannot be explained in other ways is too readily assigned.

Even so, there is some value in cultural explanations, particularly when they are applied to élite groups that interact frequently with one another, and often have shared backgrounds, as is the case with business persons, their representatives and civil servants in Britain. Dyson draws an interesting distinction between industrial cultures which stress a 'private' concept of the autonomy of action and self-sufficiency of the firm (as in Britain) and those which emphasise a 'public' conception of the firm seen as intermeshed within a network of institutional interests based on an acceptance of the central role of the state (Dyson, 1983). Self-organisation of industry can give business associations an ability to co-ordinate intra-industry adjustment. In the British and American cases, the cultural tradition of the self-sufficient firm meant that 'industrial associations did not acquire the wide range of functions and the integrative role that would have enabled them to preside over an intra-industry adjustment' (Dyson, 1983, p. 56).

It is certainly the case that industrial policy in Britain has been premised on the autonomy of the firm, and it is also true that one can find many descriptions in the literature about the 'arms length' relationship between government and business. Equally, business persons frequently complain that government does not really understand industry's needs and priorities. However, it is easy to fall into the trap of exaggerating the gap between government and business. There is, after all, a long established tradition in Britain, reinforced by civil service rules, of consulting with affected interests (see Jordan and Richardson, 1982, p. 87). Business cannot complain that it does not have ample opportunities to put its point of view across to government. Vogel's comparative study of environmental regulation in Britain and the United States suggests that business is much more of an 'insider' in the policy-making process in Britain. His study shows that in the United States business participation in policy-making largely involves lobbying, an activity directed from outside the place where policy decisions are made. In Britain, on the other hand, industry is an active and officially recognised participant in the policy process itself (see Vogel, 1986).

It could be that the elaborate processes of consultation are simply a courtly dance designed to entice business into the arms of government. This is the view taken by writers such as Nettl (1965) who see business persons as lacking a social identity of their own, and as having been emasculated through being drawn into a consensus that emanates from Whitehall. In many respects, this view is shared by business persons. In his study of the British business élite, Fidler (1981, p. 231) summarises the view of business power in Britain as follows: 'the government that is, in practice, the cabinet plus senior civil servants, controls business, not business the government'. In was apparent that British business persons 'drew unfavourable contrasts between their position and that of their French, German or even American equivalents. A particular complaint was of the enormous volume of legislation aimed at industry' (Ibid.).

The idea that business in Britain is more harshly treated by government than business in France or the United States, however firmly such a view is adhered to by business persons, is scarcely credible, and it does not square with most of the available evidence. The notion of a lack of trust and understanding between business and government in Britain is inconsistent with statements that have been made by business association leaders and officials comparing their relationships with the civil service with those enjoyed by their counterparts in other western countries. For example, a respondent in the chemicals industry project referred to in the preface stated, 'When I talk to other associations in Europe and outside Europe, perhaps there is a closer relationship between our association and government than other industries experience.'

How can this somewhat contradictory evidence about the closeness or otherwise of business and government in Britain be reconciled? First, it should be pointed out that business association officials may be closer to government than to business persons. After all, it is the job of business association officials to maintain close and regular contacts with government, and some of them are former civil servants themselves. Second, business persons in very large companies are likely to have regular contacts with government, whereas smaller businesses will not usually enjoy such contacts. Indeed, they are likely to be ideologically suspicious of government (see Scase and Goffee, 1980). Third, the existence of contacts does not mean that the form and nature of such contacts is determined by business; they are much more likely to take place on government's terms.

Are government–business relations in Britain more distant and more adversarial than in most other countries? There are plenty of mechanisms for contact which, on the whole, work well; there is much familiarity, in the sense that business association officials, leading business persons and civil servants know each other well; but there is much less mutual understanding than all this contact and familiarity would suggest. On the part of business, there is a persistent individualistic ethic which dates back to the origins of industrialisation in Britain and which is difficult to adjust in changed circumstances to engender effective collective action. On the part of government, there is a tendency to see business association as 'lobbies', legitimate interlocutors with government, but not part of the system of governance itself.

The political weakness of business

The central argument of this book is that Britain has a business sector in which there is an increasing concentration of economic power, but that business remains politically weak, making it difficult for government to enter into a partnership relationship with business even if it wanted to. This imbalance is debilitating, and potentially dangerous.

It is not easy for business in Britain either to define its interests or to select the best political strategy for pursuing them, in part because there are important divisions of interest between different sectors of business (and not just between financiers and industrialists), in part because the optimal strategy to secure a desired end is not always readily aparent or, at any rate, is the subject of dispute. The business community in Britain is capable of acting politically in a cohesive fashion if the perceived level of threat is sufficiently high, as was the case with the Bullock Report on industrial democracy in the late 1970s. In general, 'For more than a century and a half British capital has been weakly represented both politically and bureaucratically' (Leys, 1985, p. 14; see also Nettl, 1965; Brown, 1981; Tylecote, 1981). Business in Britain has not been able to get its political act together. As Leys convincingly shows, an effort was made by the CBI to get business leaders to think strategically in political terms, but met with little response. Only two of the twenty business leaders interviewed by Leys in 1983 'saw the direction of the state, the definition of national goals and of strategies for achieving them, as natural concerns of businessmen, and neither of these had ever sought a major role in leading or forming business opinion' (Leys, 1985, p. 19).

Business has not been without political influence. However, at times of crisis for the economy, leadership in the sense of developing and articulating an escape strategy has not been provided by business persons and their representatives, but by politicians with their own vision of what business needs (see Chapter 8). This is particularly true of the Thatcher Government which represents a departure from the historical relationship between business and the state in Britain of 'bargaining between two weak entities which often did not know their own minds' (Turner, 1984, p. 3). The Thatcher Government has a clear view of what is needed to secure a revival of business enterprise, although the question remains whether what British business needs is not so much freedom from the shackles of the state, but a mutually supportive relationship with government. For example, increasing import penetration in many sectors of the British economy, even relatively successful ones such as chemicals, suggests that there are deep-seated problems which cannot simply be resolved by the entrepreneurial activities of firms acting in isolation.

The political weakness of Britain makes it difficult to implement any concerted approach to the country's problems, such as might be favoured by a broad spectrum of opinion, ranging from Tory moderates to the mainstream of the Labour Party (although the position of the Liberal Party on such a spectrum is more problematic, see Chapter 8). For example, any demand-led approach to start solving Britain's unemployment problem is constrained by the propensity of earnings to run ahead of productivity gains (and, for that matter, the rate of inflation) even under conditions of high unemployment. Any attempt to solve such problems would need to start from a reform of bargaining structures rather than the imposition of an incomes policy by government (see Brown, 1980). One of the first problems that any such reform would encounter is the absence of 'employer solidarity' in countries such as Britain compared with West Germany (for an analysis of this contrast, see Tylecote 1981). Ineffective employer organisation is as much an obstacle to developing a concertative approach to economic policy problem as deficient trade union organisation which is more usually blamed. The political weakness of business is therefore a rarely acknowledged indirect cause of relative economic decline. Moreover, the inability of business to match its economic power by a capacity to enter into a constructive relationship with government and the unions may ultimately lead to political demands for more drastic curbs on the autonomy of enterprises.

2 The Power of Capital

In this chapter, alternative perspectives on the power of capital are reviewed. 'Capital' is no more of a monolith than the state, but before attempting to consider distinctions between, for example, large firms and small firms, a general overview of its power potential will be offered. In particular, the nature and extent of differences in the power position of manufacturing industry and the financial sector will be considered more fully in Chapter 4.

In providing an overview of the power of capital, a distinction will be drawn between three different perspectives: pluralist perspectives, corporatist perspectives, and those which emphasise the privileged position of capital in society. Limiting the discussion to three main perspectives does conflate a variety of viewpoints. For example, those analysts who consider that capital is a privileged interest may arrive at that conclusion from a perspective based on a model of society dominated by élite groups for whom ownership and control of the means of production is just one resource, or they may stress the central importance of patterns of ownership and control. Those working within a neo-Marxist perspective adopt a variety of views about the role of the state in protecting the interests of capital. However, as will be suggested later, although the three main perspectives may appear to be highly divergent both between and within themselves, there are also elements of convergence in their interpretations.

Pluralism

With its emphasis on the dispersal of power in society, the non-cumulative character of any inequalities in its distribution, and the way in which the exercise of power is supposedly checked by the activities of countervailing groups, pluralism remains a highly

11

influential perspective. One of the difficulties that immediately arises in using pluralism as an analytical perspective is that there is a wide variety of pluralist interpretations which could be deployed to analyse the power of capital. Lively develops a useful distinction between 'arena' and 'arbiter' pluralist approaches:

> The arbiter theory envisages government as standing above the group battle, settling the ground rules for the conflict (particularly those determining what groups and what modes of action are legitimate), ensuring the enforcement of those rules, and perhaps correcting imbalances if there is danger of particular groups growing into over-mighty subjects. The arena theory, in contrast, sees politicians merely as co-equal participants in the group battle. (Lively, 1978, p. 191)

This distinction does help us to make sense of the diversity of approach that characterises pluralist thinking. As Lively points out, the arena theory assumes 'that the given distribution of power is generally acceptable' (Ibid., p. 200). The arbiter theory could be said to assume a more interventionist state which determines 'what groups are legitimate, how they may legitimately act, and what is a proper balance between their powers' (Ibid., p. 192). Such a state might, therefore, be concerned that groups such as unions and consumers had an adequate hearing as well as business. Neither of these approaches requires the state to take any attitude towards the influence of business, although the arena approach effectively rules out governmental challenges to the existing distribution of power. Pluralist writers have pronounced on the role of business in the political process. In particular, one of the classic works of pluralism, David Truman's *The Governmental Process*, may be taken as setting out the conventional pluralist position on business as an interest.

Truman maintains that 'inequalities in the opportunities open to groups, of course, depend in large part on the structure and values of a given society' (Truman, 1951, p. 248). Critics of this position would argue that it begs the question of how that structure and those values arose in the first place and were then perpetuated. Truman's view is that the highest status in society is given to those groups whose achievements are particularly valued. The achievements of business in the United States have been such as to give it 'a status of the highest order' (Ibid., p. 249).

Truman, then, does not deny that business is a privileged interest, but maintains that that position of privilege has been earned through the efforts of business in bringing about the prosperity of American society. However, this does not mean 'that in the United States and similar societies "business" groups always enjoy a controlling advantage as interest groups' (Ibid., p. 253). Business groups have difficulty in maintaining internal cohesion and hence engaging in unified action. Moreover, 'economic power can be converted into political power only at a discount, variable in size' (Ibid., p. 258). It could be argued that the distinction between economic and political power is a misleading one, although Truman maintains that what is different about political power is that it involves eliciting consent from a heterogeneous mass of people. Truman therefore concludes that although '"business" groups in the United States currently enjoy special advantages in the use of propaganda and in other political efforts, it does not follow that they are or must be dominant or exclusive or unchanging' (Ibid., p. 259).

More recent accounts based on a pluralist perspective may be termed neo-pluralist in so far as they have moved away from the emphasis of some of the earlier discussions on interest group activity and the consequent neglect of the various interlocutors with which groups interacted, not least the state. In particular, the 'policy community' approach provides a framework for examining the behaviour of a whole range of actors within a particular political arena. Jordan and Richardson (1982, p. 94) argue that within the setting of sectors based on government departments, 'there is a tendency for policy communities to emerge. The policy community in any area is an imprecise sector likely to alter from time to time and from particular issue to issue, yet it is worth identifying as a community: in other words, it has continuity, implicit authority structures'. This approach has become increasingly influential and has been used in a number of studies in a variety of contexts (for example, see Rhodes, 1986).

This emphasis on the division of the policy-making map into 'a series of vertical compartments and segments' (Richardson and Jordan, 1979, p. 174) is perfectly consistent with the earlier pluralist contention that policy-making is carried out in a series of largely insulated issue arenas, with those actors who are influential in one issue arena generally being unable to exert a similar influence in other issue arenas. This vertical division of policy-making could be seen as an inbuilt safeguard against undue concentrations of power, although as Richardson and Jordan comment, (1979, p. 174): 'One cost involved in the increasingly close relationship between groups and government is that the policy process has if anything excluded the general public from any effective influence.' Pluralism thus starts to degenerate into something that resembles an élite political cartel.

At least the 'policy community' approach has the merit of providing a basis for examining a wider range of actors in the policy-making process than more traditional versions of pluralism. It also offers the *potential* for examining the common values and shared assumptions which underpin the procedural values that regulate interaction in a policy community and which thus bind potentially opposed actors more closely together. However, even this does not really take account of the objection that particular interests may best be served not by overt political action, but by the unstated and hence unquestioned assumption of certain beliefs about what is and what is not politically possible. Thus, Blank's (1978, p. 102) analysis of post-war British economic policy emphasises 'the creation of an interlocking network of policies which related to the preservation of Britain's role as a world power'. These included such policies as the restoration of sterling's international reserve role, and fixed exchange rates. Despite the importance of such policies which, for example, could be argued to have damaged manufacturing industry, there was 'little debate and little discussion' (Ibid., p. 103) about them.

As David Coates (1984, p. 77) observes, 'The power relationship of capital to government is of a subtler kind, less visible and more potent than simply the interaction of lobbyist and lobbied.' It is this interaction which forms the focus of pluralist analyses. Moreover, pluralism has been criticised not just for providing an inadequate account of the political process by confusing the defence of interests with their organisation, but also on the grounds that the encouragement of pluralist forms of decision-making has pathological consequences for the political system as a whole.

This attack comes from two directions and leads to rather different prescriptions. On the one hand, there are those who argue that an encouragement of group activity leads such groups to dominate the political process to the detriment of more general interests. This position has been argued by Olson (1982, p. 237) who claims that special interests are 'harmful to economic growth, full employment, coherent government, equal opportunity and social mobility'. In the British case, 'society has acquired so many strong organisations and collusions that it suffers from an institutional sclerosis that slows its adaptation to changing circumstances and technologies' (Ibid., p. 78). Such an analysis leads to the advocacy of neo-liberal solutions based on the repeal of all legislation that favours special interests and the application of rigorous anti-trust laws (see Olson, 1982, p. 236). Olson does not believe that such a policy would be enforced, but it is worth noting that neo-liberals differ from pluralists in that they regard organised interests as a sign of democratic pathology rather than health. In particular, Mrs Thatcher has been ready to condemn the influence of 'vested interests'.

Goldthorpe's analysis of the limitations of pluralism shares some common ground with Olson, although it leads to rather different conclusions. He points to the 'generally damaging effects of interest group activity on the operation of market mechanisms' (Goldthorpe, 1984, p. 322), especially the power of organised labour which makes standard techniques of macroeconomic management inoperable. One response is to transcend pluralism institutionally through corporatism which seeks to introduce a greater degree of order and predictability into relations between government and organised interests and also between those interests (Ibid., p. 324). The other alternative is to limit the beneficiaries of pluralism through 'the widening of those sectors of production in which market forces and managerial authority are relatively unimpeded' (Ibid., p. 338). Goldthorpe refers to this exclusion of a substantial part of the workforce from certain apparently well-established protections (such as the promise of full employment) as 'dualism'. Unlike Olson, his analysis of the spread of neo-liberalism draws attention to the losses incurred by particular sectors of the population, as distinct from the benefits supposedly accruing to the population at large as a result of the curbing of special interests. The question of corporatism and dualism as alternative strategies will be discussed further in the concluding chapter.

Corporatism

Some writers see corporatism as a subtype of pluralism (see, for example, Almond, 1983) and even corporatist writers state that 'Pluralism and corporatism share a number of basic assumptions' (Schmitter, 1979, p. 15). One of the difficulties in using corporatism as an analytical perspective is that despite, or perhaps because of, the number of writers on the subject, there is little general agreement on what the term actually means (see Grant, ed., 1985).

The essence of corporatism can be captured in terms of three concepts: intervention, intermediation and incorporation. One might add to these a belief in social partnership as the ideological cement which bands the disparate elements together (see Katzenstein, 1984, 1985). As far as intervention is concerned, Cawson (1982, p. 66) distinguishes corporatism as a mode of state intervention in which 'the state is neither directive nor coupled to an autonomous private sphere, but is intermeshed in a complex way which undermines the traditional distinction between public and private'. In many ways, intervention is the most problematic hallmark of corporatism, as new forms of state-organised interest relationship have emerged in retreating as well as interventionist states. (See the discussion of the innovations of the Thatcher Government in training policy and financial services regulation in Chapter 9.) However, perhaps these are better described as instances of private interest government rather than corporatism.

Intermediation refers to the particular kind of relationship that develops between the state and organised interests operating corporatist arrangements. The organised interests do not simply negotiate agreements with the state, they try to ensure that their members comply with the terms of those agreements. The state shares some of its authority with organised interests, but in return the interest groups are expected to regulate as well as represent their members. As Cawson notes (1985, p. 9), 'nowhere in the literature on interest groups written from a pluralist standpoint is stressed the reciprocity of the relationship between interest groups and the state'.

Incorporation refers to the fact that organised interests involved in corporatist arrangements are necessarily drawn closer to the state; the price of partnership is some loss of autonomy. This is particularly true for the unions who 'are required to cede or under-utilize their economic power – that is, the power they can express in collective bargaining – in exchange for the opportunity for their leaders to exert political power or, at all events, political influence' (Goldthorpe, 1984, p. 325). Corporatism does offer a mechanism for coping with the problems resulting from the increased power of organised labour. Some commentators see it largely as a social control mechanism; others (e.g. Offe, 1981) consider that it has some radical potential. What is clear is that the incorporation of labour also involves drawing the employers, usually somewhat unwillingly, into corporatist discussions which may eventually impinge on what they would regard as management prerogatives, for example, investment decisions. It should also be noted that one of the corollaries of incorporation is exclusion. Big business interests may be favoured at the expense of smaller scale enterprises; trade union members rather than the self-employed; farmers in preference to farm workers; producer groups in general to the cost of more general interests such as those of consumers.

The alleged theoretical inadequacies of corporatism, for instance, whether corporatist writers provide an inadequate specification of the state while positing a more activist role for it, need not detain us here. What is difficult is to apply a corporatist analysis to British business in the 1980s. In the 1970s, business organisations were drawn into extensive tripartite discussions about macroeconomic issues, although the effectiveness of those discussions in influencing the actions of any of the participants is another matter. In the 1980s, this macro level tripartism has largely faded away. However, there is evidence of corporatist arrangements involving business at the meso level, i.e. in particular issue arenas such as training policy, or in particular industrial sectors such as the dairy industry. A number of examples are discussed in Chapter 9, but any attempt to construct a more general corporatist system of decision-making would run up against the incoherence of the British system of business interest associations (see Chapters 6 and 7). The general explanatory ability of a corporatist perspective in studying British business is therefore limited, although it may be a useful tool in comparing the political role of business in different countries.

Figure 2.1 *Mechanisms through which a profit-seeking business can pursue its objectives*

	Economic mechanisms	Political mechanisms
Action by the individual enterprise	Purchase and sale of goods and services; acquisition and sale of assets; internal financial discipline, management of financial paper.	Use of government relations divisions; contacts with individual politicians and civil servants; donations to political parties.
Collective action by business enterprises	Cartels and cartel-like activities, e.g. control of prices, allocation of raw materials, market sharing, control of tendering.	Participation in business interest associations – peak associations, trade associations, employers' organisations, territorial associations, propaganda organisations.

Business as a privileged interest

Any analysis of business as a privileged interest has to start with a recognition of the fact that western societies operate in accordance with an underlying logic which has a presumption in favour of the interests of capital. Heilbroner (1986) argues that societies such as Britain are centrally and vitally capitalist. The business world itself is a mere vehicle through which more encompassing principles of organisation are expressed. For any given participant in the capitalist economy, what he or she has to do is laid down by the system. It is the nature of the whole system which gives a logic to everybody's behaviour, which should not be allowed to be obscured by an empirical emphasis on particular features of the system.

Such a reassertion of the centrality of capital accumulation in western societies may seem to be too sweeping for those accustomed to analyses in which hesitant qualification is equated with scholarship. However, three general points made by Causer (1978) lend support to Heilbroner's approach. First, the owners of capital control substantial economic resources, and much of what industry produces is essential to society. Second, the democratic basis of western societies paradoxically increases their dependence on private business. Governments need good economic results to retain power, and these depend on the maintenance of business confidence. Third, internationalisation of the economy diminishes the ability of governments to control business (this point is discussed further below).

Hence, even before business has to overtly 'exercise' power, there are certain equilibrating mechanisms which are embedded in the very nature of capitalist societies which constrain any serious encroachments on the privileges of business. As Marsh and Locksley emphasise (1983, p. 59):

> Capital is different from other interests because it exercises power or influence in two ways – directly through interest groups and structurally because of the crucial role boards and managers exercise over the production, investment and employment decisions which shape the economic and political environment within which Governments make policy.

In fact, business can exert power in at least four ways (see Figure 2.1): through decisions made at the level of the individual enterprise; through cartel-like collective economic action (cartels may be less blatant than in the inter-war period, but they have not entirely disappeared); through political action by the firm; and through collective political action by business through a variety of business interest associations.

What of the pluralist argument that the power of business is limited by the countervailing influence of the unions? As Offe and Wiesenthal have emphasised, whereas capital can exert power even if it is not collectively organised, labour can exercise power only through collective organisation. Capital can to some extent release itself from its dependency on labour through technical change, but labour cannot release itself from its dependency on capital for employment. The union movement is involved in pursuing interests which are based both on individualistic rationality and a collective identity, whereas 'business organisations represent a pure form of individualistic rationality' (Offe and Wiesenthal, 1985, p. 205). The combination of different logics of collective action in union organisations 'leads to an on-going contradiction between bureaucracy and internal democracy, aggregation of individual interests and formation of a collective identity' (Ibid., pp. 205–6).

In so far as labour is dependent on collective organisation for the exercise of influence, the trade union movement has been weakened in Britain in the 1980s. This is a result of a combination of circumstances, including higher unemployment, the growth of temporary and part-time work and labour laws opening up new forms of legal action which place limitations on the use of the strike weapon. One might add that the unions have also been weakened by the reluctance of some of them to make their organisations more internally democratic, and by the way in which such power as the unions have has been used on some occasions in the past (as in the 'winter of discontent').

Lindblom's analysis of business privilege

One of the most influential studies of the privileged position of business has been Lindblom's *Politics and Markets*. Lindblom finds classical liberal and pluralist thought to be grossly defective. As far as business is concerned, he states: 'Who are the main leaders in the market? Businessmen. Who are the main leaders in the exercise of privileged business controls? Businessmen, of course. Who are the main leaders in polyarchal politics? Businessmen are influential in enormous disproportion' (Lindblom, 1977, p. 200).

How is this position of privilege maintained and exercised? In Lindblom's view, fundamental issues such as private property and enterprise autonomy are kept off the political agenda. Disagreements between business and government are confined to 'an ever-shifting category of secondary issues – such as tax rates and particulars of regulation and promotion of business' (Ibid., p. 180).

How, then, are certain issues such as private property and the distribution of wealth kept off the political agenda in supposedly free and democratic societies? According to Lindblom, there is 'Early, persuasive, unconscious conditioning . . . to believe in the

note others/ongs link

media

fundamental politico–economic institutions of one's society', although he acknowledges that such conditioning 'is ubiquitous in every society' (Ibid., p. 207). Moreover, business persons 'simply try to indoctrinate citizens to overlook their privileged position' (Ibid., p. 203). In particular, Lindblom argues that business persons use the media to associate private enterprise with political democracy. Business often sees the media as unsympathetic to private enterprise in contemporary Britain. The role of the media raises a number of difficult questions which will be discussed more fully later in the chapter. In the meantime, there are certain specific features of the position of business in Britain which need to be discussed.

Concentration and economic power

Any analysis of the power position of business in Britain must take account of the high degree of concentration in the British economy. This increases the significance of decisions taken by individual firms about investment, production employment, etc. (the top left-hand box of Figure 2.1).

As Marsh and Locksley (1983, p. 38) observe, 'There are almost as many figures on concentration as there are authors on the subject.' However, the evidence reviewed by them suggests that the top hundred private manufacturing firms account for around 40 per cent of net manufacturing output, paralleled by a high degree of concentration in the financial sector. A report jointly authored by the Cabinet Office claims that 'Manufacturing enterprise in Britain is highly concentrated, one hundred firms controlling over 70 per cent of output' (Cabinet Office, 1978, p. 16). This higher figure probably takes account of the fact that it is possible to control a business whilst owning a minority of the shares, and also of the dependence of many smaller companies on larger companies which they supply with components and services. Whatever the precise measure used, the important point is that 'the great increase in the relative growth of the largest enterprises in the UK in the last twenty-five years has produced a manufacturing sector which is one of the most highly concentrated (if not *the* most highly concentrated in the world' (Utton, 1982, p. 22).

Moreover, there was undoubtedly a further increase in concentration as a result of a take-over boom in the mid-eighties. One development, connected with the so-called 'big bang' in the City of London, was the emergence of multipurpose financial conglomerates which transcended the traditional barriers between different kinds of financial services. (See Chapter 4 for a fuller discussion.) However, there was also a substantial growth in concentration in the retail sector, as well as a number of bitterly fought take-over bids in manufacturing industry.

This take-over boom should not be seen as 'accidental'. Its timing was related to such factors as a recovery in profits from the low point of the early 1980s, the development of new mechanisms for financing take-overs, and probably an element of imitation, fuelled by the perception that it was better to take over than be taken over. The general importance of mergers and take-overs in the UK is related to underlying structural factors. As an experienced businessman, Sir Hector Laing, has commented:

> Because institutional shareholders predominate in the securities markets, many managements have little real sense of identification with the objectives of their shareholders. Nor do fund managers have the expertise to solve problems of underperformance by the companies in which they hold shares so they resort to selling out. The takeover bid has thus become a widely used device to cure corporate woes. (House of Lords, 1985, p. 69)

There can be little doubt that the UK has a less effective anti-trust policy than the United States or West Germany. From time to time, there are reviews of competition policy, but the results are usually limited in terms of any impact on the trend towards greater concentration. This is not a simple matter of a lack of political 'will'. An effective competition policy would run up against another policy preference, that for 'national champions' in particular industrial sectors. As it is, British 'national champions' are often too small to compete effectively internationally (e.g. British Leyland) and a more vigorous competition policy could undermine those British companies that are able to match American and German companies on a global scale. It therefore seems likely that there will continue to be a considerable concentration of economic power in Britain's largest companies.

Internationalisation

The internationalisation of business is not something that just
affects Britain, although there are a number of specific features of
the British economy which make it particularly exposed to such a
development. Among these are the 'openness' of the British
economy in terms of the proportion of output that is exported, and
the proportion of domestic demand that is met by imports; the
role of London as an international financial centre; and Britain's
role as both a host country and a base country for major transnational companies. One consequence of internationalisation is that
it becomes more difficult for national governments to pursue
policies which seek to influence business activity in various ways,
for example, industrial policies. However, it could be argued that
there would be benefits from handling more aspects of such
policies through international institutions such as the EC and the
OECD.

It is not difficult to find indicators of the increasing internationalisation of business. For instance, the world's foreign exchange market doubled in size in the five years to 1984 to £103bn a
day, with London being by far the largest foreign exchange trading
centre (Group of Thirty, 1985). In manufacturing industry, over
half the employees of ICI in 1985 were employed outside the UK
in sixty countries. Only 25 per cent of chemicals turnover by
customer location was in the UK. The ICI Chairman in 1985, Sir
John Harvey-Jones (1985, p. 1), explained the company's strategy
in terms of the fact that 'expansion abroad has been essential in
order to maintain and improve ICI's position as the free world's
fifth largest chemical company. Not only does the United Kingdom represent less than 5 per cent of total chemical sales, but it is
growing at a slower rate than elsewhere'.

The logic of commercial success may not leave companies any
alternative other than to expand overseas. One study of the
subject concludes that, if overseas investment had not occurred,
there would not have been much additional investment in the UK,
but there would have been an adverse impact on the invisible
balance of payments (Shepherd, Silberston and Strange, 1985, p.
155). This analysis is not concerned so much with the implications
of internationalisation for economic efficiency, but rather with its
impact on the distribution of power. However responsible the

actions of particular firms are, the internationalisation of capital, especially in the financial sector, is bound to weaken the control capacity of national governments.

The role of the financial sector

One theme that has been pursued by analysts who view capital as a privileged interest is that a particular feature of the organisation of business in Britain is the dominant position of finance capital, to the detriment of both manufacturing industry and the broader public interest. For example, David Coates (1984, p. 67) argues that 'the political power of the City stands as the first major blockage to any successful strategy of industrial regeneration, let alone of socialist transformation'.

These issues will be discussed more fully in Chapter 4. The general position to be taken will be that analysts have often failed to understand the diversity of the financial sector, and the alliances that exist between certain parts of the City and large scale industry. However, the transformation of the financial services sector in the mid-eighties is leading to a form of organisation which is more unified and closer to what might be termed 'finance capital'.

The perspectives: an assessment

Elements of convergence

Despite their very different emphases, there are quite considerable elements of convergence between the three broad approaches discussed. For example, the neo-pluralist notion of 'policy communities' could be applied to what Lindblom terms 'secondary issues', leaving grand majority issues to be resolved in a different way by key actors with considerable power resources at their disposal. Although, as Marsh (1983, p. 7) points out, Lindlblom's distinction is somewhat imprecise, one could maintain, as Westergaard and Resler do, that there are two levels to the study of power. One level is that of the core assumptions of society, such as private property, which largely go unquestioned. These core assumptions set the terms of reference for conflicts and outcomes at the lower level where 'the picture will look something like the polygon of forces found by pluralist analysis' (Westergaard and Resler, 1976, p. 248).

There is also broad agreement that neither the state nor capital are monolithic entities, but are composed of a variety of conflicting interests and perspectives, some of which are more influential at particular times than others. As David Coates (1984, p. 59) notes from his perspective, the 'basic unity of class interests should not blind us to the fact that, more normally, politicians operate within a plurality of pressures from the world of capital, and accordingly face a multiplicity of potentially conflicting demands from it'. As a consequence, 'The state . . . is the focus of various, often conflicting, pressures that do not resolve easily into policies functional for capitalist interests' (Batstone, Ferner and Terry, 1984, p. 8).

The nature and limitations of business power

Despite the existence of elements of agreement between the three perspectives, there are evident disparities between them. Pluralists take a relatively benign and generally non-interventionist view of business power, although, as has been noted, there are significant differences of view among pluralist writers; corporatists consider that business can be harnessed to the pursuit of public policy objectives through collaboration with the state; whereas those who see business as a privileged interest see its power as potentially threatening to democracy and the ability of a democratic government to achieve its goals.

It is evident that business has considerable economic power, that this power is enhanced by the level of concentration in the British economy, and that opportunities for government control of business activity are undermined by its increasing internationalisation. As suggested in Chapter 1, the combination of economic power and relatively poor political organisation of business makes it difficult for government and business to enter into a mutually beneficial partnership relationship. Pluralist writers do not really address these issues; in particular, they have little to say about questions of ownership and control.

Any general picture of business as a privileged interest must be qualified in three important ways. First, it is evident that many issues are resolved in particular policy arenas or 'communities'. Although the economic power of business may be relatively constant from one sector to another, the political power of business may vary significantly. In particular, the strength of countervailing groups may vary from one policy community to another, and over time. For example, farmers have generally faced relatively weak countervailing groups, although environmental groups have started to exert a greater influence on agricultural policy.

Second, business persons are not able to determine by themselves which matters should remain in the market place and which should be taken into the political sphere. In modern conditions, this is not so much a matter of public or private ownership, as of which activities should be regulated, in what ways, and how the regulations should be enforced. Reviewing Lindblom's ideas in the context of banking regulation in Britain and the United States, Moran concludes that bankers are able to make important discretionary decisions in markets, but the range of such decisions at their command varies greatly over time. Regulators are neither passive nor marginal and 'To treat markets as arenas where business takes untrammelled decisions is thus to neglect the shaping power of regulation' (Moran, 1984a, p. 189).

Matters which business might like to keep in the market sphere are nevertheless brought on to the political agenda as a consequence of the democratic pressures which exist in western societies. As Marsh (1983, p. 7), notes 'in many West European states there are large Communist parties, or trade union movements committed either to the overthrow of the capitalist system, or extensive public ownership'. There has also been a general growth of environmental, consumer, feminist and animal welfare movements in western societies in the 1970s and 1980s, none of which align themselves with the values of business. Indeed, these groups arising from the politics of consumption may pose more difficulties for business than more traditional groups arising from the politics of production such as trade unions. It is at least possible to construct production coalitions with trade unions. This issue is returned to in the conclusion.

Once a matter is subject to political decision, the outcome for business is uncertain. This is not only because other interests come into play, but because business often has considerable difficulty in deciding what its interests are and, having made such a choice, in choosing a strategy to pursue them. This is in part a reflection of the simple fact that each profit-maximising firm has its own particular set of interests. It also reflects genuine uncertainty among many business persons about what is in the best interests of business, doubts made more difficult to resolve by the fact that most of them are so busy running their businesses that they have little time to think about wider issues (see Leys, 1985). It is not difficult for a business person to suggest what objectively would assist in profit maximisation, but a realistic business politician must consider the background against which he or she is working. He or she has to balance the long range task of changing the background against the short-run task of optimising against the given background at any time.

The third qualification that needs to be introduced is that any remarks about business privilege really only apply to big business. Small businesses operate in a completely different environment from big businesses (it is difficult to offer a precise definition of what constitutes a small business, but this difficulty should not be allowed to obscure the force of the general argument). For example, they generally find it more difficult to secure access to capital than larger businesses, and when they do the form in which the capital is provided may be less favourable (e.g. bank overdrafts secured on the personal assets of the small-scale entrepreneur). Indeed, a recurrent complaint of small businesses is that they suffer cash flow problems because of the tardiness of their large-scale customers in settling their bills. Government regulations which can be easily handled by a large business may impose a real burden on smaller businesses run by owner–managers, even allowing for their exemption from some regulations. If they have a grievance, small-scale businesses cannot generally secure direct access to a minister or relevant civil servant. Small-scale businesses also lack the degree of market protection which is provided by the *Handwerk* system in West Germany (see Grant and Streeck, 1985).

These qualifications aside, is business a privileged interest? In seeking to answer this question, it is necessary to be clear about what is meant by 'privilege'. Even the most primitive versions of pluralism did not pretend that all interests or potential interests in a society are able to exert an equal amount of influence on the decision-making process. In economies organised on free enterprise, capitalist lines, it should not surprise us that business is one of the most important interests.

In lexicographical terms, privilege refers to an advantage of some kind, although it also implies an advantage which is more durable than most. In modern usages, 'privilege' has come to carry the connotation of unjustified or illegitimate advantage. Historically, privileges were granted to parts of society which were thought to make a special contribution to its well being, and therefore deserved special rights and privileges of some kind.

It is also important to bear in mind that even if it could be established that business in some sense occupied a 'privileged' position in the political process, this would not necessarily be undesirable. A distinction should be made between the empirical question of whether or not business does have special advantages compared to other interests, and the subsequent value judgement about whether or not this is desirable.

Often, in contemporary discussions, it is assumed that the mere demonstation of 'privilege' is enough to condemn it. However, interpretations of the economic power of capital depend on the political perspective adopted. A devotee of the free market would argue that the economic power of business is both necessary and desirable. Entrepreneurs can assemble factors of production so as to make goods that people want, and hence are able to contribute to national prosperity through creating jobs, exports, etc. Freedom of action is necessary if an entrepreneurial system is to work properly; if the consequence is some concentration of wealth and power, so be it (although genuine economic liberals might take a different view on this point). In any case, free marketeers would argue, the most successful entrepreneurs often come from humble backgrounds. In so far as employees are disavantaged by such a system, they have the option of exit through becoming self-employed and hence small entrepreneurs in their own right, or they could be given a stake in their firms through share ownership schemes and the creation of a relationship between their earnings and the profit level of the enterprise.

Free marketeers would go on to argue that, in so far as the free enterprise system does not work as it is supposed to, this is the result of externally imposed constraints. Politicians impose regulations on entrepreneurs in such areas as employment law which inhibit the free movement of labour and drive up its price. Governments extract taxes which reduce the incentive to the entrepreneur, and the revenue thus obtained is diverted to less desirable, and often parasitical, activities such as levels of social security support which, it is claimed, discourage people from seeking work. An anti-entrepreneurial culture, fostered by an educational system hostile to business activity, reduces the number of individuals willing to create and maintain new enterprises. The trade unions limit employers' freedom to act, slowing down or preventing the introduction of new technology and the shedding of surplus labour.

A socialist would see things very differently. He or she would argue that employers use their control of capital to extract surplus value from the labour of workers which they expropriate as profits. Success has more to do with access to finance than genuine entrepreneurial skills. Increasingly, profits accrue to those skilled in the manipulation of financial paper, rather than to genuine innovators in the sphere of production. Examples of entrepreneurs from humble backgrounds can be found, but they are the exception rather than the rule. Workers have little interest in share ownership, and tend to dispose of shares made available to them as soon as they can realise a profit. Any scheme to relate earnings to the profits of the employing firm fails to take account of the tenuous relationship between the worker's own efforts and the success or otherwise of the enterprise.

The externally imposed constraints on employers, a socialist would argue, are in reality very limited and can simply be used as an excuse for failings in their own performance. Taxes spent on services such as education and health are providing an infrastructure of support for capital in the form of a skilled and healthy workforce. Social security only seems generous in the context of the very low wages paid by some employers. The educational system is, in general, highly supportive of existing values. Trade unions are the only line of defence that workers have. They may appear to act irrationally on occasions, but this is only to be expected in a capitalist society which is not itself run on socialist lines.

It may seem difficult to bridge these conflicting perspectives or to resolve the issues raised by them through reference to relevant evidence. Indeed, as will become apparent when the evidence relating to the relationship between business and the media is considered, many issues that arise from the role of business in society can only be resolved through a value judgement. For example, the argument that citizens are encased in a set of values favourable to business cannot be resolved by producing evidence about what the values of citizens actually are, for such evidence would not tell us how they arrived at their preferences. Even a thought experiment would not resolve the problem. For instance, supposing that a society which had previously espoused capitalist, free enterprise values decided to persuade its citizens, through the educational system and the media, that socialist values were preferable. Depending on the efficiency of the techniques used, such an experiment in re-education might ultimately be successful, although even in highly controlled state societies there are dissidents who question the teachings of the state. Such an experiment would only prove that indoctrination is possbile. It would not tell us anything about the 'real' preferences of individuals.

The use of the power of business

I would argue that it is important to consider not only where power is concentrated, but also *how* that power is used. That is not to say that one should be concerned about increasing concentrations of economic power in the hands of a relatively small number of businesses. In particular, the international financial system is developing in such a way as to place it beyond the reach of any countervailing power, whether governmental or supranational. It has so many inherent instabilities (see Grant and Nath, 1984, pp. 191–9) that it could eventually self-destruct, inflicting severe damage on the whole system of business enterprise.

However, I would argue that the central problems is whether business is able to make a constructive response to the problems facing modern western societies, not least the problem of high, long run unemployment. I am not referring here to the efforts made by individual firms to participate in schemes to help, say, the young unemployed or ethnic minority groups, worthy though such efforts are. I am referring to a strategic response by business as a whole to these problems, acting through its collective organisations in concert with government. Unfortunately, business in the 1980s seems to have been willing to abdicate political leadership to neo-liberals whose policies are arguably not in the long run interest of business or, in so far as they do not provide a solution to the problem of chronic unemployment, of society as a whole. Individual business persons and individual businesses display socially responsible attitudes, and a concern for the general condition of the society in which they operate (see, for example, the 1986 Dimbleby Lecture by Sir John Harvey-Jones). In general, business in Britain is open to the charge of not matching its considerable economic power with a discharge of its social responsibilities through a constructive political partnership with government.

Is there a media bias in favour of business?

Although the term 'the media' is generally used to refer to the wide variety of forms of printed and broadcast communication, it is important not to lose sight of the variations in the different forms of communication, and the diverse audiences which they reach. Traditionally, business organisations and firms (the latter often through corporate advertising) have tended to focus their attention on the 'quality' dailies and weeklies and specialised trade journals, but from the late 1970s onwards, as part of its efforts to convince a wider public of the importance of profitable business activity, the Confederation of British Industry (CBI) has paid increasing attention to the mass circulation daily newspapers. Even so, specialised journals remain an important outlet for statements by firms and business associations. They can use trade journals to reach enterprises in the particular industry, suppliers, customers and other target audiences such as civil servants and financiers.

A major debate about the impartiality and neutrality of television news, and of broadcasting more generally, has been launched in a series of books by the Glasgow University Media Group (including Glasgow University Media Group 1976, 1980, 1982). The group is aggrieved that 'Critiques of the economic system as such appear to be almost totally prohibited within the media framework of explanation' (1976, p. 232). The group complains that there is a tendency to blame the workforce for society's problems and has used case studies to argue that the reporting of strikes was 'quite clearly skewed against the interests of the working class and organised labour' (Glasgow University Media Group, 1980, p. 400). One might argue that it is not necessarily easy to deduce what the interests of 'the working class' are, any more than it is easy to deduce what the interests of business as a whole are. In particular, members of the working class may be more confused about their interests, and how best to pursue them, than middle class spokespersons who claim to know where their real interests lie. Nevertheless, the Media Group has raised important questions about the working assumptions of television journalists and presenters.

The Media Group claims to have established empirically that 'at least with regards to industrial and economic stories, the over-whelming use of inferential frameworks, routines and presentational techniques which favour one side of industry rather than the other exist' (Glasgow University Media Group, 1980, p. 414). How, then, is one to explain the fact that many business persons apparently believe that the media (and particularly the broadcasting media) are one of the forces in society that tend to be unsympathetic to business? A business association director commented in interview, 'The nature of much of the British media with which we have to deal is that it is not very interested in positive aspects of our industrial achievements so that all the time we are fighting for attention.' The Chemical Industries Association (CIA) commented in its 1984 activities report that 'Relationships with radio and television journalists are still weak . . . principally due to their interest in bad news.' The Media Group draws attention to the evaluative nature of many of the words used in television journalism, but such words can be used to discredit employers as well as unions. The CIA expressed concern in its 1983 activities report about the way in which 'All chemicals now appear to be "deadly"; gas escapes are all "toxic"; and . . . the phrase "firemen wearing breathing apparatus" is still used to heighten the dramatic effect.' Indeed, Lowe and Goyder (1983, p. 60) note that 'If there is cultural bias in the media, then environmental groups seem to be among the beneficiaries.'

Part of the explanation for the difficulties that business sometimes encounters in getting, as it sees it, its case fairly presented, is that television news and current affairs programmes are, however regrettably, a form of entertainment which has to compete in the ratings battle by using strong visuals, punchy reports and, in the case of television news, short items which cannot explore a subject in any depth. Even allowing for the imperatives of the medium, it cannot be said that business always gets favourable treatment from television or other forms of mass communication. The Media Group's work has been particularly concerned with trade unions but, as noted earlier, the groups that have probably gained at the expense of business through the use of the media are those in the environmental lobby. Not only has the media given some prominence to the views of environmentalists, but Lowe and Goyder (1983, p. 79) found that in a number of cases 'the intense media interest transformed what had previously been a humdrum administrative matter into a sensitive political issue'. In other words, matters which might previously have been settled by civil servants and business associations in relatively private negotiations in semi-closed policy communities are put on the political agenda by the glare of media exposure. An example in the area of consumer lobbying has been the increased attention given to food additives in the mid-1980s.

The Media Group is not beyond making its own assumptions about what should count as significant news, although in fairness it should be said that it does not regard 'neutral' news as a possibility (Glasgow University Media Group, 1980, p. 402). It notes the absence of any media analysis 'of what many saw as the key problem facing British industry; namely, the failure of substantial sections of private industry over a thirty year period to mount adequate investment programmes' (Ibid., p. 92). The view that Britain suffers from inadequate levels of industrial investment is, indeed, a widely held one which is often discussed in the media, but what is neglected is the fact that investment projects in Britain tend to generate a lower rate of return than similar projects elsewhere (see House of Lords, 1985, p. 25).

It is also worth noting that the Media Group (1980, p. 108) found that employers' spokespersons received less attention than union leaders and trade union bodies. The Media Group's explanation is that, in the context of the Labour Government's Social Contract, which was the focus of the particular study, 'it may seem logical that the news coverage concentrates upon the actors central to the debate'. Whether employers should be marginalised in a debate on a central economic policy issue is at least open to question. What is apparent from the Media Group's work is that there is no evidence that television news bulletins have provided extensive coverage for the views of employers, although clearly one has to consider the content of the coverage as well as its amount.

The preceding discussion suggests that, however well gathered and comprehensive the evidence, the controversy about bias in the media is difficult to resolve other than through a value judgement. Socialists genuinely believe that they have devised a morally superior (and more efficient) means of organising society. They believe that their methods of analysis enable them to determine what a person's 'objective' interests are. From such a perspective, the only grounds for supporting capitalism are those of self-interest. Socialists would reject attempts by conservatives and others to erect principled defences of capitalism on the grounds that it makes everyone better off than they would otherwise be, even if some are better off than others. They would question the validity of such claims, but even if it could be demonstrated that everyone was better off than they would be under socialism, socialists would not be prepared to tolerate the degree of inequality that a capitalist system entails. Thus, from a socialist perspective, only a relatively small number of owners and controllers of capital benefit from the capitalist system. Others may think that capitalism suits their own self-interest, but in fact they are deluded, because they do not understand the true realities of the economic and social system, and are prevented by the pervasiveness of capitalist values from doing so.

Why, then, is this system supported by the population at large, rather than just by the small minority of 'exploiters' who directly benefit from it? A socialist would answer that an important reason is the perpetuation of values and ways of thinking which favour the *status quo;* modern socialist thinking has placed increasing emphasis on the role played by the mass media in this process. Any attempt to challenge such a position can lead to a circular argument about whether the media creates (or, at least, reinforces) public attitudes or simply reflects existing values. What is clear is that business does not regard the media as natural allies and has had to devote increasing resources to securing what it regards as fair and balanced treatment.

Business is a strong and influential force in western societies, whose interests are deeply embedded in the working assumptions of an economic system based on capital accumulation. The nature and extent of its influence is limited by the workings of the democratic process, although the electoral imperatives of that process also creates a need for governments to retain the confidence of business. A symbiotic relationship thus develops between business and government, although its character differs considerably from one society to another. In order to understand the nature of this relationship in Britain, it is necessary to consider the various ways in which government has an impact on business. This subject is the theme of the next chapter.

3 Government and Business

A large firm will have extensive contacts with government every-day at a variety of levels and in relation to a variety of tasks. Members of the main board may be engaged in confidential discussions with a minister and his advisers about whether a new plant could be located in Britain rather than overseas. Elsewhere in the same government building, members of the firm's technical staff may be part of a trade association discussing a draft EEC directive on a particular product with civil servants. Members of the firm's financial staff may be holding a meeting to discuss the implications of proposed changes in tax law. Commercial staff may be discussing the categorisation of machinery imported from a closed foreign plant with Customs and Excise. At one of the plants, the safety arrangements for a new piece of machinery may be under discussion with the Factories Inspectorate. The person-nel manager at the plant may be discussing the possibility of vacancies with the local Jobs Centre. A planning application for a plant extension may require a site visit from the local authority.

One way of making sense of this variety of interactions (and many more examples could be added) is to define five main roles that government has in relation to business: as a policy-maker; as a sponsor; as a regulator; as a customer; and as an owner. As a maker of economic policy, government substantially influences the context in which enterprises make decisions. For example, govern-ment's exchange rate policy (or the absence of such a policy), or its view on interest rates, can have a significant influence on the profitability of a company and even its ability to survive. Decisions by government on corporate taxation, or on industrial relations law, or on public sector borrowing, all influence what enterprises can do and how they do it. This area of broad policy is, in general, the most politicised arena in which government interacts with business. Because it is so politicised, and because of publicly made policy commitments by government, it is difficult for business to change economic policies in the short run, although they can be modified beyond recognition by a 'drip, drip, drip,' process of extracting concessions from government on particular points.

The policy relationship

It would be misleading to portray the relationship between business and government in terms of a political struggle between lobbiers and lobbied. There is an exchange relationship from which government secures three types of benefit: information for policy design; consent for policy clearance; and co-operation for policy implementation.

As far as the first of these is concerned, information for policy design, the government machine in Britain operates on the basis of the collation, internal dissemination, and political use of information. Information is its raw material; hence the importance of debates over the extent of official secrecy. Information is a key bureaucratic power resource, and particular pieces of information may be hoarded by parts of the machine to be used at the most politically appropriate time.

Information is a crucial resource in the interdepartmental discussions that play a central role in the process of governmental decision-making. Departments may be able to make use of the information garnered from firms and business associations with which they are in contact to press the departmental point of view with other parts of the government machine. For example, departments concerned with particular industries may use such information to counteract arguments advanced by the Treasury. One large firm that was interviewed recalled that they had been asked by the former Department of Industry to provide papers on such subjects as the impact of exchange rate policy on industry, and the erosion of the industrial base.

Government is, of course, able to generate a considerable amount of information on its own behalf. It employs every conceivable kind of expert from vets to psychologists to marine biologists. Nevertheless, trade associations and firms have a mass of information at their disposal which may, on the one hand, forewarn government of impending political danger and, on the other, assist in the routine conduct of the policy-making process. For example, a firm may warn government that it is planning to close a plant in an area of high unemployment. A trade association can provide government with statistical information which is essential to policy-making, but which firms might be reluctant to provide direct to government. In the event of an emergency such as a strike in a crucial industry or service, trade associations will be able to advise government on the impact on their members. Assistance from trade associations may be particularly useful when government has to deal with highly technical proposals emanating from the EC. More generally, associations may be able to advise on the design of a policy so as to appeal to those affected or to minimise obstacles to its successful implementation, although this can also be a subtle means of changing policy content. However, although firms and associations undoubtedly gain some benefits from exchanging information with government, they are able to assist policy-makers by advising on the design of government measures so that they are most likely to achieve their stated objectives.

Consent for policy clearance

The notion of policy clearance refers to securing the consent, or at least the acquiescence, of affected publics to policy proposals that a government wishes to put into effect. If an affected interest strongly opposes a particular measure, they may be able to obstruct its implementation in a number of ways. Of course, there may be occasions when a government considers that it has to push ahead with a policy proposal in the face of organised opposition, because it is of such importance to its overall strategy. In such cases, government can draw on its coercive powers, but these can be rapidly depleted and should not be used lightly.

Moreover, the British system of government is one in which extensive and intensive consultation with affected interests, not least business interests, is a basic operational principle. In some cases, for example, the Food and Drugs Act, the 1981 Industrial Training Act, a duty to consult with appropriate organisations is imposed on the responsible minister by law. However, the real basis of the system is not law, but custom and practice. The basic principle is to make the consultative process as wide ranging as is practicable, although many of the letters that are sent out receive no response. In the case of the EEC's proposed jams directive, the Commission's proposal was sent out to about one hundred organisations for comment: twenty-four replied, of which six did not offer any substantive comments; and meetings during the development of the directive were confined to two food processors' organisations (Coates, Dudley, 1984, p. 152). Nevertheless, it is considered better to over-consult rather than to under-consult. As one senior civil servant explained in evidence to the House of Lords:

> We consult on any proposal those organisations which seem to be representative of the subject or interests under discussion. It is a subjective judgement on every occasion but we work on the basis that we would sooner over-consult rather than under-consult because you cannot from our position judge the importance on occasions of a particular proposal to a particular group of people. (Quoted in Coates, Dudley, 1984, pp. 146–7)

British government is characterised by highly routinised policy-making processes in which there is a close working relationship between civil servants and interest group officials operating within small and relatively closed policy communities. The study by Dudley Coates (1984) of the development and implementation of food standards laws is a classic illustration of this process at work. Food standards are largely agreed between civil servants and business association officials, although academic experts are also involved, and the policy agenda is increasingly set by the EEC.

Too much consultation with organised interests, particularly recognised 'insiders', may be objected to on the grounds that it is undemocratic. A democracy should at least be prepared to listen to what an affected interest has to say, and often the act of consultation will be sufficient to persuade an affected interest to acquiesce in a measure it does not like. The issue of the range of interests consulted is a matter for action by government. It could also be objected that paying too much attention to organised interests can lead to a form of political sclerosis which a number of writers have identified as a disease particularly rampant in Britain (see Brittan, 1975; Beer, 1982; Olson, 1982). The real problems may not be the existence of organised interests, or even the existence of organised interests with sanctions that they can use against government, but the failure of government in Britain to learn how to work in partnership with such interests.

Co-operation in policy implementation

Business associations and firms can co-operate with the implementation of government policy in a variety of ways. An association may be able to assist government in making a policy effective at the level of the firm by disseminating information about the policy and its applicability to its members. An employers' association may not only be able to publicise an industrial policy initiative to its members, but also explain its relevance to their particular needs through such mechanisms as seminars or contacts with individual member firms. Although working through an association may be the most cost effective way of contacting smaller firms, sometimes government may seek the direct co-operation of larger firms in the implementation of, for example, initiatives to train the young unemployed.

A more active form of co-operation arises when an association assumes responsibility for a task that would otherwise have to be discharged by government. For instance, an association may devise a self-regulating code of conduct in a particular problem area that obviates the need for direct government regulation. In a review of food legislation, the Ministry of Agriculture, Fisheries and Food discusses how, in some cases, the production of codes of conduct by trade associations has removed the need for statutory measures and suggests that this practice should continue to be encouraged (MAFF, 1984). Responsibility for what was formerly a public policy function may even be transferred to employers' associations, as in the case of the non-statutory training organisations which have replaced statutory boards in a number of sectors of industry. These themes are explored further in Chapter 9.

The sponsorship function

Business interests are in a rather different position from other organised interests because they have their own point of contact within the government machine, the sponsorship divisions for each industry or group of industries. The majority of these divisions are

Table 3.1 *Distribution of principal sponsorship functions across government departments, 1986*

Department	Industries covered
Department of Trade and Industry	All manufacturing and service industries apart from those covered by other departments, including aircraft, chemicals, mechanical and electrical engineering, shipbuilding, steel, telecommunications, financial, insurance and other business services
Ministry of Agriculture, Fisheries and Food	Agriculture, forestry and fisheries (in England; elsewhere, the Welsh, Scottish and Northern Ireland offices respectively); food and drink manufacturing industries and distributive trades
Department of Employment	Tourism
Department of Energy	Nationalised energy industries, oil industry, nuclear power construction industry
Department of the Environment	Construction, building materials and aggregates
Department of Health and Social Security	Medical equipment and pharmaceuticals
Department of Transport	Nationalised transport industries, domestic and international civil aviation, ports and shipping
Scottish Office	Scottish Transport Group, construction industry in Scotland, milk products

to be found in the Department of Trade and Industry, although some are scattered round other government departments (see Table 3.1). Strictly speaking, the sponsorship divisions are not just concerned with the firms and business association within their industry, but also with the trade unions as well. In practice, contacts with trade unions are somewhat tenuous.

It should not be supposed that the sponsorship divisions exhaust the points of contact for business with government. The Treasury has direct contacts with the largest firms and leading business associations. One Treasury official has commented that the CBI 'seems to be in and out of the Treasury every week' (Young and Sloman, 1984, p. 73). A former permanent secretary claimed that 'there are quite a lot of people in the Treasury who could give you a good unscripted account of what the problems of ICI are' (Ibid., p. 105). In the City, the Bank of England, although its representative role has diminished somewhat, still acts as an important mechanism for conveying the opinions of the financial sector inside the government machine. The Department of Employment has extensive contacts with employers' organisations over industrial relations questions and, since its acquisition of some functions from the Department of Trade and Industry in 1985, over small firms policy and the deregulation effort.

Nevertheless, sponsorship divisions are normally the first point of contact for firms and associations within the government machine. The larger business associations generally enjoy a good working relationship with their sponsorship divisions, and government relations staff in large firms usually see it as part of their job to know the civil servants in sponsorship divisions relevant to their firm's business. From government's perspective, the objectives of the sponsorship function have been explained by the former Department of Industry as follows:

> The basic aim of sponsorship is to help the industries to be successful, and to this end to ensure that in the formulation of policies by Government (and by international organisations such as EC and GATT) the particular interests of the industries sponsored are identified in consultation with them; and that these policies so far as possible support and promote those interests. Conversely Industry Divisions seek to ensure that their industries understand the reasons for and the implications of Government policies. (Industry and Trade Committee, 1980, p. 55)

Sponsorship divisions are thus concerned with explaining industry's needs within the government machine, and explaining government's policies to industry. In order to carry out these tasks, the sponsorship divisions are expected 'to establish a relationship of understanding and confidence not only with trade associations, but also with all leading companies in their industries' (Industry and Trade Committee, 1980, p. 55). Sponsorship divisions are expected to advise and assist trade associations and companies on any aspect of their relations with government, but also to make 'representations (sometimes at Ministerial level) to, other Government Departments and public organisations to ensure that industrial considerations are properly understood and given full weight' (Ibid., p. 55). Whether they are given full weight is another matter; this rather bland statement conceals the frustrations that can arise when an industry feels that it is suffering from the policies of departments other than its sponsoring department. An experienced food processing association official has commented:

> Too often MAFF and the food processing industries have to work together simply to ameliorate the worst effects of government policies imposed from outside. Thus, the relationship between the Ministry and industry does too often take place in an atmosphere of control and negative attitude. This has the natural but unfortunate consequence of making industry reluctant to work with Government on the kind of positive strategic work which is so obviously practised, say, in France, Ireland and Denmark, or even in West Germany. (Stocker, 1983, p. 251)

Whatever their limitations, sponsorship divisions almost act as institutionalised trade associations placed within the machinery of government, although it should be stressed that they would normally aggregate (the sometimes diverse) views of their industry and place those views within the context of government policy. However, by bringing together a variety of views, when the trade association structure in an industry is not sufficiently coherent to be able to produce an agreed view, and in ensuring that the views put forward are not so out of line with government policy as to be immediately discounted, the sponsorship divisions are enhancing the value of their representational work to their industries.

Of course, the nature and objectives of the sponsorship function do vary from industry to industry, and from time to time. The staff and other resources allocated to a particular industry will bear some relationship to its perceived importance. For example, in the Chemicals, Textiles and Paper Division of the Department of Trade and Industry in 1985, there were fourteen staff of executive officer level and above dealing with the chemical industry, ten of whom were of higher executive grade or above. In the same division, five staff, of whom three were of higher executive grade or above, had to deal with a wide range of miscellaneous industries including jewellery, furniture, toys, sports goods, clocks and watches, basketware, smokers' requisites, musical instruments, pens and pencils, fire extinguishers and sporting guns.

The way in which the sponsorship task is carried out will depend considerably on the policy objectives and strategy of the Government in office. Under a more interventionist government, which is trying to influence investment decisions taken by firms, sponsoring divisions are likely to have a 'proactive' relationship with firms for which they are responsible, initiating contacts on such matters as selective aid schemes. Under a less interventionist government, when industry is expected to stand on its own feet, sponsorship divisions are likely to have a more 'reactive' role, waiting for firms to approach them with their problems, and urging companies to find their own solutions to difficulties.

Indeed, some of the firms interviewed in the chemical industry thought that the sponsorship function had been downgraded under the Thatcher Government to such an extent that it was less useful to them than it once was:

> Sponsoring department concept substantially weakened now . . . no specialisation now, much smaller, trying to keep a relationship with many industries and failing. Sponsoring division gets very much less of attention [of this company] than used to.

> Advocacy role of DTI unquestionably diminishing and government's desire that it should diminish . . . Not just simple matter of saving money, trying to simplify government and making whole apparatus simpler, but won't be simpler from point of view of user.

The existence of the sponsorship function within government could be seen as further evidence of the structural power of capital. Cowling (1982, p. 187) argues that the laxness of past monopolies and mergers policies can in part be attributed to the existence of sponsorship divisions, concluding that 'It would seem important to challenge this institution.' Although it is true that sponsorship divisions 'represent the interests of their associated firms and industries within the state' (Ibid.), they have to carry out this task within the context of established government policy. It would be misleading to portray the divisions as bureaucratic power-houses, and their views are to some extent discounted by other parts of the government machine because of their function as institutionalised representatives. Indeed, Wilks (1984, p. 194) argues that 'the whole concept of sponsorship is to some extent a pretence . . . Sponsorship is . . . a passive, best-endeavour sort of relationship, it involves no planning and little policy-implementation capability.'

Of course, the sponsorship function is not intended to facilitate government planning of the economy, nor would it fit in with a directive state planning apparatus, but it may have unintended impacts on the system of business representation. Admittedly it is the case that that system displayed fundamental weaknesses before the sponsorship function evolved during the Second World War. However, by performing an aggregation function for business interests, and pressing a business case which takes account of current government thinking within the machinery of government, sponsorship functions do reduce the incentive to firms to rationalise and improve their representative associations. Although governments in other countries have their own experts on particular industries, they do not appear to have a sponsorship function in the British sense (nor do industry specialists in the European Commission see their job in a comparable way). By taking on part of the task of representing business interests, government is both reflecting and consolidating the political weakness of business that was discussed in the introduction.

That does not mean that if business was better organised, a sponsorship function would not be necessary. As the public affairs manager of one firm commented in interview, '[It is] helpful to industry to have [a] department playing that kind of role. Whitehall is a world of its own, has its own communication network, could thrash about for days trying to find the right person, person in the DTI can put you on to the right person immediately.' Abolishing the sponsorship function would further impair the dialogue between government and business, without encouraging business to put its own representative house in order. If business representation was better organised, more of the resources of the sponsorship function could be devoted to building up longer term relationships with firms which would assist in the explanation of the objectives and methods of government policy.

The range of business association contacts with government

As part of the research work for the International Institute of Management project on the organisation of business interests, information was collected concerning which government departments and other public bodies associations had most contact with. Associations were asked to name, in order of importance, the five executive/administrative agencies or parliamentary bodies with which the association had most intensive contact. There are a number of methodological pitfalls associated with this data. First, the project was confined to four industrial sectors, albeit chosen on the basis of a sampling matrix, and further sampling took place within each sector. (For fuller details, see Schmitter and Streeck, 1981.) The results may be influenced by the particular concerns of the sector studied. Second, the answers may reflect the particular interests of the association at the time the data was collected (1980), although there does seem to be some stability in the representational targets selected by business associations. Third, the results may be influenced by the particular responsibilities of the association official interviewed, although as this was usually the director-general or his deputy, this risk is reduced to some extent. Fourth, only ordinal level data can be produced from the information collected. Associations were asked to name up to five agencies in order of importance (although some smaller associations named fewer than five) and, in drawing up the results given in Table 3.2, a first place was given five points, a second four, and so on. This is obviously a rather crude procedure. Moreover, no attempt was made to weight the results for the importance of the association (a satisfactory procedure for doing this could not be devised). In view of all these methodological limitations, the results must be treated as suggestive rather than conclusive. Nevertheless, some interesting patterns do emerge which are worth discussing.

If one aggregates the results for all four sectors, and includes the 'peak associations' such as the CBI, the Department of Industry (as it was in 1980) emerges as the single most important point of contact for business associations with government. This is not surprising; as one former minister has commented, 'they are very close to the CBI and to industrial interests' (Williams, 1980, p. 93). The second most important ministry for association contacts was the Department of Trade which was merged with the Department of Industry in 1983. The Department of Trade and Industry is likely to be a far more important point of contact for industrial associations in general than any other department. Although the research did not cover the financial sector, it should be noted that the DTI has important responsibilities in relation to the supervision of the financial services industries.

Although references to different House of Commons committees were aggregated, the placing of the House of Commons in the cross-sectoral figures was only tenth, behind the Health and Safety Executive. Contacts with Parliament have become more important to most associations in recent years, but the bulk of the more intensive contacts are still with the executive. The task of monitoring Parliamentary activity is often farmed out by firms and associations to specialist consultants (see Chapter 5).

The most interesting results emerge when the results are broken down into the different sectors studied (see Table 3.2). It should be noted that the pharmaceuticals sector was treated as being distinct from the rest of the chemicals sector. Associations representing drug companies have a different pattern of contacts from those representing industrial chemicals companies. In all the sectors studied, except one, one ministry accounted for just under a third of the total points scored; in other words, one may draw the inference that for most associations about a third of all contacts with government are with one department. The one exception to this general pattern was the pharmaceutical industry where nearly two-thirds of all contacts were with the Department of Health and Social Security. This focus on the DHSS no doubt reflects the importance of the National Health Service as the Industry's most important customer, a relationship regulated by a special scheme for pharmaceutical prices (see Chapter 9). In all sectors, including pharmaceuticals, the sponsorship department was the most important point of contact in government for the particular industry, a finding which underlines the significance of the sponsorship system.

In the case of associations which draw members from business as a whole (the 'sector unspecific membership associations' or

Table 3.2 *Departments and agencies with which business associations
had most intensive contact by sector: rank order of first three
by points*

Chemicals
1. Department of Industry   19
2. Department of the Environment   13
3. Ministry of Agriculture, Fisheries and Food   7
Construction
1. Department of the Environment   34
2. Department of Trade   12
3. Department of Employment   8
   Department of Trade   8
Food processing
1. Ministry of Agriculture, Fisheries and Food   33
2. Department of Trade   15
3. Treasury   8
Machine tools
1. Department of Industry   15
2. Department of Employment   8
   Department of Trade   8
   British Overseas Trade Board   8
Pharmaceuticals
1. Department of Health and Social Security   15
2. Ministry of Agriculture, Fisheries and Food   4
3. Department of Trade   3
Sector unspecific membership associations
1. Department of Industry   32
2. Department of Trade   20
3. Treasury   17

SUMAs), such as the CBI and the chambers of commerce, the
Department of Industry was the focal point of contact. As might
be expected, it is the leading SUMAs such as the CBI which are
most likely to have intensive contacts with the Treasury. However,
it is interesting that there is also quite a lot of contact with the
Treasury by the food processing associations. This would appear
to reflect a deliberate strategy by leading associations in the
industry to offset the perceived partiality of the MAFF to farmers
rather than processors by developing contacts at the highest level
of government. Tim Stocker, a senior food processing association
official, has commented that ministers at MAFF have been 'according to party, an extension of Ministers of Consumer Affairs or
simply Ministers of Agriculture, and perhaps, Fisheries' (Stocker,
1983, p. 251). He concludes, 'Perhaps it is not surprising that the

Food and Drink Industries Council has turned to the Foreign
Office and Treasury to support its interest in changes in the
Common Agricultural policy' (Ibid., p. 253). Nevertheless, contacts with the sponsoring ministry clearly remain important to the
industry, particularly on more routine matters.

The regional ministries such as the Scottish Office and the
Northern Ireland Office are probably under-represented in the
table, as no Scottish or Northern Ireland associations were
selected for intensive analysis. However, in the construction industry, for example, the sponsoring ministry north of the border is the
Scottish Office which has a close working relationship with associations such as the Scottish Building Employers Federation. It should
also be noted that contacts with European Community institutions
(discussed in Chapter 10) are largely made through European level
organisations and therefore do not show up in a table of this kind.

The general picture that emerges from an analysis of the pattern
of contacts between business associations and government is of a
series of distinct 'policy communities' or policy networks, largely
focused around one ministry with a responsibility for a particular
industry. This fits in with the neo-pluralist view of the British
system of government as one that is divided up into a series of
discrete issue areas, with groups that are very influential in one
issue area exerting relatively little influence in other issue areas.
However, this picture of fragmentation must be offset by an
awareness of the importance of the Treasury in relation to decisions on macroeconomic policy and public expenditure, and the
co-ordinating role of the Department of Trade and Industry in
relation to the impact of government's policies on industry.

Quasi-governmental agencies

In addition to central government departments, there are a
number of quasi-governmental bodies that have an important
impact on the decision-making environment within which business
operates. Often they are concerned with the long-term development of policy in a particular area such as health and safety and the
immediate impact of their decisions is less spectacular than many
decisions taken by ministries, although often more important in
the long run. On the other hand, if the Monopolies and Mergers
Commission recommends that a particular merger should not

proceed, the impact of the recommendation on the firms concerned can be profound and immediate.

It is difficult to make any sensible generalisations about these quasi-governmental bodies because they are so disparate in their purposes, methods of working, powers and constitutions. For example, there are three agencies – the Manpower Services Commission (MSC), the Health and Safety Commission and Executive (HSE), and the Advisory, Conciliation and Arbitration Service (ACAS) – which are run by boards made up of a mixture of government, CBI and TUC appointees (plus other categories in some cases such as local authority or education representatives). However, one could not say that these three so-called 'tripartite' agencies are run in a similar way. The senior staff of the MSC appear to have an active policy-making role, but are also open to interventions from the responsible minister, given the high political profile of training policy in the 1980s. At the HSE, the emphasis is on a long drawn out, consensus-seeking process of drafting, consultation and redrafting in relation to new regulations. Direct ministerial interventions seem to be relatively rare, but there is extensive informal liaison and formal consultation with civil servants, business associations, trade unions and experts in local authorities and elsewhere. Non-tripartite agencies also seem to place a considerable emphasis on a British pattern of negotiations leading to mutually acceptable compromises. This is even true of competition policy agencies such as the Office of Fair Trading (see Moran, 1986a).

One quasi-governmental agency is of particular importance to relations between government and business: the National Economic Development Office (NEDO) which services the National Economic Development Council and its economic development committees serving particular (but not all) sectors of the economy. As the longest lasting embodiment of a philosophy of tripartite discussion between government, employment and unions, the NEDO network has survived periods when it seemed close to abolition or collapse. One reason for its survival has been its chameleon-like ability to adjust to the needs of the times, and to live for long periods without much in the way of political sustenance from government or industry. Thus, it was the only forum where government, unions and industry could talk together during the early years of the Health administration. From 1975 to 1979 it played an active role in the development of the Labour Government's industrial strategy. In the early years of the Thatcher Government, it provided constructive opposition within the Whitehall industrial policy network to too great a lurch towards non-interventionism in industrial policy, providing a series of documents which showed that even in countries like Switzerland the government was involved in interventionist measures.

Over time, a greater emphasis has been placed on the work of the economic development committees and sector working groups as a means of seeking constructive solutions to Britain's industrial problems, although these committees have probably been too heavily concentrated in declining industrial sectors, and too thinly spread in expanding service sectors. The Council itself has been a talking shop, although that can be of value in moving forward debates on particular issues on the political agenda, clearing away misunderstandings, and identifying areas of common ground, particularly between management and the unions. The economic development committees have tried to address themselves to specific problems, such as the adequacy of research and development in their sectors, or identifying imported products which could be made in Britain.

Nevertheless, even the most enthusiastic advocates of the National Economic Development Council and its committees would argue that its achievements have been relatively modest, although they would also claim that many of those achievements are by their nature difficult to trace. For example, Metcalfe (1984, p. 110) argues: 'If effectiveness is equated with direct executive action, Neddy is bound to be judged ineffective. But this evaluation ignores what it accomplishes indirectly by strengthening the network of relationships among organisations at the government–industry interface.'

From the point of view of firms and business associations, the Neddy network is largely seen as an additional channel for exerting influence on government, and a means of 'educating' the trade unions (or, at least, their leaderships) into a more 'responsible' attitude. A study of firms in four sectors found that there was 'a fairly universal belief' that NEDC committees 'are a convenient vehicle for making the government aware of the needs of the industry, not least because their recommendations tend to be better researched and to have a greater air of objectivity than is common with the more directly self-interested lobbying of trade associations' (Imberg and Northcott, 1981, pp. 7–8). This perception is confirmed by the NEDC's historian who admits that the Industrial Division of the National Economic Development Office has 'behaved, in a way, as a sophisticated lobby for the sectors its Committees serve' (Middlemas, 1983, p. 155).

There is little evidence that NEDC committees actually influence decision-making at the firm level, as distinct from lobbying on behalf of industrial interests. Imberg and Northcott (1981, p. 8) found that 'none of the companies in the sample could recall a single instance of a specific company investment decision being taken as a direct result of a sector working party recommendation, even though several of the companies actually had a member on the committee'. It is, of course, possible that the influence exerted may be of such a subtle character that the firms involved do not recognise that they are being influenced. However, the limited and tenuous character of the communications between NEDC committees and firms suggest that this is not the case. Moreover, the evidence of direct influence exerted by NEDC committees on government policy, particularly during the development of the 1974 Labour Government's industrial strategy, is rather more impressive than suggestions that a nebulous influence may be exerted at the firm level.

Perhaps the greatest value of the NEDC is that it provides a forum in which employers and unions can discuss economic and industrial policy issues in a more relaxed atmosphere than that provided by the process of collective bargaining. When all other lines of communication are down, which is not unusual in Britain, the NEDO committees offer a neutral meeting ground on which employers and unions can tackle the issues that divide (and unite) them. Although employers sometimes complain about the quality of the union input, particularly at sector working group level, the importance of union participation is indicated by the fact that the NEDC and its committees would certainly not have survived if the TUC boycott of 1984 had become permanent.

Government as a regulator

Government's role as a regulator of business has become increasingly controversial. In a major white paper issued in 1985, the

Thatcher Government took the view that 'Too many people in central and local government spend too much time regulating the activities of others' (Cmnd 9571, p. 2). The white paper argued that excessive regulation tended to lower profits, output and employment; raise prices; stifle competition: and deter new firms from entering markets, and others from expanding.

'Regulation' has been defined in a major study as follows:

> It is generally agreed that the term is confined to statute law and the associated delegated legislation which enables government departments or agencies to constrain the activities of firms and individuals in the private sector within the framework of the policies pursued by the government in power. It follows that regulation does not embrace fiscal measures that are designed to influence the flows of revenue and expenditure of firms and individuals through grants and subsidies, and through taxation. (Peacock, 1984, pp. 24–25)

One could make a further distinction between the exercise of regulatory powers which confer benefits, and the exercise of regulatory powers which impose penalties. Some regulatory organisations enjoy a discretion (to be exercised in conformity with statutory provisions) to allocate to particular applicants the right to provide a designated service from which a pecuniary benefit may be obtained. For example, the Independent Broadcasting Authority allocates television and radio franchises to particular contractors, and the Civil Aviation Authority shares out air routes. The winners in such allocation exercises gain a valuable benefit, the right to provide a particular service with the knowledge that competition will be limited by the regulatory body. The losers may, of course, see the process in a less favourable light.

Examples of regulation which involve the imposition of penalties may be found in such areas as health and safety at work, the safety of products sold to the final consumer, and the environmental effects of an enterprise's operations. Enterprises are required to conform to particular procedures which may not be the most profitable way of operating and, if they fail to observe the regulations, they may be prosecuted and suffer penalties.

However, this rather stark picture of penal regulation requires subtantial qualification. First, strict regulations may benefit existing firms in so far as they raise the costs of entering a particular market, inhibit foreign producers by requiring that they pass certain tests before they sell their products on the domestic market, or otherwise restrain competition. For example, in 1985 two leading manufacturers of kit cars withdrew from a code of practice devised by the Society of Motor Manufacturers and Traders, claiming that it was intended to lead to a junior form of government type approval for such cars. It was alleged that such a development would benefit an élite group of companies, while putting many smaller companies out of business (*Financial Times*, 4 June 1985).

A second point is that regulations are often weakly enforced. Enforcement resources are often limited in relation to the scale of the task, and the emphasis is often on compliance through a process of persuasion. Peacock (1984, p. 115) comments that 'A framework of negotiated compliance, rather than strict enforcement of performance standards, is the dominant characteristic of regulatory policy in the UK.' A significant strand in arguments about regulation is the claim that the regulators are 'captured' by those they set out to regulate. Faced with limited staff and statutory resources, and possible resistance from the regulated, a policy of seeking change through co-operation and persuasion, and prosecuting only when there has been a blatant breach of the regulations, may be the only practicable one that a regulatory agency can follow.

Government regulations can place a particular burden on the smaller business. Larger firms are able to employ specialists in such areas as VAT, health and safety, etc. and may even have a co-ordinating director of regulatory affairs responsible for all aspects of regulation. A study by Research Associates found that among the firms interviewed, VAT was the most frequently mentioned burden, but was generally tolerated and accepted. Employment protection law was seen as the second most serious burden. Local authority planning requirements were a relatively infrequent burden, but could be serious when they occurred. This was seen by the respondents as an area in which central government could take action. Health and safety legislation was seen as reasonable, although application needed to be more flexible, especially for small firms. Environmental regulations affected a few firms with special problems (Department of Trade and Industry, 1985).

The impact of the measures to ease the supposed burden of regulation proposed by the Thatcher Government, such as compliance cost analyses for new regulations carried out by government, will only be felt over a number of years. It should be noted that regulations affecting British industry are increasingly made by the EC, notably in such areas as environmental effects of manufacturing operations. The British concept of 'reasonably practicable means' used, for example, in the 1974 Health and Safety at Work Act, meets with less favour elsewhere in Europe. Moreover, the EC may not be content with British methods of enforcement. For instance, food legislation in Britain is generally enforced at the retail stage rather than the point of production. There is substantial support in the Community for the introduction of what is known as 'acceptance sampling' which involves the testing of representative samples at the factory or warehouse. If introduced, this would substantially change the system of enforcement for food legislation in Britain. The chapter on European deregulation in the Thatcher Government's white paper amounts to three paragraphs. Although the Government forwarded to the Commission in 1985 a list of some forty directives or regulations that had been adopted or were in the pipeline, and which were regarded as excessively burdensome, there are limits to what one member state can achieve. Significant parts of the Commission are committed to more stringent forms of regulation and countries such as West Germany cannot afford to ignore domestic political pressures for stricter environmental regulations.

Government as a customer

Government is a major customer of a number of industries, especially construction, pharmaceuticals and the defence industries. In many of these sectors, entry costs for new companies are high, and may be increased by government standards that companies have to meet before becoming recognised suppliers. Efforts have been made to increase the number of smaller companies supplying government, but it has been estimated that small firms take only 25 per cent of the market represented by £16 000 million of government spending each year on stores and services (Burns, 1984, p. 38). For many large companies, particularly in the defence sector, government is their principal customer. Dunleavy (1982, pp. 190–1) argues that in such areas as military procurement and the civil nuclear industry, 'the industry's affairs are negotiated privately by the main firms' rather than by representative organisations.

The situation of a monopsonist facing an oligopolistic (or even a monopolistic) seller is fraught with dangers, and the tensions that arise in this area reflected in the existence of a Review Board for Government Contracts. The employment of former civil servants or military officers by firms substantially dependent on defence contracts is a practice which has attracted criticism from time to time. More generally, a fear that is often expressed is that government's dependence on a small group of suppliers with a monopoly or near monopoly of specialist expertise will lead to it being exploited by profit maximising enterprises.

Moreover, there is a potential tension within government between the sponsorship role and the customer role, especially when the two tasks are performed within one department as in the case of the pharmaceutical industry. If customer departments were simply concerned with securing value for money in particular contracts, matters might be simpler. They also have a legitimate interest in securing the survival of a certain firm or industry. Broader policy considerations, such as those of defence procurement, may lead them to advocate solutions which differ from those favoured elsewhere in the government machine or, indeed, by the companies concerned. These issues are often over simplified and sensationalised, but in practice they are highly complex, and it is not easy to see where the public interest lies. For example, accusations that suppliers of drugs to the health service have made excessive profits are countered by claims on their part that they need substantial profits to fund essential research and development so that they can continue to succeed in export markets. (For further discussion of the pharmaceuticals industry, see Chapter 9.)

Government as an owner: the nationalised industries

Both their own managements and other large employers have generally regarded nationalised industries in Britain as businesses, albeit sometimes unsuccessful ones when judged by conventional commercial criteria. However, the distinctive relationship that the nationalised industries have with government, and the politically charged environment in which they operate, means that they cannot simply be treated as a special case of the close relationship that many large privately owned enterprises have with government. Government needs information, consent and co-operation from nationalised industries, as it does from private firms, for the purposes discussed earlier in the chapter. In the case of the nationalised industries, government also has certain sanctions at its disposal which, however imperfect they are in practice, introduce an additional element of coercion into the relationship.

Contacts between government and the nationalised industries have probably been the most fraught aspect of relations between government and business in Britain. The origins of this tension are not difficult to discern. Even after allowing for the major changes in the size and scope of the nationalised sector brought about by the Thatcher Government's privatisation programme, nationalised industries remain among the most important enterprises in the British economy. Their decisions on investment, wages and prices have far reaching consequences for the economy as a whole. Disputes in the nationalised industries have rapid 'knock on' effects throughout the economy as a whole, and the industries have frequently been used in the past as 'breakthrough' sectors in national wage rounds. Moreover, as increasing emphasis has been placed on reducing the rate of growth in public expenditure, the restraint of their demand for funds for investment or to meet losses has become an important element of government's attempts to control the Public Sector Borrowing Requirement.

It is therefore not surprising that successive governments, whatever their stated intentions, have intervened in the affairs of the nationalised industries. It is equally not surprising that such interventions are resented by the managements of industries who are seeking to develop and implement long-run strategies which they think are in the best interests of their industries. Despite the fact that board chairmen are often appointed from outside a nationalised industry, members of senior management have often spent their working lives in the industry, usually developing a strong loyalty to it. Their identification with the industry's corporate viewpoint tends to be increased by the inconsistency of many government attempts to intervene in its affairs.

The general picture of widespread and incoherent influence by government that emerges from reading much of the literature on

Table 3.3 *Typology of relations between government and nationalised industries*

	Commercially unsuccessful	*Commercially successful*
Important in economy	Considerable intervention, difficult relationship	Frequent contacts, harmonious relationship
Unimportant in economy	Gross neglect	Benign neglect

the subject must be qualified in two ways. First, the relationship between the industries and government differs considerably from one industry to another, and, indeed, with one industry over time. The second qualification that needs to be made to the picture of widespread government intervention that emerges from much of the literature is that intervention does not mean that ownership is translated into effective control, in the sense that government is able to ensure that the industries fulfil objectives that it considers important.

The variety of relationships

At least before privatisation became a major issue, four basic types of relationship could be discerned which can be summarised in a two-by-two table (see Table 3.3). Starting at the top left-hand corner, where an industry is of considerable importance to the economy, but loses money, and also generates complaints from individual consumers, government is naturally tempted to try to influence its affairs. A classic example is British Rail. Successive governments have subjected British Rail's investment plans to detailed and lengthy study, scrutinising much smaller investment projects than has been the case in other industries. The 1974 Railways Act gave the government rather greater powers over the railways than it had over other nationalised industries. The net result of all this activity has been a 'strategic vacuum' (McIntosh Report, 1976, p. 28) for British Rail, and an often strained relationship between the industry and government.

In the top right-hand corner of Table 3.3 government is likely to have frequent contacts and a harmonious relationship with large, successful industries. For example, British Gas has been a commercially successful industry and 'almost always enjoyed good relations with the officials of its sponsoring Department' (Select Committee on Nationalised Industries, 1977, p. xi). Industries of this type are rather liable to be the subject of privatisation attempts. Where these involve selling off profitable parts of the business, as with British Gas's oil fields, they may introduce a new element of strain into a previously harmonious relationship. However, much will depend on the attitude of the management of the particular industry. British Telecom's management, for example, appeared to be more welcoming towards privatisation than the management of British Gas.

Government is naturally going to spend less time on the industries in the bottom half of Table 3.3 which are not of central importance to the economy. A small, successful industry is likely to be left largely to its own devices, provided that it meets financial targets. Thus the British Airports Authority did not think that 'there is any lack of trust or mutual understanding between the British Airports Authority and the Department of Trade, our sponsor' (Select Committee on Nationalised Industries, 1977, p. ix). Government was able to monitor the Airport Authority's performance through a financial target and discussions on its corporate plan. There are worse things that can happen to a nationalised industry than being treated by government with benign neglect. Nationalised industries in this category come the nearest to operating in normal commercial conditions.

The least enviable position is that of the small, commercially unsuccessful industry in the bottom left-hand corner of Table 3.3. For example, the British Waterways Board does not even report to one of the main sponsoring departments for the nationalised industries, dealing instead with the Water Division of the Department of the Environment. The British Waterways Board has complained that their industry 'is in the Department's view of no matter – an embarrassment to be tolerated only until it can be got rid of' and that 'the absence of anyone in the Department committed to the Board's future prosperity continues to have an adverse effect on the Board's ability to make real progress in any sphere' (Select Committee on Nationalised Industries, 1977, p. xxiii). A report had been with the department for over a year and had apparently not been considered, and a board member who died in November 1975 had not been replaced by 1977. Small, unsuccessful industries can find themselves in a situation of gross neglect.

The limits of government control

The official historian of the post-war nationalisations comments that 'having regard to the powers given to the ministers by the nationalisation Acts . . . it is remarkable how much independence the Boards were able to retain' (Chester, 1975, p. 1040). In Chester's view, the most important limitation on the powers of government was 'the fact that the technical and expert staffs were employed by the Boards' (Ibid., p. 1041). This observation is confirmed by Foster who, drawing on his experience of working in the Ministry of Transport, came to the conclusion that the boards of the nationalised industries enjoyed a very great practical independence. 'In the end the Boards have mostly their own way' (Foster, 1971, p. 78).

The McIntosh Report, commissioned by the 1974 Labour Government to review the role of the nationalised industries, found that 'civil servants believe that the power of appointment is the most important single mechanism for effecting changes in corporations' performance' (McIntosh Report, 1976, p. 34). Foster is sceptical about the value of the power of appointment, but much depends on how it is used by the Government in office. The Thatcher Government has used it to appoint chairmen and board members who are considered sympathetic to its way of thinking. Apart from the fact that the Government has a different doctrinal approach from its predecessor, 'it was felt that some existing Chairmen and board members had become weighed down by the threat of union militancy and entrenched in the belief that Treasury cash was always on demand to bail out over-manned and unproductive industries' (Centre for Policy Studies, 1984, p. 7). Nevertheless, even with a government with a strong sense of ideological direction, the recruitment process is evidently somewhat haphazard. Governments 'have consistently found it difficult to attract the right individual to serve as a board Chairman or Director' (Ibid., p. 17).

The unsuccessful search for a conflict reduction formula

If many of the mechanisms of government control are less effective than they might appear to be, this only adds to the tensions between government and the nationalised industries. The fundamental problem is that there is a lack of agreement about what the objectives of nationalisation are (see Grant and Nath, 1984, pp. 63–5). There is no doubt that the boards of the industries see themselves primarily as commercial undertakings (McIntosh Report, 1976, p. 23). The Government, for its part, imposes certain social objectives on a number of the industries, although in principle these can be covered by subsidies specifically provided for uneconomic but socially desirable tasks. Intervention in the pursuit of government macroeconomic objectives is a greater source of tension. A striking example of such an intervention was the Heath Government's attempt to hold down nationalised industry price increases as part of its counter-inflation strategy, with consequences for the financial structures of the industries that took years to sort out.

Various attempts have been made throughout the post-war period to devise a formula or structures that would allow a mutually acceptable division of responsibilities between the industries and government, or at least a mechanism for resolving conflicts as and when they arose. None of the formulas that were produced really worked. By the late 1970's, the McIntosh Report found relations between government and the nationalised industries characterised by a lack of trust and mutual understanding, confusion about roles, the absence of a systematic framework for reaching agreement on long-term objectives and strategy, and no effective performance measurement system (see McIntosh Report, 1976, p. 8).

A fundamental difficulty that any review of the role of the industries faced was that they had originally been conceived as public trusts which would be run by a disinterested body of men and women who, freed from the constraints of having to make a profit, would easily be able to discern the public interest (see Tivey, 1982). In practice, the conflicting pressures on boards meant that they had little time or inclination for a platonic pursuit of the public interest. One response by government was to move away from the original idea of the industries breaking even (which led to a misallocation of resources in the economy as a whole) and to impose a surrogate profit target for at least the more viable industries. However, this effort to introduce greater commercial discipline always ran up against the twin problems of how one compensated boards for the consequences of government intervention, and what penalty one could impose on boards that did not meet their targets (given that dismissal was legally difficult and politically risky).

As far as the first problem is concerned, governments have not been slow to intervene, but have been reluctant to meet any additional costs incurred as a result by the industry. Recalling a period when the Central Electricity Generating Board was required to reduce its coal burn in anticipation of a miners' strike at a cost of £15 million, a former chairman of the board notes, 'On what industrialists would regard as a comparatively straightforward matter, namely payment for costly Ministerial intervention in the affairs of a public enterprise, there are no clear ground rules' (England, 1985, p. 88). As far as the problem of dismissal is concerned, board chairmen have been eased out or have not had their contracts renewed, but the real justification has often seemed to be political unacceptability rather than managerial inefficiency.

Reflecting on his long experience in the electricity industry, England (1985, p. 89) concludes:

> I am sure there would be less conflict and confusion if, whenever industry and government met, those in the discussion on both sides tried to maintain with absolute clarity the basic principles that the Minister and the department are interested in the broad strategies and the way forward for the enterprise, whereas the board of the enterprise is totally responsible for running and managing the enterprise itself.

Relations between sponsoring departments and nationalised industries are themselves often too fraught and complex to allow for any guidance to be derived from basic principles; what makes matters even more difficult is the involvement of a range of other actors. The McIntosh Report argued that there was a wide range of legitimate interests apart from government that had a stake in the affairs of the industries, including the trade unions, consumers and, in some cases, suppliers and local authorities. If these interests were brought into the policy-making process, rather than being left outside, it would, the report argued, be possible to produce a more stable and effective policy framework. The mechanism proposed for implementing this approach was a two tier board with a Policy Council containing representatives of a variety of interests. This proposal was not popular with the nationalised industries and was never brought into operation.

A significant aspect of the McIntosh proposals was that they represented a break with the original conception of the boards as a disinterested group of persons pursuing the public interest (although the original boards contained a considerable sprinkling of trade unionists). Indeed, the 1974–79 Labour Government did attempt to make the boards more 'representative' by appointing individuals connected with a variety of interests, most notably in the Post Office where there was an experiment in trade union participation at board level, with consumer 'representatives' as well. (For an assessment, see Batstone, Ferner and Terry, 1983.) One consequence of this approach was that the management of the industries were encouraged to regard themselves as a separate 'interest', a tendency which was apparent even before McIntosh in the formation of the Nationalised Industries Chairmen's Group.

Although the failure of a variety of attempts to find a satisfactory formula to regulate relationships between government and the nationalised industries did not, of itself, produce the Thatcher Government's ideological thirst for privatisation, it did make the defence of the industries more difficult. The relationship with the industries had increased government's workload considerably, and a tempting solution appeared to be to get rid of at least most of them. The temptation was increased by the poor commercial performance of many of the industries (see Pryke, 1981), consumer dissatisfaction with the services that they offered, and socialist disillusionment with their failure to change the situation of the workers.

Despite some difficulties in preparing industries for privatisation, and criticisms of the way in which the sales were handled, the privatisation programme went ahead. Indeed, it came to occupy an increasingly prominent place in the Thatcher government's shop window as other policies were modified or ran into difficulties. Even so, by well into the Government's second term, a number of industries remained in public hands and continued to present all too familiar political problems. If the Government won a third term, the only nationalised industries left might well be the railways, the Post Office, the Coal Board (although profitable mines could be sold off) and the least commercially attractive parts of the British Steel Corporation. Such a shrunken nationalised sector would be of less central political importance, although it would still pose difficult problems from time to time.

Nationalised industries as political actors

The increasing realisation of the nationalised industries that they have distinctive interests as institutions which have to be defended politically has been paralleled by trends in British political life which have left the industries 'relatively friendless' (Tivey, 1982, p. 46). Conservatives are, at best, unsympathetic, and, at worst, hostile, to the industries; the Labour movement has been disillusioned by their tendency to behave like any other large enterprise; and the Alliance parties are critical of their centralisation and their record of service to the domestic consumer. However, this increasing lack of enthusiasm for the nationalised industries across the political spectrum is to some extent offset by advantages that institutions enjoy in the task of political representation compared with membership groups: 'Institutions have greater latitude – more discretionary resources and more autonomous leadership authority – to enter the political arena. Institutions have less need to justify their political efforts by reference to membership approval or demand' (Salisbury, 1984, p. 68).

Nationalised industries, acting individually and collectively, have a number of ways in which they can seek to influence government, apart from the normal contacts between a board chairman and his sponsoring minister. The relations between a sponsoring division and a nationalised industry necessarily differ from those with a privately owned industry (particularly one not dependent on government contracts) because of the element of control underlying the relationship. This is unavoidable because public funds are involved, although a frequent complaint of nationalised industry chairmen is that ministers and civil servants are too interested in questioning them over details and not enough over questions of broad strategy.

It would therefore seem that sponsoring divisions are unlikely to be as much help to nationalised industries as they can be to private industries. However, one qualification has to be made to this picture. The Treasury has a strong interest in the nationalised industries because of the large sums of public expenditure involved and has a significant proportion of its staff involved in monitoring the industries. There can be occasions when the sponsoring division will act as a useful ally of the industry to fight off the Treasury within the government machine. Whether this happens will depend on the general state of relations between the sponsoring department and the industry and on the department being convinced that the industry has a good case on the particular issue. It cannot be relied on as a general mechanism for redressing the representational inadequacies of the industries. Moreover, as England (1985, p. 89) notes, the word 'Treasury' can be used by civil servants as an alibi which ties their hands. His solution for cutting the knot is to ask for a Treasury official to be present at the next meeting.

Government relations divisions in the nationalised industries

It would appear that publicly owned enterprises are even more likely to have government relations divisions or their equivalent than privately owned firms. (The role of such divisions in private firms is discussed in Chapter 5.) One study found that eight of the nine nationalised industries contacted had government relations divisions, a higher proportion than for large private companies (Slatter, 1983, p. 73). Admittedly, such divisions are not usually called 'government relations divisions', but have some other description such as 'parliamentary affairs', 'government committee' or 'corporate affairs'. They seem to perform similar functions to equivalent divisions in privately owned companies: monitoring relevant political developments; co-ordinating the enterprise's response to them; maintaining lines of communication with politicians and civil servants; and disseminating relevant information within the enterprise and providing support for line managers. Even relatively small nationalised industries often have government relations divisions.

The importance of the government relations function in nationalised industries is not surprising. After all, they operate in a highly politicised environment and are even more affected by government decisions than most private companies. Hence, they have a particular need for a sophisticated 'in house' mechanism for understanding, and responding to (or, even better, anticipating) changes in the political environment. In organisational terms, government relations divisions in nationalised industries are similar to those in privately owned firms, that is, they are usually small, high level units reporting direct to the board or one of its members and composed of staff in mid-career (although sometimes staff nearing retirement may be involved). Asked to comment on the differences between the government relations function in a private sector and a public sector enterprise, a government relations manager in a nationalised industry replied, 'In [an] equivalent private firm not different at all. Maybe we have to have closer contact with government.'

As has been indicated, what is different about the function in the nationalised industries is not their organisation or their tasks, but the more politicised environment in which they operate. What would be normal commercial decisions in a private sector company acquire a new sensitivity. For example, a government relations manager commented in an interview that his nationalised industry had to be aware of the political sensitivity of advertising budgets: 'Somewhere out there is a line, if we go beyond it we receive more criticism.'

It should also be noted that privatisation has increased the sensitivity of the political environment within which nationalised industries operate. This is not just because of the partisan controversies over the desirability of privatisation (nationalised industry managements have generally been in favour), but because it sets up new tensions between the industries. Where two industries are in competition and one of them is privatised, officials in the industry remaining in the public sector may consider that they are disadvantaged by having to operate under different and more restrictive ground rules.

Organised representation of the nationalised industries

When the CBI was formed in 1965, nationalised industries were admitted as associate members, the CBI taking the view that there were many areas where the interests of the boards of nationalised industries as large employers of labour and as concerned with a wide range of managerial functions coincided with the interests of privately owned industry, and that advantage would accrue to both from their common membership of the CBI. (CBI Annual Report, 1965, p. 7)

In 1969, the industries were admitted as full members and they have taken an active part in the work of the CBI. Two nationalised industry representatives serve on the top level CBI President's Committee, and a number of nationalised industry representatives have served as chairmen of CBI committees. For example, Lord Ezra, formerly chairman of the National Coal Board, was for many years chairman of the CBI's Europe Committee. Area staff of the industries have been considerably involved in the work of the CBI's regional councils. Nationalised industry managements see this involvement in the CBI as serving a number of purposes, including keeping in touch with trends in business opinion in the private sector and the symbolic function of, as one manager put it, of demonstrating that they wanted 'to be part of the industrial scene'. It should also be noted that the nationalised industries have often exerted a moderating influence on CBI policy, particularly in the area of industrial relations. For example, at the 1985 conference an Electricity Council representative spoke against a resolution calling for new legislation on industrial relations (the resolution was overwhelmingly defeated).

Although the nationalised industries have close links through the CBI with privately owned industry, the fact that they have an identity of their own is reflected in the existence of two organisations confined to publicly owned industries, the Nationalised Industries Chairmen's Group (NICG) and the Association of Members of State Industry Boards (AMSIB). The NICG grew out of a lunch club organised for the chairmen of major industries by Lord Robens of the National Coal Board in the 1960s. In 1975 the membership was enlarged to encompass the smaller industries, and in March 1976 the informal organisation became a Group (see Tivey, 1979). It only has a staff of two and 'A main function of the NICG remains internal – that of enabling chairmen to talk among themselves' (Tivey, 1982, p. 43). However, the Group obtained access to the highest levels of government, although the Conservatives have been less enthusiastic about the idea of the nationalised industries as a collective interest than their Labour predecessors, and the process of privatisation has to some extent undermined the political unity of the industries.

Nevertheless, the NICG successfully fought off proposals by the Thatcher Government to extend its controls over the operations of the industries, including powers to remove directors. In a parliamentary written answer explaining the Government's decision, the Chief Secretary to the Treasury noted that useful progress had been made in discussions with the NICG about increasing effectiveness and commercial viability. These talks would continue and the progress made would be borne in mind in future legislative proposals in respect of any individual public corporations were brought forward (*Financial Times*, 16 November 1985). Moreover, the NICG could provide the nucleus for a future organisation of *industries* rather than *chairmen* if the nationalised industries were asked by a future Labour Government to leave the CBI.

The AMSIB represents something over half of the executive members of state industry boards below the level of chairman, 'and was formed in 1976 to represent their interests in view of the Government's continued refusal to implement the 1974 salary recommendations of the Top Salaries Review Body' (Select Committee on Nationalised Industries, 1979, p. 108). The AMSIB has close, informal relations with the NICG, but the former body's principal concern is with the pay and conditions of appointment of executive board members. In many respects, the AMSIB could be described as a very exclusive white collar trade union, but it has no negotiating rights with government, although there have been extensive informal contacts.

In many respects, the relationship between government and the nationalised industries shares some of the negative features which characterise the relationship between government and the private sector, in particular a lack of mutual trust and understanding and, despite extensive consultative arrangements, a tendency for the relationship to be adversarial rather than one based on partnership. Indeed, in a book which is generally critical of the adversary politics thesis, Gamble and Walkland (1984, p. 37) note that there has been a 'constant party dogfight over not just the size but the legitimacy of the public enterprise sector, and one result has been the erratic handling of nationalised industries – their methods of accountability, their investment and pricing policies, and their relations with Government'. The political weakness of business is not compensated for by an effective capacity on the part of government to engage with business, even in those sectors where it has mechanisms of control at its disposal.

4 Banks and the Financial Sector

The economic strength and political influence of the financial services sector is an important feature of British business which merits separate treatment. The financial sector is often referred to as the 'City', but although this is a convenient shorthand, it was always something of a misnomer, and has become even more so as financial institutions have moved away from the 'square mile' in search of dealing rooms which give them the space to cope with round-the-clock international trading.

The financial sector is made up of an 'institutional structure of short term markets (or exchanges) in commodities, securities, money and services' (Ingham, 1984, p. 60). The banks (the clearing banks, the merchant banks and, of course, the Bank of England itself) have played a crucial role in this system of financial intermediation. Other key actors have included the Stock Exchange, providing the focus of the securities market; the various commodity markets and exchanges; Lloyds and the insurance market; the insurance companies and pension funds; unit trusts and investment trusts; and the building societies. There is also a case for considering the accountancy profession as a part of the financial sector which exerts a key influence on industry; this point is developed further below. There has also been a growing integration of financial services and the commercial bar; for example, two recent Governors of the Bank of England were practising barristers before entering the mainstream of banking. More generally, the growth of regulation and litigation is pushing barristers up the corporate hierarchy.

In the mid-1980s, the financial sector was undergoing major changes, the full consequences of which could not be predicted when writing in 1986. These changes were encapsulated in the so-called 'big bang' of 27 October 1986, which liberalised the securities markets through the ending of minimum commissions and the traditional distinction between brokers and jobbers. Giant institutions, both British and foreign owned, were formally enabled to acquire full control of stock exchange firms. The 'big bang', although the product of a particular political deal (the Goodison–Parkinson agreement) has to be seen against the background of longer run changes in the financial sector, spurred on by greater international competition and the development of new technology facilitating continuous global trading in financial paper. These changes can be traced back to the end of sterling convertibility in 1958, the subsequent rise of the London Eurodollar market, and the exposure of traditional financial institutions to competition from foreign (especially American) banks. In 1971, the Heath Government quietly introduced changes 'in the way banks were to compete for business and were to be regulated by the authorities' (Moran, 1984b, p. 2). The consequences of these changes were in many respects more significant and far reaching than those introduced by the Industrial Relations Act.

> They were designed to reverse a century-long trend to cartels and other restrictive practices within the banks; to change a system of monetary control in which credit was largely rationed by administrative decision into one in which price was the decisive influence; and greatly to increase the part played in the banking system by competition and the free market. (Moran, 1984b, p. 2)

In effect, these changes ended the distinction between wholesale banking (merchant banks/accepting houses) involved in the procurement of finance, and retail deposit-taking banking (the clearing banks).

This process of change has continued and has prompted the introduction of a new system of investor protection (discussed in Chapter 9). The extent of the transformation may be illustrated by considering the case of the building societies. These were not 'City' institutions in so far as their origins were in the provinces (the largest from Halifax in Yorkshire). In their original form, they were non-profit-making, mutual aid institutions but, over time, they have come to behave like commercial bodies, seeking

growth through expansion and merger. Their traditional reputation was one of cautious conservatism; by borrowing cheaply from
small savers they were able to fund the expansion of home ownership in Britain. The inflationary conditions of the 1970s heightened
their political profile, and brought them into a close negotiating
relationship with government about the interest rates they charged,
institutionalised through the Department of the Environment/
Building Societies Joint Advisory Committee on Mortgage Finance. Their main contact with government was with the Department of the Environment; their principal significance was within
the housing policy community.

In the 1980s, the building societies underwent a number of
important changes. They started to develop what amounted to
retail banking services, while the clearing banks moved into the
mortgage market. Money was raised on the financial markets as
well as from small savers. Wholesale funding increased from 0.5
per cent of total deposits in 1982 to 6.3 per cent in 1985, including
£1.125 millions raised in Eurobonds. The BSA interest rate cartel
was abandoned, and competition between societies intensified.
Their increasing importance in the financial system was exemplified by the shift in their 'sponsor department' from the Department of the Environment towards the Treasury.

Legislation before Parliament in 1986 would enable building
societies to become public companies, thus finally eroding their
original identity as mutual benefit organisations. In practice, the
conditons attached to the legislation make it unlikely that many
societies will be able to take up this option. The Building Societies
Bill allows building societies to diversify into real estate, un-
secured personal lending and insurance broking. Even more significant in terms of their role in the financial sector, the Government
announced that they would be allowed to administer personal
pension contracts, which could involve the management of equity
and gilt investments. The societies were thus given the opportunity
to become multipurpose financial institutions. Their emergence
into the financial mainstream was symbolised by the 'poaching' of
a senior member of the Halifax's staff by a City of London finance
house.

What was happening to the building societies exemplified a
broader trend: the breaking down of traditional barriers between
different types of institutions and markets through a combination

of deregulation and market forces. One consequence was the emergence of large financial conglomerates performing a wide range of functions. The clearing banks provided one basis for such operations. For example, Midland Bank decided in 1985 to bring together its Group Treasury, the merchant bank Samuel Montagu (it had first acquired an interest in 1967, taking complete control in 1985), and the stockbroking firm of W. Greenwell & Co. in an Investment Banking Group. The complementary nature of these functions can be illustrated by the management buy out of the Mecca Group. Samuel Montagu acted as an adviser, and underwrote the equity element of the consideration, which was placed by Greenwells, whilst Samuel Montagu provided the banking facilities which made up the balance. The investment banking side of Midland is also able to use modern technology to engage in twenty-four hour global trading in the money and foreign exchange markets.

The retail banking side of Midland's operations serves private individuals and smaller businesses, while the corporate banking business provides a comprehensive range of services to larger customers. This can include involvement in financing major projects. The fourth side of the business, international banking, provides a range of international banking services for corporate, governmental, institutional and retail customers, as well as taking responsibility for international risk assessment and monitoring. In 1980, Midland took a majority shareholding in West Germany's largest private bank, Trinkaus and Burkhardt. It is strongly involved in the international private banking market, particularly through Swiss subsidiaries such as Handelsfinanz Midland Bank. An office in Mayfair provides what is described in the Midland's annual report as 'a discreet international private banking service, operating through the main world financial centres'. These private banking activities supplement the services provided by Trust Corporations in the Channel Islands, Isle of Man and Cayman Islands.

It might seem that the emergence of financial conglomerates heralds the final establishment of 'finance capital'. However, although they represent a further concentration of economic power within the financial sector, one must be cautious about using this term. Ingham rightly criticises the argument that it emerged in the inter-war period (Ingham, 1984, pp. 195–9). Indeed, the term itself is a problematic one (see Ingham, 1984, pp. 32–6). It is also misleading if one accepts Ingham's argument (Ibid., p. 5) that 'the key to understanding British economic development lies in the recognition of the essentially *commercial* (and not simply financial) character of the City'. Indeed, it wil be argued later in the chapter that the real problem on the agenda is not so much the conventional one about the supposed dominance of the financial sector, but the destabilising features of some of the changes that are taking place in the international financial system. According to one account, deregulation in capital markets 'is beginning to look suspiciously like a bankers' ramp with a fuse attached – shades of the 1920s' (*Financial Times*, 9 May 1986).

What must be emphasised is that the emergence of enterprises straddling traditional boundaries in the financial sector has not produced a new political unity of purpose. As Moran states:

> To state a truism: the City is not a united interest; the financial services industry is less united still. Hostility, suspicion and competition divide sector from sector and firm from firm. Deregulation, structural change and uncertainty about the results of the 'Big Bang' have intensified this traditional culture of alien suspicion. (Moran, 1986a, p. 29)

Later in the chapter some of these sectoral divisions within the financial sector will be examined in greater detail. It is first necessary to examine the argument that the financial sector exerts a greater influence in Britain than industry; that manufacturing has been subordinate in political terms to finance. In economic terms, what is often remarked upon is the absence of a relationship; large British firms generally raise the greater part of their investment capital from retained profits. It should be noted that arguments about the hegemony of the financial sector have an 'efficiency' as well as a 'power' dimension: the two types of argument tend to overlap. The 'efficiency' arguments focus on what is seen as the contribution of the nature of the financial sector, and its relationship with manufacturing industry, to relative economic decline. Among the arguments advanced are the lack of a close relationship between banks and industry; the dominant role of institutional shareholders interested in short term portfolio management rather than the longer run viability of an enterprise; and the absence of adequate funding arrangements for smaller concerns.

These 'efficiency' arguments are not the focus of this particular study, although they unavoidably creep into the analysis. However, three brief comments may be made. First, a close relationship between industry and finance is not necessarily desirable. It can lead to the easier translation of a financial crisis into an industrial crisis or vice versa, and it assumes that financial institutions actually have some worthwhile advice to transmit to industry. Second, the gap between industry and finance is often exaggerated, as is their closeness in other countries (see Grant, Paterson and Whitston, forthcoming). Third, it could be argued that underinvestment in Britain has been more of a demand-side than a supply-side problem. Many firms sit on 'cash mountains', considering that they can obtain a better return from gilt edged stock than from their own enterprises.

Finance and industry

In analysing the relationship between finance and industry, a rather sceptical view will be taken of the argument that there is a deep divide between finance and industry in Britain. In so far as such a division does exist, it does not manifest itself in overt conflict. Even so, two important observations need to be made. First, London is an unusually 'international' financial centre. In the other two great centres, New York and Tokyo, international banking, for example, has a far more developed domestic base. In London, the volume of international business overtowers the domestic system. Second, institutional domination by finance in the sense of 'victory' in open political struggles is not common. For instance, it is difficult for the financial sector to overturn new taxation measures announced by the Chancellor in his Budget speech. There is evidence of ideological domination in the sense of the shaping of policy debate by the 'internationalist' assumptions of the leading parts of the financial sector. Part of the problem is that these assumptions have often gone unchallenged in the past. They are, therefore, open to influence through political criticism and open to change through political action.

The division between finance and industry has conventionally been presented as having historical origins in the way in which the Industrial Revolution was financed by individual entrepreneurs, compounded by the subsequent development of the City as an international financial centre and its consequent preoccupation with finding a profitable outlet for British capital abroad. However, Ingham argues that too great an emphasis on overseas investment can distract attention from the financial sector's commercial activities. He notes, 'Since the 1830s . . . the City's earnings from the foreign exchange and money markets, freight and commodity broking, and – spectacularly in recent years – insurance have exceeded the income from overseas investments' (Ingham, 1984, pp. 35–6). It should be added that the commercial services provided in London are heavily oriented to international markets.

As Ingham points out, many of the writers on this subject have failed to take 'the basic step of closely examining the nature of the City's activities' (Ibid., p. 33). One consequence is a tendency to present the financial sector as more monolithic than it actually is and to ignore the fact that some parts of the City may be closer to industry than others. This is particularly true of the clearing banks who do not wish to accumulate bad debts through the collapse of significant numbers of their industrial customers.

Analysts have overlooked the significance of the development of a professional corporate treasurer function within large firms. A survey by the Association of Corporate Treasurers reported in 1985 found that 50 per cent of the treasury departments surveyed had been in existence for less than ten years (*The Accountant*, 7 March 1985). One of the most important tasks of the treasurer is to manage a company's relationship with its suppliers of financial services. The development of a professional treasury function has given companies a more sophisticated appreciation of the rapidly changing range of financial services available to them. More generally, corporate treasurers may be seen as a means of bringing the financial and industrial sectors in Britain closer together. The Governor of the Bank of England commented in 1983:

> By the nature of their job, corporate treasurers embody the link between industry and finance, and they are therefore especially well placed to increase the degree of understanding between the two . . . I see a key role here for corporate treasurers, on the one hand in explaining financial constraints and opportunities to their own companies; and, on the other, in explaining to finan-

cial institutions the objectives and policies of their own companies and in specifying the precise financing requirements which they entail. (*The Treasurer*, December 1983, p. 9)

Radical analysts are prepared to admit that 'in the last two decades the relationship between industry and the City has grown closer' but maintain that the 'relationship is not as close as elsewhere in the advanced capitalist world' (Coates, David, 1984, p. 65). Radical observers regard what they see as the dominance of finance capital as a fundamental pathology of the British economic system. It is seen as leading to enormous concentrations of power in the hands of the financial institutions, but, more importantly, it is argued that the financial sector has been able to impose policies which are in its interests on government, but which damage the economy as a whole:

> City interests prevailed over industrial ones in the opposition to free trade after 1906, in the decision to return to the gold standard in 1925, and in the way in which the 1931 financial crisis was handled. City interests benefited disproportionately from the retreat from planning after 1948, and from the way in which successive post-war governments strove to maintain a world role for Britain based on the use of sterling as a reserve currency, on the liberalisation of capital markets, and on the maintenance of the sterling area. (Coates, David, 1984, p. 62)

Coates admits that the City has not always had its own way. For example, for most of the post-war period, real interest rates have been negative. Tolliday (1984, p. 59) reminds us that in the inter-war period, the Governor of the Bank of England, Montagu Norman, 'had a clear shared interest with the government in industrial regeneration since it was felt by many in the Bank that continuing industrial decline imperilled the stability of the Gold Standard and Britain's world financial power.' Moreover, much of the autonomy, and hence the power, of the financial sector has depended on its ability to exercise a largely unsupervised self-regulation. The rapid pace of change in financial markets in the 1980s, combined with a number of financial scandals in the 1970s and 1980s, created pressures for greater regulation of the financial sector, even if the proposals adopted did not go as far as many critics of existing arrangements wanted.

Even if they are reluctant to accept that 'The traditional British division between City and industry is being closed' (Moran, 1983, p. 67), advocates of the view that there is a major divide between finance and industry have to contend with the difficulty presented by the fact that there is little evidence of open conflict between finance capital and industrial capital. It should be remembered that industrialists sit as non-executive directors on the boards of financial institutions, and financiers are to be found on the boards of many industrial companies. Indeed, Useem (1984, p. 53) argues that 'the interlocking directorate forms a national transcorporate network overarching all sectors of business'. In particular, the experience of multiple directors 'even transects the industry/City divide' (Useem and McCormack, 1981, p. 384). It is also worth recalling that companies which are interested in growing through take-overs have a particular interest in cultivating good relations with the financial sector.

In terms of political representation, the financial sector and manufacturing industry have been coming closer together in recent years, with increasing numbers of financial firms and institutions (even the Stock Exchange) joining the CBI. Most of this increase in financial sector membership occurred in the late 1970s. It is doubtful whether the financial institutions joining the CBI did so because they now saw it as their main spokesman; rather they wanted to give their support to a revitalised organisation battling with a Labour Government. The chairs of key CBI committees continue to be drawn very largely from manufacturing industry. Nevertheless, Leys suggest that the recruitment of so many non-manufacturing members may have diluted the organisation's commitment to manufacturing industry:

The fact that non-manufacturing companies supply nearly 30 per cent of the organisation's membership and funds acts as a significant restraint on its representation of manufacturing interests. This restraint was operative in 1980 when many commercial and all financial companies were benefiting from high interest and exchange rates. (Leys, 1985, p. 14)

Against this background, it is not surprising that when the CBI passed a motion at its 1978 conference rejecting the notion that there was any conflict between finance and industry, what was more significant than the anodyne motion itself was the fact that the debate attracted very little interest. As far as business itself is concerned, the supposed divide between finance and industry is something of a non-issue. Although differences may come to the surface more in private than in public (Fidler, 1981, p. 229; Grant and Marsh, 1977, p. 69), or when a particular firm encounters difficulties, financiers and industrialists seem to recognise that what unites them is more important than what divides them.

Of course, this absence of overt conflict could be written off as a case of false consciousness, the result of a failure by industrialists in particular to discern how their objective interests differ from those of the financial sector. As long as a conflict of interest remains unrecognised by the parties to it, its practical importance is likely to be limited. A more sophisticated explanation of the absence of conflict is advanced by Longstreth (1979, p. 188) who argues that the real divide is not between finance and industry, but between finance and multinationals – with a common interest in the export of capital – and domestic industry.

Longstreth advances an interesting modification of the usual broad brush distinction between finance capital and industrial capital. However, as Ingham points out, Longstreth fails to identify the boundaries of what he regards as a dominant 'fraction' of capital. Nor is it clear from Longstreth's analysis whether the two interests must necessarily be opposed, or if this just happens to be the case in Britain (Ingham, 1984, pp. 29–30). It is also desirable to avoid the temptation of trying to refine the distinction further, a process which leads to a long but not very informative list of so-called 'fractions' of capital which is open to further subdivisions and additions. For example, Strinati distinguishes between national based, industrial monopoly capital; small-scale or petit-bourgeois capital; foreign (mainly American) multinational capital; and money capital (Strinati, 1982, p. 204). It will be argued in Chapter 5 that a more interesting and useful categorisation is one that attempts to look at the different corporate political philosophies of firms.

The political influence of the financial sector

Although one must not exaggerate the division between finance and industry, there is a distinctive financial sector, and it is able to exert considerable political influence. In part, this is achieved by

informal links between financial interests and the Conservative
Party, channelled through individual MPs with City links and
through such mechanisms as the Conservative backbench finance
committee. The Governor of the Bank of England has traditionally acted as the City's representative to government, whilst in the
1970s and 1980s the trade associations of the financial sector have
undergone a process of revitalisation and professionalisation.

These developments are discussed further below. However, the
real key to the influence of the financial sector resides in its
'exceptionalism' (a phenomenon which also helps to explain the
special treatment of agriculture, see Chapter 7). By 'exceptionalism' is meant the long-standing freedom of the financial sector
from extensive government intervention and the way in which
issues which might be awkward to it have not appeared on the
political agenda. For example, the Eurocurrency market developed in London with far less regulation than in the United States.
More generally, Moran notes that the City's power has rested not
on a crude capacity to influence overt policy, but on ability to
convert matters vital to its interests into non-decisions: 'they were
not matters thought to be the concern of bureaucratic politics in
Whitehall or partisan politics in Westminster' (Moran, 1983,
p. 54). This privileged treatment cannot be explained simply in
terms of City 'hegemony'. As Ingham emphasises (1984, p. 37),
'During the twentieth century, the policies which the City had
advocated have also been favoured by the Treasury and Bank
because of their favourable impact on their own *independent
practices* and *institutional power*.'

The influence of the financial sector can only properly be understood in terms of the broader acceptance of particular orthodoxies
by policy actors outside the financial sector. For much of the
post-war period, British industry was handicapped by an excessively high exchange rate for the pound (it was further decimated
by the pound's appreciation in value between 1978 and 1981).
When the Labour Government came into office in 1964, it quickly
rejected the option of devaluation. Given the size of its majority,
that was not a surprising decision. However, in the summer of
1966, with a substantial mandate from the electorate, it chose
deflation rather than devaluation, a decision which can be seen as
the start of the erosion of the post-war commitment to full employment. It was finally forced into devaluation in 1967.

This unhappy sequence of events was not simply the result of incompetence by Labour politicians (indeed, if they lacked anything, it was courage rather than competence). They were acting on the advice given to them by their senior civil servants, and those civil servants were reflecting established wisdom in the Treasury and the City (even though it was challenged by many economists). Blank convincingly argues that the post-war conduct of British economic policy was dominated by the defence of sterling prompted by the foreign policy goal of trying to maintain Britain's status as a world power. He comments (1978, pp. 120–1):

> Rather than searching for the influence of one department, the City, or the bank, it is more useful and accurate to think in terms of an 'overseas' or 'sterling' lobby within the government and administration. This lobby shared the belief that Britain's international position and responsibilities constituted the primary policy objectives and that the international role of sterling was vital to this position.

When the position of the financial sector is threatened, it has a number of sanctions at its disposal. One of the most potent is the gilt edged 'strike', a co-ordinated refusal to buy government stock. Moreover, the attention given by the media to such indicators as the sterling exchange rate or movements in the FT stock exchange index also allows City 'opinion' to exert a subtle influence on policy-making. 'In these instances it is not the actual ownership (or even possession) of assets by City organisations which is important but rather their privileged access to the "mood" of the markets' (Ingham, 1984, p. 230).

Nevertheless, it should not be supposed that the financial sector will be able to preserve its autonomy. The 'golden hellos' used to attract staff in anticipation of the 'big bang' have attracted criticism even within the Conservative Party. The financial sector in Britain has functioned largely on the basis of trust, reinforced by informal social sanctions which can have a powerful influence among individuals with a shared background. However, such informal sanctions are no longer sufficient against a background of rapid innovation in financial instruments and increasing internationalisation. There has been increasing concern about the pace and direction of change in the financial sector fuelled by the Johnson Matthey affair and events at Lloyds. The *Financial Times* admitted in an editorial (19 December 1985):

> The City of London stands at a lower point in the public's esteem than it has for many years. Fraud allegations dominate the national newspapers and are an increasing preoccupation in Parliament. Standards of behaviour in the financial markets have slipped to the point where transactions which used to be undertaken on trust now have to be scrutinised by teams of lawyers.

The financial sector has to change if it is to maintain its position in world markets. It is generally recognised that liberalisation carries with it considerable risks. Discussions with financiers suggested that there is some concern about the rate at which new forms of financial paper are being introduced. The self-regulatory arrangements for the financial sector embodied in the Financial Services Bill largely preserve the City's traditional autonomy from external intervention. It would probably take only one major scandal or crash to change that.

The Bank – Treasury relationship

The Bank of England–Treasury relationship has been the fulcrum of contacts between the financial sector and government. Until the 1970s, financial interests largely relied on the Bank to express their views to government. The Bank thus has a dual role as government's representative in the City (the Treasury's 'East End branch' as it is sometimes jokingly called), and as a voice for financial (particularly banking) interests within government. The Governor in office in 1970, Sir Leslie O'Brien, GBE made it clear in evidence to the Select Committee on Nationalised Industries that he was not an undiscriminating advocate of the financial sector's interests. He filtered their advocacy (Select Committee on Nationalised Industries, 1970, pp. 273–5).

Since the 1970s, the role of the Governor as a general representative of financial interests has diminished in significance. Sector-specific trade associations have become far better organised and more significant intermediaries in government–financial sector relations than was previously the case. Increasing government intervention in the financial sector, exemplified by the growing role of the Department of Trade and Industry in financial matters, brought to the surface tensions between the Bank of England's representative and public roles. As Moran (1983, p. 61) explains:

> The Bank remains, rather in the manner of a conventional sponsoring department, an important means of expressing City interests in government . . . But no significant City interest now feels it necessary to approach central government only through the Bank of England; and the powerful clearing banks, who a couple of decades ago, would not have ventured into Whitehall except in its company, now look upon it as just one way among many of influencing public policy.

That is not to say that the Bank–government relationship is no longer a significant one. Apart from the high level contacts between the Governor of the Bank and the Chancellor and, on occasion, the Prime Minister, Bank of England staff are extensively represented on various government advisory committees. The Bank plays an important role in the management of the money markets, the foreign exchange markets and the placement of gilt-edged stock. The latter task is of particular political significance and offers a good illustration of the sharing of tasks between the Treasury and the Bank.

Over three-quarters of the national debt in the mid-1980s was funded by gilt-edged stocks (British Government and government-guaranteed stocks listed on the Stock Exchange). The day-to-day management of gilt-edged stock is in the hands of the Government Broker (traditionally the senior partner of Mullens & Co.) He is in contact with the Head of the Gilt-Edged Division in the Bank of England. The legal authority to make issues is in the hands of the Treasury. In practice, the Treasury and the Bank work closely together, with the Bank 'aiming to provide the monetary conditions desired by political decision. There is informal and frequent contact between the Head of the Gilt-Edged Division and the Treasury Under-Secretary in charge of the Home Finance Division by telephone, in writing and in meetings' (Wormell, 1985, p. 22). In addition to these daily meetings, there is a monthly cycle of consultation based on each month's money stock data, which is discussed by the Bank and the Treasury. One of the issues discussed will be the implications for interest rates.

The Chancellor of the Exchequer receives a daily report on the gilt-edged market. Developments in the market are also carefully assessed in the financial press. This will include discussion of the impact of any political events, for example, an unfavourable by-election result for the government which might influence assessments of political risk. Although the market is clearly influenced by the attempts of players in it to maximise their own returns, it is also very sensitive to political developments, and, on occasion, may be a means of signalling an adverse City response to such developments. It should be remembered that issues are continually maturing. These have to be redeemed in cash creating a need for new stocks to be sold.

A reluctance on the part of the City to buy new gilts can thus have a considerable impact on government decisions. In May 1978, the then Labour administration faced what appeared to be a crisis. As a member of the cabinet at the time recalls, 'The City was in a jumpy mood and we were not selling Gilts' (Barnett, 1982, p. 146). The Chancellor advocated measures to control the money supply and an increase in the National Insurance Surcharge. No immediate statement was issued, and there were worries about how the markets would react. Attempts by the Opposition to build up a crisis atmosphere were unsuccessful, 'and we later heard that the mood in the City had improved, with £450 million of Gilts being sold in an hour' (Ibid., p. 147). This particular episode was thus handled successfully from the Government's point of view, but it illustrates the extent to which governments have to heed developments in the gilt-edged market.

It should not be supposed that the financial sector is necessarily unhappy with a Labour Government. As one City commentator remarked during the lifetime of the 1974–79 Labour Government, 'we are already served by about as good a conservative Government as we are likely to get' (*Financial Times*, 29 November 1977). In the spring of 1977, a poll taken by stockbrokers Rowe Rudd showed that over two-fifths of investors thought that a Conservative Government would be bad for share prices. The City's mood only really changed after the 'winter of discontent' of 1978–79 showed that Labour had no special ability to prevent industrial unrest. Contemplating the possibility of a new Labour Government, Samuel Brittan commented in 1986, 'Cripps, Callaghan, Jenkins, Healey, were all – or became – sound money Chancellors' (*Financial Times*, 15 May 1986).

Sectoral financial associations

Sectoral associations in the financial sector have the past often been little more than gentlemanly clubs performing restricted range of functions, or, at best, running a cartel. However, in the 1970s and 1980s there has been a noticeable improvement in the professionalism and sophistication of such bodies. A number of factors have contributed to this trend, including the replacement of specialised, often family controlled, businesses by large financial conglomerates; a series of failures in the old mechanisms or representation; the limitations of the Bank of England as a representative of financial interests; and the new pressures generated by EC membership (see Moran, 1983). Thus, 'The Committee of London Clearing Bankers . . . has in recent years been transformed from a trade association operating restrictive practices into a highly efficient lobbyist in Whitehall' (Moran, 1984b, p. 12). In 1985, an enlarged group called the Committee of London and Scottish Bankers was formed. This grouping represented the Bank of Scotland, Barclays, Lloyds, Midland, National Westminster, Royal Bank of Scotland, and Standard Chartered. The US bank, Citibank, which is a clearing bank is not included because it does not meet the full membership requirement of being a publicly quoted, British-owned recognised bank operating branch networks in the UK. The other principal banking organisation, the British Bankers' Association (BBA) 'was roused from a dormant state in 1972 to lobby for the wider interests of all bankers, especially in Brussels' (Moran, 1984b p. 12). The lobbying functions of the clearing bankers' committee have now been absorbed by the BBA which has thus emerged as the principal representative organisation for bankers. (For further discussion of the EC activities of this organisation, see Chapter 10.)

In the area of insurance, the formation of the Association of British Insurers (ABI) in 1985 gives insurance companies operating in Britain a potentially more effective representative body. Before its formation, there were more than ten insurance associations. There were three associations covering life assurance, as well as others such as the Accident Offices' Association and the Fire Offices' Committee which reflected the days when insurance companies operated a tariff system for their general insurance business. This heterogeneous structure made it difficult to present a common industry front to government, Parliament and the

media. The fragmented system of associations led to the abandon-
ment of the introduction of an insurance complaints system and an
industry advertising campaign.

The process of rationalisation took several years and was not
without its difficulties. The British Insurance Association commissioned a report from PA Management Consultants to review the
structure and possible alternatives which was delivered in 1983.
The PA Management report started from the premise that insurance is seen by the outside world as one industry. The new
structure should build on this perception, however mistaken.

The main division in the UK insurance industry is between
short-term (general insurance) and long-term (life and pensions).
This is reflected in the existence of a Life Insurance Council and a
General Insurance Council in the new ABI structure, each with
their own specialist committees. The councils, together with three
officials, form the ABI board. Life companies were worried that,
despite these carefully constructed arrangements, the ABI would
be dominated by the major composite insurance groups.

Most companies were persuaded to accept the new structure and
the ABI's members account for more than 90 per cent of business
transacted in the UK insurance company market. However, many
newer linked life companies have refused to join, just as they
refused to join the Life Offices Association. The giant Co-
operative Insurance Society left the British Insurance Association
in 1984 and has not joined the new association. The Associated
Scottish Life Offices has been maintained as a separate association
of the chief executives of the Scottish life companies based in
Edinburgh. It is clear that the ABI, with its integrated secretariat,
provides a much more streamlined structure for the representation
of the British insurance industry.

The exception to this general picture of an enhanced importance
for sector associations is the Building Societies Association. It has
lost its carter function, and the close relationship it had with
government over mortgage interest rates in the 1970s. Increasing
competition between member societies within the BSA, and greater divergence in their interests and activities, may undermine the
BSA's coherence. An internal review of the functions and operations of the BSA was under way 1986.

It should be noted that in addition to working through industry
trade associations, many of the larger financial institutions such as

clearing banks and major insurance companies have their own government relations divisions and parliamentary specialists. These maintain direct contacts with government and Parliament. The roles and functions of such units are discussed more fully in Chapter 5.

Accountants

Accountants are not confined to the financial sector; the are to be found in industry, in government and in local authorities as well as other public bodies such as the National Health Service. Indeed, an accountancy qualification often seems to be a necessary qualification for a wide range of jobs in the public and private sectors. This is perhaps not surprising when one considers that

> The expertise of accountants plays a dominant and pervasive role in the regulation of modern industrial societies. Their skills are deployed not only to quantify and audit the performance of all types of organisations but also to budget, cost and generally regulate the flow of stocks, cash and behaviour within them. (Willmott, 1985, p. 44)

Even though accountants are confined to the financial sector, they may be seen as a group professionally concerned with the application of financial standards of judgement. Indeed, it is possible to argue that one of the features of British industry is its *internal* dominance by financially oriented standards of conduct adhered to by accountants who occupy key positions in many firms. (The segmentation of accountancy bodies, whilst offering another illustration of fragmentation in 'British organisations, does not undermine the general point being made.) Many British firms are relatively decentralised in all matters except financial control. Operating units are required to meet financial standards in such matters as cash flow, profit margins, etc. Applications for investment funds to head office have to meet stringent financial criteria. Relatively little pressure is exerted from the corporate centre in relation to such matters as efficiency of production (except when it shows up in financial results), employee relations and quality control. There is, therefore, a constant pressure to cut corners to meet short-term financial targets. One consequence may be a neglect of preventive maintenance, which seems to be a feature of British factories by comparison with their German counterparts (see Daly, Hitchens and Wagner, 1985).

It might be objected that a preoccupation with the 'bottom line' is an invariable accompaniment of a capitalist system of production. However, accountants do not seem to enjoy so much prestige, or occupy as important decision-making roles, in major competitor countries. Lawrence notes (1980, p. 76) that 'With regard to accountants, there is a definite difference between Britain and Germany.' There is simply no equivalent of the chartered accountant in West German industry. 'The book-keeping is done by clerks and the higher level functions of financial control, often discharged by qualified accountants in Britain, will these days be in the hands of graduates in business economics in Germany' (Lawrence, 1980, p. 76).

Accountants have been somewhat neglected in discussions of the influence of the financial sector. Accountants do not, of course, necessarily agree with each other, even about the technical procedures associated with accounting. However, their pervasiveness gives them the potential for considerable influence within enterprises. Their role in reinforcing finance-driven perspectives of how an enterprise should be operated may be of greater importance than some of the issues which have conventionally preoccupied analysts and relations between finance and industry.

Conclusions

It is clear that the mechanisms through which the financial sector exerts influence have been changing in the 1970s and 1980s. Whether such changes represent a shift in the influence of the financial sector is a more difficult question to answer. As has been noted, the financial sector has significant sanctions at its disposal, has a range of formal and informal channels which it can use to influence government and the political process and, above all, has considerable autonomy in the conduct of its affairs. It is in this last area that it is most vulnerable to external pressure, particularly if it is unable to demonstrate that it can put and keep its own house in order.

The debate over the role of the financial sector in Britain has to some extent been obscured by an exaggeration of the divisions of interest between finance and industry (and by the implicit message that a closer relationship would necessarily be beneficial). In so far as industry has been able to exert less political influence (or enjoy less autonomy of operation) than the financial sector, much of the blame lies with industry itself. As Ingham notes (1984, p. 232), 'Industrial capital's weaknesses should not be seen exclusively (and somewhat tautologically) as the corollary of the City's manifest strengths; the former's chronic inability to get its proposals implemented also has quite distinct and independent bases.' In particular, 'industrial capital in Britain has exhibited a very low level of organisation and solidarity' (Ibid., p. 233). This is a point that will be returned to throughout the book. The success of a particular CBI campaign, the strength of a particular sectoral association, the effectiveness of an individual government relations division does not amount to an effective identification and articulation of industry's interests as a whole.

Whatever the deficiencies of the financial sector within Britain, they are eclipsed by developments taking place internationally which, of course, profoundly influence the City of London. It could be argued that the international financial system is slipping beyond the control of any national government or international institution. A global capital market is emerging. In particular, 'securitisation' is increasing whereby lending is channelled through markets in tradeable paper instead of through the banking system. It is open to question whether securitised paper would be generally marketable if several creditors of a single debtor tried to liquidate their holdings at once.

Moran (1986b) takes the relatively optimistic view that, rather than traditional restraints on unscrupulous behaviour being eroded by the progress of capitalist culture, the progress of capitalism raises rather than lowers standards. This is because of the impact of public regulation and the domination of markets by bureaucratically organised corporations. Public regulation of financial markets may be improving, but institutions such as central banks find it difficult to keep up with the pace of financial innovation. The Cross Report, published by the Bank of International Settlements (BIS) in 1986, argues that with more credit flowing outside normal banking channels, we will see less supervision in the future. Moreover, the BIS Group, chaired by Sam Cross of the New York Federal Reserve, argued that many of the new instruments proliferating on the markets were underpriced in relation to their inherent risks.

Future debates on the financial sector will therefore have to pay more attention to the international context in which it operates. There have, it is true, been moves towards a restoration of international financial co-ordination in the 1980s. The first step was taken with the Plaza Hotel agreement of September 1985 between the Group of Five countries which led to the dollar being talked down. There is not going to be a restoration of the old Bretton Woods system of fixed exchange rates, but there may be a use of exchange rate targets. The degree of integration of the world's capital and financial markets would seem to require some form of control of capital movements if there was an international effort to regulate exchange rates. However, what kind of system could cope with the fact that 'the outstanding stock of Eurocurrency liabilities now substantially exceeds the annual value of world trade and amounts to something not far short of 30 per cent of total OECD output'? (Artis and Ostry, 1986, p. 4).

The interlocking of the system means that a crisis in one part of it can have serious and speedy repercussions elsewhere on parties uninvolved in the initial upset. Given the erosion of the checks and balances in the system, the risks of a catastrophic incident are high. One hopeful sign is that the United States seems willing once again to exercise world economic leadership, a role which no other country is really equipped to play (with the possible exception of West Germany). One immediate problem is the erosion of the world trading system, and the agenda for a new GATT round. There is no doubt that this is 'the weakest link in the chain of multilateralism' (Ibid., p. 75).

On the national level, 'the integration of world capital markets implies a set of constraints on national policy-making' (Ibid., p. 5). In particular,

> the sensitivity of mobile capital to the prospect of gain or loss is liable to mean that a country whose policy seems unduly adventurous, and in some way prone to inflation, will be heavily punished by the withdrawal of funds, which will result in extensive reserve losses under a fixed exchange-rate regime or in a

severe exchange-rate depreciation under a regime of floating exchange rates. (Ibid., p. 5)

One implication that can be drawn is that a future Labour Government would have to be sensitive to the opinions of the international financial community, of which the City of London is an important part, in carrying out its policy programmes. Global financial markets set limits on the autonomy of domestic governments. As well as devising effective national regulatory systems, governments would be well advised to work together to improve international economic co-ordination so that they are able to exert some influence on the world's financial markets, as well as seeking to ensure that international supervision is as effective as possible.

5 Large Firms and the Political Process

As Dyson has commented, 'The politics of the firm has been neglected' (Dyson, 1983, p. 35). This is unfortunate, given evidence that direct interactions between firms and government, without the intermediation of a business interest association, are of increasing importance in the British political process. One indication of this development is the increasing use by very large firms of specialist government relations divisions to co-ordinate their interactions with government. The functions and operations of such divisions are extensively discussed in this chapter. Both large firms and medium sized firms have made increasing use of political consultancies, mainly for their contacts with Parliament, and the work of such consultancies is also reviewed here.

The high degree of concentration in the British economy (see Chapter 2), and the persistence of an individualistic enterprise ethic (see Chapter 1) contribute to the development of direct contacts between large firms and government. Another important factor has been the tendency for the industrial policies followed by both Labour and Conservative governments since the launch of the Industrial Strategy in 1975 to emphasise a more 'bottom up' approach which stresses the value of direct contact with firms. As a senior civil servant has commented:

> What I now detect is that, as compared with the 1960s, the era of the National Plan which was imposed from the top, and where sectoral implications were carefully worked out with the help of trade associations, in the 1970s there has been a greater realisation that government must also have contact with individual companies, to complement its relations with industry's collective bodies. That principle is now generally accepted and quite a lot of progress has been made. (Mueller, 1985, p. 105)

The firm: organisational and political variety

It is clear that firms vary considerably in terms of the range and character of the markets they serve, their patterns of ownership, their personnel policies, and, most important from a political perspective, their forms of internal organisation. Firms vary considerably in their degree of centralisation and the way in which control is operated from the centre. In some enterprises, functions such as personnel, purchasing, marketing, etc. are highly centralised, and only day-to-day production–management decisions are left to the plant level. In other cases, the enterprise is highly decentralised, with considerable autonomy being given to the product division or subsidiary company.

In a decentralised company, political operations may be conducted at two levels. The corporate centre may lobby on behalf of the company as a whole, either through a government relations division or more personal contacts. The subsidiary units will then work through the appropriate trade association(s). Such a structure can and does lead to different parts of the company pursuing conflicting policies. However, even in a relatively centralised company operating units may cherish their political autonomy. One relatively centralised 'top ten' company that was interviewed admitted that it did not know how many trade associations it belonged to.

Nevertheless, those firms which are in regular contact with government do develop their own corporate political philosophies which are in large part a reflection of broader corporate philosophies. It is argued that a distinction can be made between 'tripartite' and 'capitalist aggressive' firms. The 'tripartite' firms are likely to have a relatively bureaucratised relationship with government; the 'capitalist aggressive' firms are more likely to have a personalised relationship. In other words, the 'tripartite' firms will probably conduct their relations with government through government relations divisions, whereas the 'capitalist aggressive' firms will make more use of personal contacts. The 'tripartite' firms are likely to be strong supporters of associative activity, whereas the 'capitalist aggressive' firms may be unenthusiastic about it. The 'tripartite' firms tend to see associative activity as much a social obligation as something from which they derive a calculable net benefit; the 'capitalist aggressive' firms are likely to make a calculation of costs and benefits, estimate them as negative and refuse to participate. Finally, the 'tripartite' firms are more disposed to take a moderate stance on such matters as the conduct of employee relations, are more likely to favour moderate social policies generally, and such innovations as electoral reform. The 'capitalist aggressive' firms are unlikely to take such a stance on public policy issues.

These categories may be made clearer by examining two examples, ICI and GEC. ICI has enjoyed good relations with government for a long period of time. The company's official historian comments, 'there was a continual dialogue between ICI and Government, sometimes with the Government looking for action from ICI . . . and sometimes with ICI seeking help from Government' (Reader, 1975, p. 473). Reader goes so far as to suggest (Ibid., pp. 475–6) that 'the large corporation, of the size and style of ICI, stands midway between a company in private business, properly so-called, and a public corporation'. Certainly, one minister in the 1945 Labour Government suggested that it was easier to get co-operation from ICI than from the then British Electricity Authority (Williams, 1982, p. 133).

ICI was one of the first firms to have its own government relations division and has always been a strong supporter of associative activity by businessmen. It has been very active in the CBI and a large number of sector and product associations. Although company policy is not to make political donations, its leadership has tended to be moderate in its political outlook. When Sir Michael Clapham of ICI was President of the CBI from 1972 to 1974, the organisation went through the most liberal phase in its history. The ICI chairman at the time of writing, Sir John Harvey-Jones, is known to be a supporter of the Social Democrats in his personal life.

GEC provides a considerable contrast to ICI. Its government relations are conducted on a highly personal basis by its managing director, Lord Weinstock, who has been 'careful to cultivate the support of both ministers and civil servants' (Williams, 1983, p. 138). In effect, he has been his own government relations division. The political editor of the *Financial Times* has observed of his performance: 'During the past twenty years he has had access to all levels of government often including prime ministers. In the process he has won considerable respect and influence as the highly effective head of one of Britain's largest and most successful companies' (*Financial Times*, 28 March 1984). Something of the flavour of his relations with government is conveyed in what are claimed to be the minutes of a meeting with senior civil servants and other industrialists to discuss a possible merger between GEC and Rolls-Royce. According to the published account, the then Sir Arnold is claimed to have said that 'either he ran the new company or it would never be formed' (Kellner and Crowther-Hunt, 1980, p. 321). Lord Weinstock took his opposition to the Thatcher Government's proposals for the liberalisation of British Telecom to the floor of the House of Lords, although some observers considered that the fact that he had to act in this way was a sign that his influence in Whitehall was beginning to wane.

If GEC is distinguished from ICI by its more personalised handling of government relations, it is also distinguished by its lack of enthusiasm for associative activity; indeed, there could hardly be a stronger contrast. GEC was a member of the old Federation of British Industries, but left the CBI a couple of years after its formation. It has subsequently left the Engineering Employers' Federation as well. Finally, GEC cannot be said to be associated with a tripartite political stance, but rather has a reputation for the determined pursuit of profits. It has been criticised for sitting on a large cash mountain, which it invests in gilt-edged stock and other financial outlets, but its reply to these criticisms is that it would never fail to take advantage of a worthwhile opportunity for investment in manufacturing.

It is difficult to generalise about why a particular firm should adopt a 'tripartite' or a 'capitalist aggressive' corporate political philosophy. Often the explanation seems to reside in the historical development of the particular firm and the influence of key individuals at crucial points in its history. The creator of ICI was Sir Alfred Mond, a firm believer in an enlightened labour policy and instigator of the conciliatory Mond–Turner talks with the TUC in the aftermath of the General Strike. It could be claimed that ICI today is still influenced by the legacy of Mond's philosophy. Similarly, GEC in its modern form is the creation of Lord Weinstock and bears the imprint of his personal philosophy.

Table 5.1   *Distribution of government relations divisions by size of company, private sector industrial companies only, UK*

Size (category based on rank by turnover) (Source: The Times 1000)	Number of firms with government relations divisions in size category	Percentage of firms in size category with government relations division
0–10	9	90%
11–20	3	30%
21–50	7	23%
51–100	6	12%
100–199	8	8%
200–299	1	1%
300–399	1	1%
400–499	1	1%

Forms of political activity by firms

There is a clear and direct relationship between size of firm in terms of turnover and the possession of a specialist government relations division (see Table 5.1), a relationship confirmed in independent research by Slatter (1983). Government relations is understood as a specialist function within a firm which seeks to provide strategic co-ordination of its relations with government and other external actors, and to offer 'in house' advice on the conduct of such relations. The function may have a number of titles other than 'government relations' such as corporate affairs or public affairs, but it must be distinguished from units or individuals performing a traditional public relations function. The writer's list of government relations divisions, used to compile Table 5.1, is certainly not complete, but it is as comprehensive as possible. It is based on contacts with civil servants, individuals working in government relations divisions, political consultants and on lists of specialists attending Industry and Parliament Trust seminars; assistance was also provided by the Royal Institute of Public Administration.

It should not be supposed that having a government relations division and being actively involved in business interest associations are mutually exclusive activities for large firms. The evidence suggests that large firms tend *both* to have government relations

Table 5.2 *Firms holding at least one CBI committee chairmanship between 1965 and 1980 by size of firm*

Firm size group (based on turnover rank at the end of period)	Percentage of firms in size groups holding at least one chairmanship
1 – 10	70%
11 – 20	40%
21 – 49	23%
50 – 99	18%
100 – 149	10%
150 – 200	4%

Source: *The Times 1000* for size data; author's calculations based on *CBI Annual Reports*.

divisions and to be active in business interest associations. Estimates made available to the author suggest that large firms may devote between 1300 and 1700 man days a year of the time of senior management to business interest and association activity. As Table 5.2 shows, holding a CBI committee chairmanship between 1965 and 1980 (a demanding role) was related to size of firm measured by turnover in a similar way to the incidence of government relations divisions.

The cost of subscribing to a business interest association for a large firm is so small in relation to turnover that it is hardly worth bothering about as an item on the firm's budget. However, the cost rises when one takes account of the attendance of senior executives at meetings. In 1981, it was difficult to find a candidate who could spare the necessary four or five days a week to be President of the CBI and three front-runners turned the job down because of pressure of work, although one of them eventually accepted (*Financial Times*, 15 April 1981). Nevertheless, involvement in an organisation can confer additional benefits as well as additional costs. Explaining why he joined the President's Committee of the CBI when he had heavy and demanding responsibilities at British Leyland, Sir Michael Edwardes has stated (1983, p. 260), 'It was essential to contribute to commercial and trade and economic politics, and furthermore I learned a great deal in the process of contributing.' Business interest associations are regarded by many business persons as a valuable source of information about competitors and

Table 5.3 *Percentage of firms influencing decision-making process by different methods*

Method	Percentage and number
Industry associations only	44% (41)
Industry associations and government relations divisions (and consultants in eight cases)	38% (35)
Does not attempt to influence	10% (9)
Government relations divisions only	5% (5)
Consultants only	2% (2)

Source: Derived from R. Slatter, M.Phil thesis, University of Oxford, 1983.

their managements, about developments in the industry and about political developments more generally; for junior management, they can serve as a form of training, introducing the manager to wider decision-making considerations and thus helping to prepare him or her for a corporate role.

Large firms are often able to pursue their own particular interests through business interest associations in a way that they could not do on their own behalf. One of the 'top ten' firms stated in interview that they derived three main benefits from business interest association activity. First, there was a whole series of questions where it was necessary to have an industry view, for example, on international trade matters. Second, although the firm could look after its own interests with the British Government, this was not possible on the European level; it was necessary to have associations for European Community representation. Third, there were a number of consultative bodies in Whitehall dealing with technical matters of great interest to the company: it could not sit on them as Company X, but it could sit on them as Company X, representing Association Y.

An important study by Slatter (1983) shows that very few firms rely solely on government relations divisions for the conduct of their relations with government. Slatter sent a questionnaire to the top hundred industrial companies, plus the major nationalised industries and leading companies in the financial services sector, obtaining an overall response rate of 66 per cent. As Table 5.3

shows, 44 percent of responding companies worked only through industry associations, as against 38 per cent who worked through a combination of industry associations and their own government relations divisions, a minority of this category making some use of consultants as well. Only five enterprises worked solely through their government relations divisions and four of these were nationalised industries. It is therefore clear that business interest association activity remains important even to the largest firms.

Some large firms make substantial donations to political parties and this subject is discussed more fully in Chapter 8. However, it should be made clear at this stage that only a minority of the top hundred companies make political donations. Such donations are made in the belief that the election of a particular party would benefit the company, rather than as a means of securing influence. Making political donations may be of some benefit to medium sized companies rather than large companies in so far as they could give them access to ministers (e.g. at party functions) which they could not otherwise enjoy.

Government relations divisions

Which companies have government relations divisions?

As has been pointed out, size is the best single predictor of whether a company will have a government relations division. As Table 5.1 shows, the government relations function is almost universal in the ten giant companies, and its incidence falls off rapidly below that level; it is relatively rare outside the top hundred industrial companies. In the financial sector, the government relations function is generally well developed in clearing banks, but less so in insurance companies. They are even more rare in accepting houses, discount houses, investment trusts and property companies (see Slatter, 1983, p. 73).

However, size by itself is not an adequate explanatory variable as there are many large companies which do not have government relations divisions, and some companies outside the 'top hundred' which do. The most important other explanatory variable is undoubtedly the extent and character of state involvement in the sector in which the firm operates. This involvement manifests itself particularly in terms of regulatory activities which impinge on the autonomy and profitability of the individual firm, and also in the extent to which the industry is used as a major source of tax revenue, and whether government is a major purchaser of the industry's products. The oil industry is substantially influenced by government decisions about taxation, exploration rights, environmental standards, etc. and at least eight companies in the industry have government relations division. It is the only industry in which maintaining contacts with individual companies is formally defined as part of the sponsorship function in the *Civil Service List*. A government relations executive in the oil industry who was interviewed commented:

> In the oil industry, it's not a case that we have a choice, the politics of energy and oil draw us into very close relationships with government. Government has discretionary powers over various aspects of the oil industry. Much of what I do is the result of policies enforced on us by legislation that pulls us into relationships we would not pursue by other means.

Many of the considerations which apply to the oil industry also apply to the closely related chemicals industry (many companies cross the boundary between the two) and five companies based in chemicals have government relations divisions. The prevalence of government relations divisions in companies with substantial interests in tobacco (three) and in alcoholic drinks (three) reflects the extent to which these sectors are used by government as sources of tax revenue and, especially in the case of tobacco, government's wish to place restraints on tobacco advertising for health reasons. Companies producing electronics products of various kinds are likely to have government relations divisions (at least four do) because government is often an important customer, and because of the interest of government (and the EC) in stimulating 'industries of the future', thus drawing firms and government into a close relationship.

The more internationalised a firm's operations are, the more it may feel that it needs a capability for gathering information about the stability of the regimes in the countries in which the company has invested or is thinking of investing. Of course, no large firm can stand aside completely from the greater internationalisation of politics, particularly the greater complexity introduced into the decision-making environment by Britain's membership of the EC. The balance between a firm's domestic and international activities may have more of an impact on the way in which the government relations function is discharged, rather than on whether such a function exists at all. Different political problems face transnational companies, notably those operating in parts of the world, such as South Africa, which are likely to expose them to criticism from cause groups of various kinds. Transnational companies have relatively little organisational capacity for defining and defending their collective interests as transnational companies, however influential they may be individually. Outside the Multinationals Panel of the CBI, and certain informal arrangements, transnationals have no distinctive organisation to defend their particular interests against increasing outside criticism. In the absence of such a collective capacity, individual transnationals may feel that they need their own means both to anticipate criticism and to defend themselves against it.

Although it is possible to make a number of sustainable generalisations about which types of company are likely to develop a government relations function, 'the specific socio-political issues of concern to those companies with government relations functions do vary significantly' (Slatter, 1983, p. 95). Slatter's research suggests that not only may the issues of concern vary between classes of companies, but they may also vary widely within a particular category.

Industries in which a government relations function is less likely to be found in large companies – although examples can be produced in each case – include retailing, food processing (other than alcoholic drinks) and construction. Apart from construction, which has government as a major customer, these industries do not have a high political profile. Moreover, many such firms conform to a pattern, noted by Litvak in Canada, of 'large, old fashioned corporations that question the need, let alone the value, of such an area of activity' (Litvak, 1981, pp. 49–50). Construction and food processing companies are very generous donors to the Conservative Party and many of them appear to place quite a lot of emphasis on personal contacts with ministers. In the construction industry, members of the founding family are still on the board of a number of companies and government relations may be one of

the personal tasks of a director, thus conforming to the old
'establishment' style which has been displaced in most companies.

Why did the function develop when it did?

ICI developed a government relations function as early as the
1950s, but in most British companies the function was introduced
in the 1970s, others developing it later in the 1980s. Interviews
with firms suggested that many of the reasons for the introduction
of a distinct government relations function at a particular time
were specific to the individual company – a threat of nationalisation or a Monopolies Commission investigation, a chance conver-
sation between two directors on a long distance flight, the
application of the thinking of an American parent company to the
British subsidiary. Clearly, it was not accidental that managers in a
number of firms decided at around about the same time that it
would be desirable to have a specialist industrial relations capability. Obviously, they were responding to changes in the external
environment, albeit perceived in different ways. However, four
major common factors did emerge from the interviews: a long run
increase in government intervention in the economy; events in
British politics in the mid-1970s; long run changes in the British
political system; and imitation.

There was a general consensus among the government relations
executives interviewed that, whatever specific changes may be
made, continued government intervention in business is unavoidable and therefore needs to be coped with by firms in a permanent
and sophisticated way. As one government relations executive put
it, 'Government is so much involved now in things that involve our
business, whether its agreement to establish a new plant or a
decision to limit imports or establish new guidelines on [a matter
specific to the company] – one needs a much better idea of what is
going to happen to apply influence.'

The unstable economic and political situation in Britain in the
mid-1970s convinced a number of companies that they need an 'in
house' capability that would enable them to understand what was
happening and the implications for their firm. As one respondent
commented:

Started not with Labour Government but with 1970–74 Conservative Government, comes back to [the] old myth that [a]

Conservative Government is our government. [We] got a rude shock in 1970-74, sort of action [one] might have expected from Labour Government. Also companies were under pressure because of the economic situation, particularly from 1973 onwards. So much breaking over them, they were floundering, angry, upset, many companies reacted against it.

Long run changes in the British political system can be subdivided into three categories. First, there are general changes which produce a sense of instability and insecurity and give firms a need to analyse the significance of changes for their businesses. In many ways, this is a similar influence to that exerted by the economic and political climate in the mid-1970s discussed above, but in this case the changes are seen as more long run in character. Another respondent commented:

In Britain today, we have a declining economy, a political process that looks less precise than in the past, different set of pressures in society, all become apparent in [the] last decade in more dramatic way than in [the] past . . . now infinitely more complex, [an] appreciation that in order to compete effectively we need professional capable of analysing situation and helping to secure means of satisfying objectives.

Secondly, an important long run change is the disappearance of the 'establishment' in the sense in which it existed in the 1950s when much could be settled by a company chairman having a word in his club with a government minister. Matters are occasionally still settled in an informal way, but as one respondent commented, 'The whole area has become more complex, twenty years ago all that a major chairman needed to do was to meet the Chancellor at his club, have a word in his ear and say "This isn't on."' It probably never was quite as simple as that, but the conduct of relationships between business and government has changed over the last thirty years, if only because the London clubs are not the important meeting places they once were.

A third long run change has been the growing importance of 'cause' groups of various kinds such as environmental groups or consumer groups. A respondent referred to the social changes that had led to an increasing sophistication and success on the part of such groups. He commented:

When we think of strategies, we have to take that into account. In relations with government departments, if you had government on your side, that was all that mattered seven or ten years ago, now not simply enough, necessary to understand these groups, how you might deal with them – 'deal' in inverted commas – by confrontation or compromise.

The fourth general factor is simply that of imitation: the more companies develop a government relations function, the more other companies may feel that they need to follow their example. One respondent pointed out that there was much more communication between companies internationally than had once been the case, if only through intermediary channels such as management experts, and awareness of the rapid development of the government relations function in the United States diffused relatively rapidly. Seminars at the Corporate Responsibility Centre or the Industry and Parliament Trust have provided companies with an opportunity to learn about the government relations function and to discuss their experiences with other companies without giving away commercially sensitive information.

The organisation of the government relations function

The government relations function was not a large one in terms of staff employed in any of the companies visited. The largest unit was in a company with a total government relations staff of fourteen, including secretaries, although that was a Europe-wide operation. In many companies, the function was staffed by just one executive. However, a more typical pattern would be two or three executives in mid career, placed in a distinct government relations unit located relatively high up the company's decision-making structure. Companies differed in their practice as to whether government relations was organised separately from public relations, although often both functions were part of a corporate affairs, external affairs or public affairs division.

The range of tasks performed

The definition of the government relations function used in this book (p. 96) makes a distinction between tasks relating to the external environment and tasks relating to the company's internal needs. Clearly, there is a close link between the two sets of tasks. For example, monitoring political developments is concerned with the analysis of the external environment for internal purposes. The performance of the strategic co-ordination function of government relations involves, among other things, ensuring that information and advice provided by a government relations division within a company is related to the more effective handling of the company's external relations. Nevertheless, the internal/external distinction is of some assistance in analysing what government relations divisions do.

As far as external relations are concerned, practice varies from company to company in terms of how much contact with government is actually channelled through the government relations division itself, although it is extremely unlikely that all contacts would be handled in this way. The function of a government relations division is to co-ordinate the large number of contacts a company has with government at a variety of levels. One respondent stressed that it was very important that at least some of the work should be done by the division itself and that it should not be confined to a co-ordinating function, however important that was. At a minimum, most units keep track of contacts between the company and government, so that if an executive or director is meeting a particular politician or civil servant, it is known whether he or she has met anyone from the company before and, if so, for what purpose. Some companies have quite sophisticated 'senior executive calling programmes' to ensure that contact is maintained with ministers, shadow ministers and key civil servants.

There is considerable variation in the extent to which EC questions are handled by government relations divisions. At one extreme, one of the companies interviewed did not cover the EC as part of its government relations work because 'A large number of directors don't see how we fit into it although we trade with Europe.' At the other extreme, some companies had offices in Brussels with specialist staff. However, in nearly half of the companies interviewed, a limited interest or none at all was taken in EC matters by the government relations division. This is, of course, an area in which even large companies rely to a considerable extent on their trade associations. In part, this is because the Commission encourages discussions with European level representative organisations, as distinct from direct contacts with companies, although such direct contacts do take place right up to Commissioner level. Another consideration is that maintaining a Brussels office is expensive; £100,000 annually according to the CBI (*Financial Times*, 9 April 1984). Thus, it is mainly giant transnationals such as Esso and Unilever that have public affairs representatives in Brussels. A compromise solution is to have a London based executive who spends a number of days each week in Brussels; for example, Marks & Spencer sends a representative to Brussels for three days a week (*Financial Times*, 9 April 1984).

The internal services that government relations divisions provide for their own line managers can be divided into three categories: the dissemination of information through newsletters and briefing papers; 'hand holding' in terms of providing guidance to line managers faced with a task with political implications (e.g. appearing before a Parliamentary committee); and building up the political capabilities of line managers. All these tasks amount to providing a rudimentary political education to line managers who have little understanding or experience of political matters.

The limitations of the government relations function

Since the early 1970s, government relations divisions have been formed in a considerable number of large firms operating in Britain. They are clearly an important new factor in the conduct of relations between business and government. However, one must be careful not to overstate their importance. Such divisions often face two particular limitations: a lack of integration in the decision-making process in many firms; and an absence of control over the firm's involvement in business interest associations.

Integration into the firm's decision-making processes

Before they can contribute effectively to a firm's decision-making processes, most government relations divisions have to overcome a credibility problem within the company. Directors and executives may agree that the political environment has a considerable impact on the firm's profitability, and ultimately its survival. Nevertheless, they may be suspicious of a function which cannot point to a quantifiable result on the bottom line; they may argue that political forecasting is even more unreliable than economic forecasting; and that even if political outcomes can be forecast, there is little that a company can do to influence the course of events. As one house magazine commented in a feature on the company's government relations unit, 'there may still be colleagues who are keen to know how a small team of retired diplomats and young economists contribute to the business of a multi-national insurance group'. It was clear from the interviews that a number of government relations units had experienced or were experiencing difficulties in establishing their credibility within the company, a finding confirmed by subsequent informal discussions with government relations executives at seminars. A number of units appeared to depend on the personal patronage of a board member, which would be lost if he left the board.

A number of companies visited were clearly taking the incorporation of political considerations into their corporate planning process more seriously. As one respondent commented, 'Ten years ago the political situation was a footnote to the business analysis, now a more fundamental part.' Another respondent remarked, 'Our planning staff are doing the econometric guessing, but we also need an input on social and political guesses.'

Government relations divisions and business interest associations

If government relations divisions are seeking to provide strategic co-ordination of a firm's political activities, it might be supposed that their responsibility would extend to the firm's participation in business interest associations. In fact, this is generally not the case; most associational activity is dealt with by members of line management. There are a number of reasons why this should be the case. Clearly, the personnel department has a particular interest and expertise in employers' organisation activities. Many trade association activities concern highly technical questions and demand the participation of the relevant expert from the firm's staff, although this does not remove the need for some overall co-ordination.

Of more general importance is the location of government relations divisions within a company and, in a sense, their relative weakness within the organisation. Government relations units are generally near, but not at the top of, a company's organisational structure, often staffed by high fliers in mid career. They thus generally have access to directors and top managers (particularly if they are in the same building and have access to the highest level dining facility), but this access does not enable them to co-ordinate the behaviour of higher ranking personnel. Participation in major CBI committees and the leading committees of key trade associations will generally be the responsibility of these senior managers. Conversely, there will be many specialist committees within trade associations (or specialist trade associations) that are the concern of a particular product division or subsidiary company. Given the decentralised character of many British companies, it will be difficult for the government relations division (which is unlikely to have a large staff) to exercise much influence over these activities. Indeed, as one respondent commented, 'No one in [the] company has any idea how many trade associations [this] company belongs to or what their worth is.'

Even if the company decides that it does want to co-ordinate its business association activities, the internal political costs of doing so may be too great. Another respondent commented that subsidiary companies were 'determined to hang on to what they have . . . I have to be very careful, I co-ordinate on occasions'. One firm which has devoted considerable effort to co-ordinating its business association activities does so through a division which is completely distinct from its government relations function. In another case, where a company chairman found that a product division was advocating a policy line in one of its trade associations which was contrary to corporate policy, the chairman decided that the trade association structure required changing rather than the company's own arrangements! (It was subsequently reformed.) What all this suggests is that the political activities of a firm are highly complex, being handled at a number of levels through a variety of channels, with attempts at co-ordination generally being weak.

Political consultants

There has been a considerable increase in recent years in the number of political consultants offering services to firms and business associations. The 1984 directory of the Public Relations Consultants' Association (PRCA) lists twenty-six firms offering some kind of specialised political consultancy service, although there are a number of firms that are not PRCA members. The most frequent form of specialisation is in parliamentary affairs, although there are some firms that offer advice on relations with local authorities, whilst one specialises in 'privatisation'.

Why should firms or associations wish to use a consultancy rather than develop their own expertise in political relations? First, for a medium sized firm, the likely volume of work may not justify the development of an 'in house' government relations division. Similarly, a smaller trade association may prefer to subcontract much of its work, especially parliamentary work, to a consultancy. However, it is clear that many larger firms and associations also make use of political consultants. Perhaps they are convinced by claims such as those made by Charles Barker, Watney and Powell, almost certainly the largest political consultancy with a staff of sixteen in 1985, who state in their promotional literature that government affairs departments or MPs retained as advisers cannot provide 'the breadth of experience, availability and expertise of a recognised independent parliamentary consultancy'. Even a trade association with its own parliamentary unit, or a firm with a government relations division, may find it too complex a task to keep up with the interests of over 600 MPs, not to mention peers, and may therefore use a consultancy for advice and information.

David Wedgwood, who runs a specialised government relations consultancy, categorised his work in an interview under two main headings, 'intelligence' and 'operational'. Under 'intelligence', three main tasks were carried out:

1. Monitoring – checking parliamentary papers, reports by party research departments, political journals, etc. for material relevant to clients.
2. Intelligence – providing background information and interpretation, sometimes providing digests of material for clients.
3. Research – a need for more in-depth research might arise from the results of monitoring or from the discussion of future plans.

Another consultant confirmed that much of the work was humdrum, routine monitoring of parliamentary reports for issues that might affect clients. Charles Barker, Watney and Powell have additional staff who carry out this task when Parliament is sitting. They provide a daily information service for their clients, involving extracts or the whole document covering subjects of interest. This is sent out daily by post, although urgent material is sent by telephone and telex or conveyed by dispatch rider in the London area. Advance warning is given of relevant parliamentary questions.

David Wedgwood identified three main tasks under the 'operational' heading:

1. Counselling – a question of keeping the client in the picture, he may want more feedback or to talk to a sympathetic MP.
2. Passive representation – getting the client together with MPs, civil servants, pressure groups.
3. Active representation – where there is a specific objective in mind; getting something raised, launching a piece of legislation or trying to check or stop it.

The UK consultancy service provided by Charles Barker, Watney and Powell deals primarily with putting over a particular case to decision-makers at Westminster, and to civil servants. As they explain in their promotional literature, 'This involves promoting, opposing or amending legislation, briefing MPs at appropriate moments, suggesting useful parliamentary questions, encouraging unofficial "interest" groups and assisting with deputations and approaches to Ministers.' It is clear that offering an intensive service of this kind can be difficult and time consuming: for example, technically correct amendments to bills may need to be drafted at standing committee stage, which often involves working to a strict time limit. Consequently, consultancy services are not cheap, with a standing fee often being supplemented by a 'taxi meter' rate.

Charles Barker, Watney and Powell provide the secretariat for several All Party Parliamentary Committees including the Parliamentary Information Technology Committee and the All Party Motor Industry Group. This kind of work, by its nature, is not very profitable for a consultancy, but all party groups provide an opportunity for the exchange of information, and can help a consultancy to build up a reputation for expertise in a particular area. There has been some controversy about the role of all party groups, and this topic will be returned to later.

A number of consultancies have started to offer an advisory service on EC matters, but this is not an easy area in which to work, for number of reasons. First, British companies are not always as interested in Community affairs as might be supposed. This could be because Community proposals generally take a long time to come to fruition, and companies often wake up to their implications only when an adverse directive is about to be implemented by the UK Government. Second, maintaining an office in Brussels, with sorties to other relevant locations such as Strasbourg, is expensive, although some consultancies get round this problem by retaining someone on a part-time basis. Third, consultants have to be very careful not to upset relationships between European level industry associations and their British affiliates. Nevertheless, despite all these difficulties, as Charles Barker, Watney and Powell point out in promotional literature, 'permanent company representation in Brussels is costly and reliance on European trade associations can result in a company's position being lost by inter-company trade-offs'. It is likely that in the future companies will make more use of consultancy services which cover the European level of decision making.

Should consultants be controlled?

Consultants do not find it difficult to obtain access to MPs, peers and other decision-makers. One consultant has claimed that he was able to have a brief favourable to his client placed in a minister's weekend red box (House of Commons, 1985, p. 8). However, many consultants focus their attention on Westminster where doors are generally open to them because they provide information which MPs, with their limited research facilities, cannot readily obtain elsewhere.

Reputable consultants are always careful to explain who they are working for when they contact an MP. Nevertheless, there has been growing concern about the role of political consultants. In part, this has been a reaction to a growth in the amount of parliamentary lobbying, and to its greater professionalisation and organisation. There have also been particular incidents which have given rise to concern. The Public Relations Consultants Association was formed in 1969 in response to widespread concern about a case a couple of years earlier concerning a public relations consultancy which was retained by the then military government in

Greece. In 1985, the Leader of the House of Commons rebuked a public relations consultancy for offering to pay the travelling expenses of the Commons Select Committee on the Environment to enable it to examine an advanced system for disposing of radioactive waste in Sweden. Mr Biffen made it clear that it would be improper for any select committee, conducting an independent inquiry on behalf of the House, to accept funding from an interested private party (*Financial Times,* 6 April 1985). An inquiry into the role of Parliamentary lobbyists had already been started by the Select Committee on Members' Interests in 1982 and a report was eventually published in 1985. The recommendations of this rather disappointing report are discussed more fully later in the chapter.

It should be pointed out that those consultancies which are members of the PRCA are required to subscribe to a fifteen point code of consultancy practice which requires them to publish a list of their clients, state whether they employ or retain any MPs, peers or councillors, and what their annual fee income is within a number of bands. Member firms of the PRCA are not allowed to propose to their clients any action which would constitute an improper influence on government or the legislature, and are not allowed to offer inducements to legislators to favour clients. Member firms are not permitted to serve some announced cause while actually serving an undisclosed special or private interest. Any infringements are considered by the PRCA's Professional Practices Committee; three or four cases a year brought by dissatisfied clients or disgruntled practitioners might be considered by the committee. It should also be noted that consultancies which were interviewed made it clear that there were certain kinds of business they would not handle, such as, for example, work from the South African Government or the government of the South African 'homeland'. Even if they were not influenced by ethical considerations, they would not wish to damage their carefully nurtured reputations.

Of course, not all political consultancies are members of the PRCA. There are three or four moderately sized political consultancies which are not PRCA members and which, as it happens, have attracted a considerable amount of press publicity. There may also be fifteen or twenty one or two person consultancies which are not PRCA members. It is not implied that firms which are not PRCA members do not adhere to high ethical standards.

However, it has to be said that there have been instances when the behaviour of self-designated political consultants has fallen below the standards expected of members of the PRCA. In addition, some non-PRCA members, whilst they behave ethically, have a rather brash or abrasive style. Telling the newspapers 'how we put one over on the minister' does not help other consultants, even if it is a good self-advertisement.

One 'grey area' is that of consultancies run by MPs or peers. Members of Parliament are, of course, permitted to act as paid or unpaid advisers to trade associations and firms, and many of them do so, often on a large scale. Doig noted in 1986:

> The practice of hiring MPs as consultants has mushroomed in recent years. Today, out of 650 MPs, 150 now hold 280 consultancies between them. Of these, 99 are 'Parliamentary consultancies' – that is, they are hired to advise on Parliamentary affairs or represent interests in the House because of their skills and availability. Of the remainder, 39 own or are employed by consultancy or public relations firms, 20 act as consultants to financial firms, 102 are with commercial firms, and 18 are with public bodies. (Doig, 1986, p. 39)

MPs are required to record paid consultancies in the register of members' interests which is published annually, but this practice does not resolve the question of whether MPs should own, or be directors of consultancies. Sometimes the underlying issues are raised in a tangential way. For example, there have been complaints by MPs about overcrowding in the Palace of Westminster; at different times, this concern has focused on the use of American students as research assistants by MPs, or the alleged misuse of meeting rooms. As Jordan comments, 'That complaint is about members, more or less, selling access to the House' (Jordan, 1985, p. 178).

It has been suggested that some all party groups (or 'registered groups' as some of them are now styled) were formed largely to take advantage of parliamentary meeting facilities and the status of being a parliamentary group. There are probably around eighty such groups linked to a common interest, such as industry, and about a hundred based on an interest in an overseas country. Following a debate in October 1984, a motion was passed restricting the use of the term 'parliamentary' in relation to all party groups.

There is reason to believe that the facilities used by Parliamentary 'lobby' journalists may sometimes have been misused. For example, a lobby journalist could obtain parliamentary documents earlier than they would be available from the Stationery Office and without charge; they could then be passed to a commercial client. The Deliverer of the Vote (a Commons Official) has stated:

> There are several organisations, one particular one which we regard as extremely suspect in regard of its activities within the House because we do not believe that they in fact perform the correct duties of Lobby correspondents – they are acting as an agency and obtaining an enormous amount of documents from us. (House of Commons, 1985, p. 77)

Following a Commons debate in December 1985 which discussed recommendations in a report from the Select Committee on Members' Interests, new registers have been established for journalists, for secretaries and research assistants, and for parliamentary groups. Pass holders in these groupings are required to record any other gainful occupation where their privileged access to Parliament is relevant. However, as the Institute of Public Relations has remarked, 'Some of the abuses of Parliamentary access currently being practised stem from the difficulties of obtaining public information . . . there should be speedier and easier access to public documents from the Houses of Parliament' (House of Commons, 1985, p. 36). The Sales Office provides a service to Parliamentary Agents who require it in connection with private bills, to public bodies who have an interest in legislation going through the House, and to any other public body which can convince the Deliverer of the Vote that they have an entitlement to a service other than that provided by the Stationery Office. If Commons documents were put on sale to the public at the time that they are made available to MPs, less firms and trade associations might need to employ consultants to obtain information speedily to which they are surely entitled.

Reference has been made to a number of recommendations made by the Select Committee on Members' Interests on the issues raised by the expansion of professional parliamentary lobbying. The committee proceeded from the premise that 'It is the right of any citizen to lobby his Member of Parliament and if he considers that his case can be better advanced with professional assistance he has every right to avail himself of that assistance' (House of Commons, 1985, p. iii). It could be objected that what is at issue are not the rights of the citizen, but the purchase of influence by the privileged, although in practice all that is usually being bought is advice on who to approach and how to present a case effectively. It should also be remembered that an ill conceived piece of legislation which does not take account of legitimate objections may not only harm the owners of an enterprise, but also the workers who derive their livelihood from it.

The central issue that the committee had to face was whether there should be some form of register of lobbyists, and it is the rejection of this idea which is the most disappointing feature of the report. Registration could help to ensure that all consultancies adhered to standards of the kind required of PRCA members. However, the committee seems to have been influenced by a letter from the Leader of the House in which he argued that 'it is unconstitutional for a limited number of bodies or individuals to be given formal preferential access to Parliament to present their own views or the views of others' (House of Commons, 1985, p. 82). Whether there is a difference of principle between giving certain journalists preferential access to Parliament as members of the Lobby or the Press Gallery, and giving preferential access to registered lobbyists who adhere to a code of conduct, is open to question. In any event, the PRCA envisaged a licence to practice that would extend across the whole field of public relations consultancy practice, not merely in relation to Parliamentary work.

The committee was also concerned about the problem of defining a lobbyist. They took evidence from the United States which showed that the Supreme Court had defined a lobbyist in terms of payment; having the lobbying function as his principal purpose; and seeking to influence the passage or defeat of legislation through direct communication with a member of Congress. Critics of the law who want more regulation of lobbyists are concerned about the way in which the Supreme Court limited the reach of the statute to persons whose principal purpose is to influence legislation (see House of Commons, 1985, p. 15). However, these definitional difficulties are not insuperable. If consultants who registered were given an entitlement to use certain facilities in the Palace of Westminster, rather than confining such privileges to journalists, the inducement to register would create a form of self-definition.

Whatever the defects of such an arrangement, it is surely preferable to a situation in which some consultants are subject to the discipline of PRCA regulations, but others are not required to disclose who they are acting for, and who within them or advising them holds public office. The absence of regulation may lead to suspicions that abuses are more frequent than they actually are, discrediting not only consultants, but the whole political process.

Conclusions

There does seem to be a trend towards a greater involvement by firms in political questions, a trend that has not been reversed or even halted by the Thatcher Government; indeed, privatisation and the shedding of state functions raise issues which have to be considered by firms, both individually and collectively. Moreover, the trend towards greater regulation of firms in the environmental, consumer protection and safety and health areas continues unabated, if only because of EC initiatives.

This greater involvement had made many firms aware that they need to develop a more sophisticated appreciation of how political issues affect them, and a capability to take political action when necessary, even if they are sceptical about formal techniques of political risk analysis. As was discussed earlier in the chapter, one way of developing an ability to interpret political developments and relate them to the achievement of the firm's business objectives is through the 'in house' government relations division. However, such units often have problems in building up confidence in their expertise within their companies. Firms often turn to consultants as well, partly because of their specialist knowledge of such arenas as Parliament or local government, but also because a consultant can bring a greater breadth to a task because he or she is simultaneously handling a wider range of problems. A consultant can also be freer of the constraints which can arise from internal company politics. In addition to their development of government relations divisions, and their greater use of consultants, firms continue to rely on the various business associations to which they belong as a means of influencing public policy, and it is the work of such associations which forms the focus of the next two chapters.

6 The CBI and Other National Intersectoral Associations

The most publicly prominent representatives of business are the national intersectoral associations claiming to speak for business as a whole, most importantly the CBI, but also the Institute of Directors (IoD) and the Association of British Chambers of Commerce (ABCC). Prominence is not the same thing as influence, and in many respects the sector specific trade associations and employers' organisations probably achieve more of concrete value for their members. Nevertheless, one must not underrate organisations such as the CBI, and British business is better organised as a collective interest at the national level than in the United States or Canada, where there is no one organisation that is regarded as the principal spokesman for business.

In a book written by the author with David Marsh, completed in 1976, the conclusion was reached 'that the CBI had relatively little impact on the major issues which have dominated British politics since its formation . . . it has been able to extract detailed concessions which are of benefit to its members' (Grant and Marsh, 1977, p. 207). In particular, we argued that the CBI as an organisation representing manufacturing industry lacked 'a direct sanction equivalent to the political strike or to the City's ability to move vast amounts of capital out of the country' (Ibid., p. 213).

It could be argued that our book was published just at the time that the CBI was undergoing a major revitalisation, and therefore, although our conclusions might apply to the first decade or so after the organisation's formation in 1965, they did not apply to its second decade. In the mid-1970s the CBI had experienced a major trauma, coinciding, and in part prompted by, one of the worst

117

periods of crisis in Britain's post-war history. During the 1970–74 Heath Government, the CBI had done its best to help the Government, most notably by designing and implementing a voluntary price restraint initiative in 1971–72 which did help to restrain manufacturing prices. This initiative was followed by the imposition of statutory price controls, leaving many of the CBI's members feeling cheated.

Nevertheless, the CBI did its best to help the Government with its initiative in tripartite economic policy-making launched in 1972, but the Government often seemed more concerned with the views of the TUC than with those of the CBI. This was not surprising when one considers that the Government had to win over the TUC from a hostile stance, whereas it already had the qualified support of the CBI, but a further complication was the antipathy of the Prime Minister to the CBI. In his study of the Heath Government, Holmes quotes Lord Armstrong as stating in an interview that the Prime Minister 'was often rude to the CBI – he thought they talked rubbish', and a senior policy adviser commented, 'I've been to a number of dinners between Heath and industrialists and Heath always abused them – he never got on with them' (Holmes, 1982, p. 51).

This difficult period culminated in some widely reported remarks made by the CBI's then director-general, Campbell Adamson, a few days before the general election of February 1974, which were interpreted as a repudiation of the Government's Industrial Relations Act. The possibility that these remarks might have contributed to the narrow defeat of the Conservatives was too much for some companies, already irritated by what they saw as Adamson's liberalism, and a number of leading firms resigned or suspended their membership. Under the presidency of Ralph Bateman (1974–76), the CBI took a more combative attitude to the Labour Government than to its Conservative predecessor, but Bateman confessed that 1975 had been the CBI's 'most difficult' year (CBI Annual Report, 1975, p. 5).

The real transformation of the CBI as an organisation was brought about under the presidency of Lord Watkinson (1976–78), who was joined as director-general in February 1976 by (later Sir) John Methven. In January 1976, the CBI Council received the *Report of a Committee of Enquiry into the CBI's Aims and Organisation* (often known as the Plowden–Partridge report) which was intended to point the way 'to stronger interpretation and execution of CBI's role and purpose' (CBI Annual Report, 1976, p. 23). Among the practical consequences of this report were the creation of a President's Committee of top level industrialists to offer advice on strategy and tactics, and a decision to seek a higher public profile for the CBI, reflected in the launching of an annual conference in 1977, and the creation of a Parliamentary unit.

One should not exaggerate the consequences of these changes of style. The CBI did obtain more television coverage, and more coverage from papers such as the *Sun* and the *Mirror* to which it had previously paid little attention; the zenith (or perhaps the nadir) of this strategy was reached with the appearance of the president on the popular radio programme, the Jimmy Young Show. The annual conference had a certain novelty value, and attracted additional media publicity for the CBI. The fear that it would lead to backwoodsmen propounding reactionary views in public that would embarrass the CBI was largely confounded, but the majority of overwhelmingly male business persons turned out to be rather dull and hesitant speakers in public. The conference did bring out into the open differences of political emphasis between business persons, and also reflected a shift to a more 'hard line' approach that was also apparent at the time in the Conservative Party.

However, like the Conservative Party conference, the CBI conference did not take any binding decisions (it did not even have a voting system that reflected the varying importance of different firms), it simply 'communicated a mood' to the organisation's leadership. Policy formation within the organisation was sometimes influenced in a rather indirect way, but awkward decisions, such as that to back proportional representation, did not have to be pursued. The CBI Council remained the formal ruling body of the CBI, although its size meant that in practice policy was hammered out in the various specialist committees, with the President's Committee providing general guidance on strategy and tactics. The conference's main value was as a platform for expounding the CBI's views. It did not turn business persons into public figures in a way comparable to some of their trade union counterparts. An NOP market research survey in 1979 found that barely one in ten of those interviewed could identify the CBI's director-general, compared with two-thirds who recognised Len

Murray of the TUC, and 87 per cent who identified Rod Stewart, a popular singer.

During this period, the CBI made a vigorous effort to expand its membership, particularly among groups that had not previously joined the organisation such as auditors, advertising agents, accountants and stockbrokers. As suggested in Chapter 4, one consequence may have been to diminish its value as a voice for manufacturing interests, as distinct from business as a whole. In any event, the recruiting campaign was a success, and by 1982 the CBI had 18 000 direct members, compared with under 12 000 in 1972. The CBI no longer publishes detailed membership figures in its annual report which allowed outside commentators to observe the ebb and flow of members (see Grant and Marsh, 1977, p. 38). Probably many of the new members were relatively small firms. However, as Lord Watkinson commented in 1976, the CBI 'primarily resolves at present around the pivot of the hundred top manufacturing companies' (Watkinson, 1976, p. 146). It is the CBI's apparent ability to speak for these major companies in a highly concentrated economy that is the main source of its influence with government.

One of the main disappointments of the revitalisation of the CBI in the late 1970s was the failure to boost employer solidarity through a strike fund. The incoming president, Sir John Greenborough, noted in the 1978 annual report, 'employers must find ways of working together for greater solidarity, so that they are not picked off one by one' (CBI Annual Report, 1978, p. 3). This led to a proposal for a strike insurance fund launched in 1979, but not enough large companies were prepared to back the idea and it was shelved. Larger companies felt that the scheme might not be commercially beneficial, especially if too many small companies made calls on the fund. Personnel directors feared that the fund might exacerbate relations with the trade unions, and that belonging to it might stigmatise a company.

It is also apparent that not all Lord Watkinson's ideas for reforming the CBI, set out in his *Blueprint for Industrial Survival* published in 1976, were put into effect. Watkinson bluntly stated, 'it is surprising and greatly to the credit of successive presidents and director-generals that the CBI actually represents anything' (Watkinson, 1976, p. 146.). One of his central themes was that the CBI must seek to change the course of events rather than just reacting to them, and certainly the policy programmes produced by the CBI in the late 1970s and 1980s were as comprehensive, and probably better researched and documented, than anything of an equivalent character produced by a political party, although there was an understandable tendency to 'mudge and fudge' on issues like incomes policy which divide businessmen. However, it cannot be said that the CBI achieved Watkinson's vision of each senior minister having a 'CBI shadow, in a manner somewhat similar to the practice followed by the opposition in Parliament' (Ibid., p. 147).

The CBI and the 1974–79 Labour Government

Whatever the limits of the organisational reforms of the CBI – and there is no doubt that as an organisation it was in much better shape by the end of the 1970s – the period of the 1974–79 Labour Government was one of considerable success for the CBI. It was able to persuade the Government to introduce tax relief on stock appreciation that turned out to be worth thousands of millions of pounds to companies; the Government's whole industrial strategy was modified from one of state intervention to co-operation with industry, so that even a proposal for a watered down form of planning agreement was dropped; and it saw the eventual defeat of the devolution proposals which the CBI regarded as a major threat to British business. Above all, the CBI waged a successful campaign against the implementation of the Bullock proposals on industrial democracy.

It was also, rather unusually for a business interest association, able to mobilise its members to frustrate government policy. In February 1978, the Government announced its intention to insert clauses in its contracts with private sector companies pledging adherence to its pay limits. For five weeks, the CBI persuaded most of its members not to sign new contracts containing the clauses, forcing the Government to make substantial modifications to its policy. The CBI hailed this cohesion 'as a most important milestone on the road to improved employer solidarity' (CBI Annual Report, 1978, p. 3). Unfortunately for the CBI, in July 1978 its members refused to repeat the action when the Government reintroduced the clauses for the new pay round. CBI members were reluctant to be seen to be opposing pay restraint, although the Government was eventually obliged to drop the clauses after a defeat in the House of Commons.

The experience of the 1974–79 Labour Government might seem to suggest that the CBI is a more influential organisation than was allowed for in the Grant and Marsh study. In a sense, this is the case: the CBI was more successful in 1974–79 than it was either under Labour from 1965 to 1970, or the Conservatives from 1970 to 1974. As one CBI activist was reported as commenting: 'The representational game that the CBI is in, is a con trick based on propaganda and self-confidence. What Methven has done is to give the CBI head office and its leading people the self-confidence they lack to pursue that con trick' (*Financial Times*, 6 November 1978). Nevertheless, it would be as dangerous to generalise about the potential for political influence of the CBI on the basis of the experience of the 1974–79 period, as it would be to generalise on the basis of the 1965–74 period. First, there is reason to believe that certain special conditions were present in the 1974–79 period which are unlikely to be repeated. Second, the CBI has underlying structural weaknesses which place limits on its ability to exert political influence.

In many respects, the CBI was pushing at an open door between 1974 and 1979. Many members of the Labour Government sympathised with its objections to the policies adopted by the Labour Party in opposition. In particular, Harold Wilson as Prime Minister had little time for extensive state intervention of the kind envisaged by Mr Benn, and worked hard and successfully to influence industrial policy in a direction which would be more acceptable to businessmen. As far as the Bullock Report was concerned, many members of the Cabinet were lukewarm about its proposals to say the least, and the trade union movement was itself divided about the desirability of industrial democracy and the form that it should take. However, with the desertion of many leading members of the Labour right to the Social Democrats, any future Labour Government is likely to be more determined to implement an interventionist strategy. Nevertheless, it has to be admitted that an interventionist strategy which stops short of wholesale nationalisation necessarily relies to some extent on the co-operation of business, and therefore draws government into a bargaining relationship with organisations such as the CBI.

A second special factor was that for much of its term of office, the Labour Government lacked a parliamentary majority. The CBI has always been able to make use of the House of Lords to modify legislation in a way that benefits its members, but between 1975 and 1979 it was also possible to defeat the Government in the House of Commons. Towards the end of this period, the CBI built up an effective lobbying system modelled on that of the National Farmers' Union and had a number of successes in influencing Liberal, Nationalist and Ulster Unionist members. The CBI could replicate such successes under a future Labour Government that was dependent on parliamentary support from other parties, a not impossible scenario.

However, for the greater part of its life the CBI has faced Conservative Governments, and in many respects these pose greater problems for the organisation than Labour Governments. With a Labour Government the CBI is usually quite successful at obtaining detailed concessions through 'behind the scenes' lobbying if such lobbying is not successful, it can openly attack the Labour Government in a way that is bound to please its members. Rather greater problems occur with a Conservative Government. The CBI President from 1980 to 1982, Sir Ray Pennock, was warned by Sir John Methven that 'holding presidential office under a Tory Government would be much more testing than under Labour, much more searching and much more vulnerable'. Sir John commented, 'Because the vast majority of our members support it, we must strive consciously and sensitively to avoid any semblance of undermining the Government in the process' [of criticising it] (*Financial Times*, 26 May 1982).

The CBI and the Thatcher Government

These underlying difficulties manifested themselves in the CBI's relationship with the Thatcher Government, particularly in the first couple of years. The combination of a world recession and the Thatcher Government's policies, especially its willingness to allow the exchange rate to appreciate substantially, led to a drop of 6.5 per cent in industrial production in the UK in 1980, and a drop of 4.0 per cent in 1981. (Commission of the EC figures.) The fear of many companies that they might be forced out of business produced increasing criticisms of government policies among CBI members, notably in hard hit regions such as the north west and the West Midlands. Responding to these fears, the new CBI director-general, Sir Terence Beckett, made a speech at the 1980 CBI conference which promised a 'bare knuckle fight' with the Government. The speech received a standing ovation, but did not go down so well with some CBI members who resigned from the organisation, thus repeating the 1974 crisis. The CBI's standing was not improved when, the day after the conference, the president and the director-general went to Downing Street to inform the Prime Minister of the worries of industrialists, only to emerge on the pavement apparently empty handed and declaring that Mrs Thatcher's performance had been 'magnificent'. As one of the industrialists who took his firm out of the CBI commented, 'They went in like Brighton rock and came out like Turkish delight.'

Under the presidency of Sir Campbell Fraser (1982–84), the CBI drew closer to the Conservative Government, too close for the liking of some members. Nevertheless, the CBI did appear to have reached a *modus vivendi* with the Government, and could thus criticise it on specific issues without appearing to undermine its basic policies. As Sir Ray Pennock put it, 'We have now got the Government to understand the realities of industry without being so loud as our more vociferous members might want' (*Financial Times*, 4 November 1983).

In private the CBI was more candid in its criticisms of government policies than in public, particularly in discussions between CBI officials and the Department of Trade and Industry, which continued its traditional role of being the Government department closest to the CBI. For its part, the Government made a number of policy concessions to the CBI, most importantly on the abolition of the employers' national insurance surcharge. However, in the same Budget, the Government made changes in capital allowances against corporation tax which the CBI considered 'would cause serious problems for many companies' (CBI Annual Report, 1984, p. 9).

Tensions between the CBI and the Government continued to surface from time to time. In the summer of 1985, after complaints by the CBI about the high level of interest rates, the Chancellor, Nigel Lawson, told companies that they must borrow less and curb wage rises. The CBI responded by complaining that high mortgage rates were 'an increasingly sensitive factor in wage bargaining' (*Financial Times*, 27 June 1985). At a meeting of the National

Economic Development Council in September, the Chancellor tried to stop Sir Terence Beckett from making a highly critical statement calling on the Government to 'untie our shoelaces' and allow British businesses to compete on equal terms with other countries. After an intervention by the TUC general secretary, Norman Willis, Sir Terence was allowed to finish his statement, but the Chancellor did not allow any debate on broad economic issues (*Financial Times*, 26 September 1985). Despite these occasional public disputes, it is clear that some Tory moderates felt let down by the CBI, who they considered could have been more vigorous in resisting Government policies damaging to manufacturing industry. Sir Ian Gilmour complained that the CBI 'has become little more than an adjunct of the Conservatives' (Gilmour 1983, p. 195).

Structural weaknesses of the CBI

Although the CBI managed to patch up its relations with the Thatcher Government, the organisation's underlying structural weaknesses remained or were exacerbated by new developments. When I interviewed firms for the study of the CBI with Marsh in the mid 1970s, a number of firms, especially large firms, indicated that the CBI embraced too broad a spectrum of interests to be an authentic representative of their own particular interests, and had to make too many compromises to enable it to be a forceful critic of government policies.

This criticism of 'stifling breadth' re-emerged when I interviewed large firms for my work on government relations divisions in the early 1980s. Indeed, it had even more validity than in the early 1970s, considering the way in which the CBI has broadened its membership since then. For example, a respondent in one major company commented, 'CBI is pretty useless, too broad a range of members to reach any worthwhile views'. Another company commented, 'our relations with CBI are friendly, but we're not very active . . . CBI has to represent a range of companies. As an oil industry and American international company, we have special interests that may not align with those of the CBI'. An American owned company that was not a CBI member commented:

CBI we regard as being totally non representative of British industry. We would not find it easy to readily conform to statements made on behalf of industry by people who tend to speak for British industry . . . If member of CBI, being represented in policies with which you may not agree, then [would be] forced to participate in committees to see policies are on lines we want. Can do without that.

Some foreign owned companies prefer to keep a low political profile in Britain, but many British companies (and some foreign ones) have allowed their leading managers to spend company time serving on CBI committees. At the same time as he was reorganising British Leyland, Sir Michael Edwardes found time to serve on the CBI President's Committee. He explained his reasons as follows:

It is no longer sufficient for companies to concentrate on internal efficiency and merely to shelter as far as possible from any adverse influences in their external environment. It is not essential to be outward-looking, to get in amongst these so-called external influences and try to bring about beneficial change, instead of acting defensively and accepting the political economic and commercial environment as immutable? (Edwardes, 1983, p. 260)

Although the CBI does receive valuable contributions of expertise from many of its member firms, its relationship with the chaotic system of industry level associations is more tenuous than one would hope for in a properly organised hierarchical system of industrial representation. Indeed, it might more properly be termed an 'umbrella' association rather than a 'peak' association. The Devlin Report (1972, p. 10) on industrial representation recommended that 'the CBI ought to derive its representative power primarily from its place at the head of a hierarchy of associations'. Devlin felt unable to recommend that the CBI's membership should be confined to associations, and the compromise that was put forward of restricting CBI membership to large firms was generally unpopular and simply alienated smaller firms from the report. Unfortunately, the unacceptability of the Devlin proposals to business finally quenched the enthusiasm that the CBI had had in the 1960s for rationalising the secondary system of industrial associations.

One of the strengths of the CBI has always been its ability to produce detailed, well thought out critiques of every aspect of government policy that has any relevance to the problems of business. Indeed, its capacity to undertake research to back its case has been enhanced in the 1980s. Its Industrial Trends Survey is widely regarded as the most authoritative reflection of the views of industrialists on economic prospects. In November 1984, the Industrial Trends Survey suggested that official figures for many manufacturing output were too low: a fortnight later they were revised upwards (CBI Annual Report, 1984, p. 9). From 1984, the Industrial Trends Survey was supplemented by a Distributive Trends Survey. The CBI's Pay Databank provides regular information on the level and content of pay settlements and changes in working time arrangements. Assessments of the economic situation, together with forecasts of economic prospects, are published regularly in the CBI Economic Situation Report and form a basis for the development of CBI policy.

All these activities add to the CBI's ability to make an effective contribution to the debate on economic policy. However, it should be noted that financial difficulties in the early 1980s, brought about in large part by the recession, led to the organisation's staff being cut back from 480 to 360. It is difficult to say what impact, if any, this had on the CBI's effectiveness, but it could undermine its ability to 'chip away' at government policies it considers unhelpful, an ability which has arguably been its real strength. Moreover, these cuts came at a time when the CBI was taking on new burdens, notably an 'unprecedented concern with local politics. Initially this interest focused on the question of the rates but the campaign has broadened out into a wide-ranging concern with the functioning of local government' (May, 1984, p. 34).

The CBI's competitors

Perhaps the main threat to its credibility that the CBI has faced in recent years has been the emergence of competitors on the national scene in the form of the Institute of Directors (IoD) and the Association of British Chambers of Commerce (ABCC). Neither of these is, of course, new organisations; indeed, they predate the CBI and its predecessors. The ABCC was founded in 1860 and was for a time the only national spokesman of business interests in Britain (see Ilersic and Liddle, 1960), and the IoD was founded in 1903, receiving its royal charter in 1906.

The IoD has undergone a complete transformation in recent years, to an extent that has evidently irritated the CBI from time to time. 'Ask them how many launderette owners they have as members,' one CBI official is reported to have said (*Sunday Times*, 29 August 1982). The IoD organises individual directors rather than firms or associations, so it is perfectly possible for a business person to be involved in both organisations. In the 1970s, its image was largely that of a club for businessmen, providing good lunches, cheap executive health checks, and an annual jamboree at the Albert Hall when directors listened to speeches while eating out of lunch boxes. However, under Walter Goldsmith as director-general (succeeded in 1984 by the former head of the Prime Minister's policy unit, Sir John Hoskyns), the Institute of Directors obtained a new reputation as an effective lobbying organisation, although the attractive selective benefits remained. Goldsmith claimed, 'A few years ago I think it could justifiably be said that we had not done the homework to back up our policies. That is no longer true' (*Sunday Times*, 29 August 1982).

The IoD's new importance was not only a reflection of its larger staff and new orientation, but also the fact that it tended to be a more loyal supporter of the Thatcher Government than the CBI, trying to talk up the economy at a time when the CBI's prognostications appeared to be more doom laden, and always ready to back new initiatives to curb the power of the unions. Government ministers often found what the IoD had to say more ideologically acceptable than the hesitations and reservations of the CBI, and the IoD is 'widely regarded as a major influence in shaping the Tory employment legislation' (Lewis and Wiles, 1984, p. 75). Sir John Hoskyns, outlining his strategy as director-general, commented, 'I . . . see the present Government as the first one we've had since the war with a chance of tackling the fundamental problems' (*The Director*, July 1984, p. 40).

The Thatcher Government also turned to the chambers of commerce movement as an authentic spokesman of the views of business, particularly smaller businesses. However, much of the

Table 6.1 *Staff and resources of national business associations in 1980*

	Income	Staff
CBI	£6 569 807	480 (approx)
IoD	£2 775 000	92*
ABCC	£231 153	12

* Includes seventeen in *The Director* publications.

attention has been concentrated on the local chambers rather than the ABCC. Many of the larger chambers are better resourced than the ABCC, and not all of them are even ABCC members. The Devlin Report commented, 'the ABCC overestimates its value and effectiveness at the top' (Devlin Report, 1972, p. 12). Nevertheless, under the Thatcher Government, the ABCC has been in the limelight rather more, and has been exerting influence in areas other than ones in which it has been traditionally strong such as taxation. In 1985, the ABCC published a policy paper on industrial decline which was considerably at variance with the Thatcher Government's approach to the problem. It attacked the lack of government policy towards industry, argued that the development of services should be treated as complementary to recovery and not as a substitute for it, and criticised the conception that high technology industries could take over from 'smokestack' industries which could then be allowed to die off.

Of course, one should not exaggerate the importance of the revitalisation of the IoD and ABCC. The CBI is still a better resourced organisation with a far larger staff than either the IoD or ABCC (see Table 6.1) and, although the latter two organisations may be able to exert greater influence on particular decisions, they cannot match the CBI in the breadth of its expertise and coverage of issues. Nevertheless, a survey carried out by EPIC (an industrial communications company) in 1984 found that 47 per cent of the managers and 58 per cent of the trade unionists interviewed thought that the CBI's influence over government had waned. Seventy-three per cent of the trade unionists and 30 per cent of the managers interviewed agreed that the IoD had more influence on government policies than the CBI.

However, well the CBI organises itself, the greatest impact on its ability to exert influence comes from the willingness of the government in office to bargain with the CBI, and this varies not only from one administration to another, but over time within one administration. At the same time, the CBI also has to decide what its strategic approach to bargaining with government is going to be. In the early 1970s, it was committed to tripartite bargaining with government and the unions; in the 1980s, it was less willing to value consensus as a goal in its own right. As Sir John Methven admitted in 1978, 'We've drawn away from tripartism . . . People have got to believe this place is independent. It is crucial' (*Sunday Times*, 5 November 1978). Methven explained the change of strategy as follows:

> The great difference between now and 1974 is that we have learnt that secret trilateral negotiations between unions, employers and Government don't work for us. They don't work because we are the weakest of the three. The TUC is master of arguing in public and negotiating in private . . . We have to argue the public case, to provide a national voice for industry that will influence public opinion and help to shift the Government that way. (*The Observer*, 5 November 1978)

However, that change of strategy should not be seen as irreversible. Even the CBI is capable of shifting on its anchor, of veering with the tide. In 1985, there were signs that the organisation was responding, if not to a new tide, at least to a fresh wind blowing from a quarter which it had not done for some time. In the spring of that year, the CBI published a consultation document, *Change to Succeed*, which was interesting as much for the questions it posed, as for the answers it provided. The criticisms of the excessive attention paid by government to the PSBR figure, or the calls for spending on cost effective capital projects in the public sector, were consistent with earlier CBI pronouncements. Even such 'wet' comments as that unemployment represents 'a tragic waste of human potential', is a 'social evil' and that 'Business cannot be divorced from the community in which it operates and support for free enterprise will wither if it seems that it provides no response to the challenge of unemployment' (CBI, 1985, p. 38) were not so surprising. I know from private conversations that many businessmen are genuinely worried about the damage that prolonged, large-scale unemployment is doing to the social fabric of Britain; unfortunately, many of them are reluctant to voice their worries in public for fear of giving aid and comfort to the Labour Party.

What was new and interesting about the document was its concern with questions of political reform. In effect, the CBI was suggesting to its members that they should consider lobbying for a series of constitutional changes such as the abolition of Budget secrecy, fixed term Parliaments and a Bill of Rights. A reference to proportional representation was particularly significant as in many ways it is the bell-wether of a more moderate, consensus building approach to Britain's problems. The CBI recalled the 1978 conference decision in favour of proportional representation and, although cautioning that the conference does not commit the whole organisation, noted that 'some members have said there are reasons to re-examine the situation' (CBI, 1985, p. 36). This statement could be seen as a concession to a small but influential group of businessmen, some of them declared Conservatives, who have been discreetly campaigning for proportional representation. (Among the members of this group were Sir Graham Wilkins of Beecham, Sir Adrian Cadbury of Cadbury–Schweppes and Sir Richard Cave of Thorn–EMI, as well as a number of prominent City figures.) Even so, it is interesting that the CBI has decided to revive an issue which by its own admission 'was not followed through' (CBI, 1985, p. 36) after the original conference decision.

The CBI and the TUC

The broader significance of employer–union relations

An examination of the course that relationships between the CBI and the TUC have taken also permits the exploration of two broader themes which are related to the central concerns of this book as a whole. One theme is the absence of employer solidarity in Britain. William Brown (1981, p. 79) comments, 'British employers are remarkable by comparison with other Europeans for their lack of solidarity.' Brown goes on to show that this does matter because the voluntaristic, decentralised British bargaining system has 'appalling power as an amplifier of inflation' (Ibid., p. 98). Government has then tried to solve these problems by imposing incomes policies, which not only fail to work but also place strains on the democratic system as a whole (Ibid., p. 98; see also Grant and Nath, 1984). The fact that inflation has not been as central a problem in the first half of the 1980s as it was in the 1970s does not mean that it will not recur in changed labour market conditions.

As noted earlier in the chapter, the CBI tried to build up employer solidarity in the late 1970s by introducing a strike fund. Sir John Methven, the CBI director-general, made it clear at the time that his thinking on the subject had been influenced by the operations of German employers. However, one cannot impose solidarity from the top down; it has to be nurtured and sustained by appropriate attitudes shared by the generality of employers. It could be argued that it is really only possible to build such solidarity in circumstances where employers trust one another to behave in a responsible fashion and to avoid unnecessary disputes with the unions. German employers are used to building co-operative relationships with the unions because of the whole legal framework of industrial democracy obliges them to do so (see Streeck 1984), although it should be added that it is easier to operate within such a framework in an environment where there is not the constant risk of inter-union disputes. However, there are deeper reasons for employer solidarity in Britain which predate post-war legislation. As Tylecote (1981, p. 33) points out:

We have to ask who gains, and who loses, from a firm's decision to participate in a strong employer organisation. The greatest gainers are the *other* firms – will the firm have their interests at heart? In Germany, yes, because of the Unternehmer tradition of solidarity, and the power of the banks with a stake in the whole industry; in Britain, there is no such cement to bind firms together.

Tylecote sees the poor organisation of British employers as a factor of central importance in explaining inferior British economic performance compared to West Germany; the question of poor economic performance is an implicit concern of this book. He comments, 'Germany resembles Britain in some important ways . . . but there is a crucial difference, which makes *any* econometric explanation difficult: the character of the employers' (Ibid.,

p. 155). Tylecote compares what he sees as the individualistic and short-sighted way in which British employers make decisions on wages (and other matters) with the ability of German employers to act collectively and for long-term objectives. The leaders of British employers, unlike their German counterparts, did not tour the country in the 1970s organising employer resistance to wage demands. 'On the contrary – they demanded that the government stop punishing firms for breaking the incomes policy (in Germany such punishment would have been administered by the employers' organisations themselves)' (Ibid., p. 162).

The two main themes that have been mentioned, the lack of employer solidarity and poor economic performance, are related to the specific question discussed here, the relationship between the CBI and the TUC, or rather the absence of an effective working relationship for much of the period since the formation of the CBI in 1965. Admittedly, there are those who would argue that the less the CBI has to do with the TUC the better. Certainly, the way in which the trade union movement conducts its own affairs often induces despair in those who believe that there is an important and constructive role for the movement to play in improving economic performance.

If one examines 'successful' liberal corporatist polities such as Austria, it is apparent that a key feature of the arrangements is an effective working relationship between organised capital and organised labour (see Katzenstein, 1984). The state may play a facilitating role but, on the whole, it stays in the background (see Marin, 1985). As Lehmbruch has observed, 'liberal corporatism as we understand it presupposes a clearing between unions and employers with regard to the overall goals of public economic policy' (Lehmbruch, 1979, p. 173). A properly functioning tripartite arrangement depends on the existence of the base line of the triangle: the employer–union relationship at the national, insectoral level.

Of course, in Britain bilateral policies operated by the CBI and TUC have been 'notably absent' (Brown, 1981, p. 99). There is no reason to suppose that they will be possible in the future. Indeed, the possibility of a major split in the ranks of the TUC, with perhaps the formation of a competing body, suggests that there is a risk that such employer–union co-operation may be more difficult in the future. The CBI might find co-operation with a moderate, breakaway trade union federation an attractive prospect, but that would not amount to effective employer–union co-operation of the kind found in Austria.

It might be argued that it does not really matter any more whether the CBI and the TUC are capable of having an effective working relationship. Britain in the 1980s has moved away from tripartism towards a state-led effort to redefine the place of trade unions in society. However, although the bargaining climate may have been fundamentally altered, tripartite arrangements may not have been completely wiped off the political agenda. The Labour Party's economic policy proposals published in the summer of 1985 envisage discussions on national economic issues between government, CBI and TUC. The state of CBI–TUC relations may become a live issue again.

CBI–TUC relationships

Before the CBI was formed in 1965, industrial relations matters were dealt with by the rather secretive British Employers' Confederation. An important motivation for the formation of the CBI was that it would be 'the right medium to enable employers to get closer to the TUC' (*The Times*, 15 September 1965). This hope seemed to be realised with the formation of a Joint Committee of the CBI and TUC in 1967, but regular and formal dialogue ceased after the passage of the 1971 Industrial Relations Act. However, contacts at staff level continued. Discussions at leadership level resumed after the election of a Labour Government in 1974 (*The Guardian*, 4 April 1974). (For a more detailed account of relations in the period up to 1974 see Grant and Marsh, 1977, pp. 150–2.)

In the late 1970s, the CBI started to take a harder line towards the unions, enchoing the shift of attitude of the Conservative leadership. Sir John Greenborough frankly admitted in 1978, 'Of course what we're trying to do is to create a countervailing power to the unions' (*The Observer*, 5 November 1978). There was a shift from an emphasis on the need to seek dialogue with the union movement to 'the need to review the role and power of the trade unions – a most sensitive topic but one which must be tackled' (CBI Annual Report, 1978, p. 3). The CBI took the view that abysmally poor profitability was related to an imbalance of bargaining power between employers and unions which favoured the unions. In order to produce proposals for redressing this perceived imbalance, the CBI set up a high-powered Balance of Power Steering Group chaired by Sir Alex Jarratt.

This group was involved in the ill-fated strike fund, but also recommended that the CBI broadly support the 'softly softly' strategy of industrial relations reform being followed by the 1979 Conservative Government's Employment Secretary, James Prior, which was embodied in the 1980 Employment Act. Some employers pressed for a tighter clampdown at the 1980 CBI conference. However, at the 1981 conference the Government was warned to tread carefully on further industrial relations legislation. Summing up a debate on employment law, Mr Chris Walliker, chairman of the CBI's Midlands Region noted that many industrialists were worried about changes in industrial relations law coming too far from the extreme right. He commented. 'I hope the new Employment Secretary does not put as much emphasis on the closed shop as the Conservative associations of Cheltenham Spa or Ascot do' (*Financial Times*, 3 November 1981).

The CBI generally supported the further changes contained in the 1982 legislation. At its 1983 conference, a cautiously worded resolution supporting further changes in industrial relations law was passed, although some delegates thought that the motion was too adversarial and others thought that it displayed exessive caution. Certainly, employers were united in condemning the type of militant trade union leadership shown in the miners' strike of 1984–85; one practical step that the CBI took in the dispute was to write to chief executives of companies urging energy savings to enhance the ability of the electricity industry to maintain power supplies indefinitely. Employers were also intrigued by the possibility of 'no strike' agreements which stressed the observance of procedures and the role of arbitration. However, there were uncertainties, and some differences of opinion, on whether there should be further legislation on, for example, strikes in essential services. In its 1985 strategy document the CBI was obliged to hedge its bets on further government action:

It is arguable that the situation has now been reached where any further legislative reform would intervene directly in industrial relations, in a way which has hitherto been regarded as

unacceptable. However, it may be that the need to improve
competitiveness makes it important that we consider such change.
(CBI, 1985, p. 47)

Apart from the CBI's stand on employment law, which was
broadly supportive of the Government's step-by-step approach, its
relations with the TUC were badly damaged by the collapse in
1980 of a draft agreement on the introduction of new technology
which was seen as a first step towards a more comprehensive
agreement covering technological change in industry. Despite
agreement between the leadership of the two organizations, it was
opposed by rank-and-file members of the CBI who 'chose to kill
the agreement because they were then in a favourable situation for
introducing technical change and saw the possibility of a national
agreement as making the introduction of new technology more
rather than less difficult' (Richardson, 1982, p. 355). In a careful
analysis of the episode, Richardson shows that there was a failure
on the part of the CBI to clear the agreement with its membership
as it was being formulated, and a reluctance to force the policy
through against significant minority opposition (Richardson,
1982). Drawing a general lesson from this episode, Richardson
comments: 'When we see the TUC and CBI as organisations
lacking the necessary strength to support tripartite or bipartite
structures, we are implying that their leaders do not have the
necessary attitudes or they possibly lack the necessary power, or
political skill, to implement agreements' (Ibid., p. 354).

Misunderstandings of this kind against the background of the
Thatcher Government's economic and industrial relations policies
not surprisingly led to a further deterioration in CBI–TUC relationships, even at staff level. Sir John Methven, in a posthumously
published interview, is reported to have said that Len Murray, the
then general secretary of the TUC, rejected all attempts to establish a personal working relationship with the director-general of
the CBI. (*The Guardian*, I May 1980). Reviewing the situation in
1983, an analysis in the *Financial Times* (4 November 1983)
commented:

The main reason for the CBI is plainly to have a relationship
with Government: it also used to have a relationship with
organised labour. Now, that relationship is even more patchy

than the recovery: it exists in tripartite form, like the National Economic Development Council and the Manpower Services Commission (but only in the latter does it amount to anything much): otherwise the two staffs never walk the few hundred yards across New Oxford Street to exchange views.

The TUC's assistant secretary, David Lea, commented: 'Many employers were glad to see unions on the floor, and there was the view that profits could get up off the floor – where they were too – and leave the unions down there' (*Financial Times*, ibid.). However, the 1984 crisis over continued TUC participation in the NEDC, resulting from a TUC boycott of the Council in response to the ban on trade unions at the Government Communications Headquarters, seems to have concentrated the minds of the CBI and TUC and brought them into a working relationship again. Together with the TUC and the National Economic Development Office, the CBI explored ways of making the Council 'more relevant to the economy's needs' (CBI Annual Report, 1984, p. 10). A paper on the reform of the Council was prepared jointly with the TUC and presented to the NEDC when the TUC returned in December. CBI worries about government policies may also have contributed to a revival of the CBI–TUC joint committee.

Nevertheless, the whole history of the CBI–TUC relationships since 1965 leads one to be cautious about the chances of an effective working relationship being constructed between the two organisations. As Richardson (1982, p. 351) points out, 'If tripartism is to work then it must probably be preceded by a bipartite consensus between the CBI and the TUC.' Such a consensus still seems unlikely. Although the preceeding discussion has concentrated on the CBI because of the focus of this book, it should not be presumed that all the faults and mistakes which have prevented the development of a better relationship with the TUC have been the responsibility of the employers.

A further complicating factor has been the divisions within the TUC about whether trade unions should accept money provided for union ballots by the Thatcher Government under their trade union legislation. Although the immediate expulsion of two leading unions (the engineers and the electricians) was avoided by a last minute compromise at the 1985 TUC, the underlying tensions remain. The possibility of a new trade union federation which might also embrace the breakaway miners' union based in Nottinghamshire has not entirely receded, although by mid 1986 it seemed less likely. Even so, the general secretary of the Electrical, Electronic, Telecommunication and Plumbing Union, Eric Hammond, did address a fringe meeting at the 1984 CBI conference and suggested that his union might seek CBI membership. The audience at first thought that this was a joke, but Mr Hammond stated that he intended to study the CBI's constitution to see if there was a way in which a trade union could join (*Financial Times*, 8 November 1984).

This rather bizarre idea has not been taken further, but there is a risk that if a breakaway trade union federation emerged, some industrialists might see it as in their interests to develop a closer relationship with it than with the TUC. However, what would be seen as meddling in the internal affairs of the union movement would probably be resented by union leaders and would further damage, perhaps beyond repair, the CBI's tenuous relationship with the TUC, which is likely to remain the body that organises the greater part of the trade union movement. If the CBI and TUC were able to develop a durable dialogue, it would be a sign of greater maturity on the part of both organisations.

7 Sectoral and Local Business Associations

As well as being represented by national intersectoral associations such as the CBI, businesses belong to a considerable variety of associations serving a sector of the economy or particular locality. The sectoral associations range from those serving particular products, through subsectoral organisations, to well-resourced associations serving, for example the motor industry or the chemical industry. The farmers have been a particularly influential sectoral group and are the focus of a section of this chapter. At the local level, businesses are represented through chambers of commerce and trade. In addition there are associations which represent importers and (less common) exporters.

The overall pattern of business representation in Britain at the sectoral and local level is characterised by high differentiation and low integration of the various associations which claim to speak for business. Even when product and subsector associations are affiliated to a sector-wide association, the relationship between the different levels is often a rather tenuous one. This situation is both a cause and consequence of the political weakness of business identified in Chapter 1.

One notable weakness is the relationship between the CBI and the sector and subsector associations; in many ways, the CBI could better be termed an 'umbrella' rather than a 'peak' association. It will be recalled that the CBI organises both business associations and firms, although firms provide by far the greater part of its revenue. A firm can belong to the CBI direct, and bypass its sector association, or it can rely on its sector association's affiliation to maintain contact with the CBI, although many firms are both direct members of the CBI and of their sector associations. An association director commented:

In Germany trade associations pyramid up to the BDI and it is
not possible to by-pass the second or third tier associations and
come directly to the BDI. This produces a very tidy hierarchy of
decision taking and commitment. In distinction is the anarchy in
the United Kingdom where [the] CBI is a hybrid organisation . . .
Far from giving solidarity this encourages free loading and
by-passing of the second and third tier associations. I am not
surprised that we are not more efficient in the British trade
association business – I am amazed that we are as efficient as we
are in fact taking account of the anarchy which is encouraged by
the composition and constitution of the CBI.

This chapter, then, attempts to treat in a systematic way phenomena which are essentially unsystematic. It will not be possible
to discuss in detail the special features of business associability in
particular sectors, other than farming. (For detailed case studies of
the four sectors studied in depth in the IIM project, see Grant
1983a, 1983b, 1983c, 1983d; Sargent, 1983a, 1983b.)

Explaining the pattern of business associability

The pattern of business associability at the sectoral and local level
in Britain has evolved over a period of 200 years. The oldest
association studied in the IIM project, the Birmingham Chamber
of Commerce, was founded in 1812. The overall pattern of sectoral
and local associations is therefore the product of a long drawn out
historical development. For example, a considerable number of
the associations studied were founded during the Second World
War, often at the behest of government. These organisations
survived after their original wartime function had disappeared. A
considerable amount of inertia is built into the system of business
representation, and associations often continue in existence long
after they have outlived their original function and, often, it
seems, without acquiring any new one. It will not be possible to
examine the historical development of the pattern of business
associability here, but a number of useful studies are available
(Blank, 1973; Kipping, 1972; Middlemas, 1979; Turner (ed) 1984;
Wigham, 1973).
Provided that one always bears in mind that the pattern of

sectoral and local associations is in the nature of a palimpsest, it is possible to explore the factors affecting the shape and character of the system in two ways. First, one can examine the factors that affect the overall patterning of the system of business associability. Second, one can look at the calculations that the individual firm has to make in deciding whether to join, or remain in membership of, a particular association.

As intermediary bodies, business associations have to retain the support of their membership and at the same time a credibility with government and other interlocutors such as trade unions. Schmitter and Streeck (1981, p. 50) have formalised the Janus-like character of business associations by introducing a distinction between the 'logic of membership' (the characteristics of members) and the 'logic of influence' (the characteristics of state agencies).

Sources of differentiation between businesses

An examination of the logic of membership draws our attention to variables which differentiate businesses, and therefore make it more difficult for them to combine in organisations with broad domains. It might seem that the most important of these factors would be competition between firms. However, one should not exaggerate the obstacles that competition places in the way of business associability. Firms that are competing vigorously in the market place will not usually see that as a hindrance to co-operation to deal with common problems posed by government or EC measures, or by trade union action. In many industries, competition is in practice relatively limited, with firms satisfied with retaining a stable market share. Sensitive commercial data which could be of use to competitors, such as data used for calculating competitive performance statistics, can be kept confidential by association staff or even processed by an outside body. In practice, competition is less important as a hindrance to collective action by business than common differentiating factors such as size heterogeneity, product heterogeneity, and technological heterogeneity. Social cohesion is one membership characteristic which could act as a unifying factor, but it seems to have little impact on the contemporary organisation of business interests in Britain.

A line of cleavage which poses persistent problems of organisational design and maintenance for business associations is that between small and large firms. Small firms may serve different markets from large firms and thus be faced with very different problems. In many industries they are suppliers to larger firms, a relationship which can give rise to tensions which prevent common organisation. Small-scale business persons are often attracted to a world view in which they see themselves as the authentic representatives of the virtues of free enterprise (see Scase and Goffee, 1980). It is therefore not surprising that there are a number of national organisations claiming to representing smaller businesses, notably the National Federation of the Self-Employed and Small Businesses.

Nevertheless, in many sectors of industry, small businesses are found in the same organisation as larger businesses, so there must be factors that draw them together, as well as influences that pull them apart. One explanation is that larger businesses cross-subsidise the provision of services of various kinds by business associations which are of particular value to smaller firms; the membership of the smaller firms gives the association a more 'representative' character. However, a comparative study by the author and Wolfgang Streeck of the construction industry in Britain and West Germany found that state influences on the market could either exacerbate or reduce tensions between large and small firms (Grant and Streeck, 1985). In other words, the logic of membership is itself conditioned by the logic of influence (see also van Waarden, forthcoming).

Product heterogeneity can manifest itself in a number of ways, including the use of different raw materials, different production processes, and market segmentation. For example, product heterogeneity is a significant influence on business associability in the food processing industry (see Grant (ed.) forthcoming). The industry uses food as a basic raw material, but that raw material may differ considerably in its origins, the machinery and techniques required for its processing, the packaging of the product, and the product market which it faces.

Particular product interests need not, of course, lead to the formation of distinct associations. They can be catered for by internal differentiation within a sector or subsector association by the formation of product sections, or through serviced affiliates of such associations. Even so, it was not until 1984 that the food processing industry had an organisation that could speak for the sector as a whole (the Food and Drink Federation) and there is still substantial differentiation at the subsector and product level. The Food and Drink Federation had been preceded by the Food and Drink Industries Council, formed at the time that Britain joined the EC. As Stocker (1983, p. 247) comments, 'Before the change in UK agricultural support policy to what may be called the intervention system, the need for a concerted food and drink industry lobby on the main direction of agricultural policy was probably not proven.' A shift in the distribution of state functions between national and supranational level, and consequent changes in policy, initiated changes in the system of business associations. Logic of influence factors thus tended to wash out logic of membership factors.

The existence of competition between firms does not, of itself, inhibit the formation of business associations to pursue identifiable common interests. However, it may produce a highly fragmented association structure in certain cases. When competition is based on different technologies of production, a firm cannot rely on a satisfying strategy of securing a stable market share because a particular technology may be wiped out by a competing one. Firms which have invested in the capital equipment necessary for a particular technology cannot easily switch to a different one, and this problem is compounded when the use of the technology depends on craft skills which require skilled labour. A classic example is the roofing industry in Britain which has eight associations serving the builders of different types of roof (e.g. flat or pitched) or different types of roofing material (e.g. metal or mastic asphalt).

Last but not least, it should be remembered that large firms in Britain are often organised on the basis of product divisions which have a considerable degree of autonomy, including the choice of which business associations to belong to. For example, ICI's agriculture division is closely involved in the work of the British Agrochemicals Association, its pharmaceuticals division participates in the work of the Association of the British Pharmaceutical Industry, and its paints division is prominent in the Paintmakers' Association. The relative independence of product divisions helps to explain why large firms in Britain are organised in a number of associations specialised by product or market segment, and why they do not press for mergers of related organisations.

State influences on the organisation of business interests

Government interventions to encourage or stimulate the rationalisation of the system of business associations in Britain have been hesitant, sporadic and generally ineffective. The Department of Trade and Industry did second a civil servant to act as secretary of the Devlin Commission on Industrial Representation, set up in the early 1970s by the CBI and the ABCC, but the report's recommendations for reform proved controversial in business circles, and no significant changes resulted from the report. There have been some government initiatives at the sectoral level. Support was given to the CBI's eventually unsuccessful attempts to reform the chaotic representational arrangements in mechanical engineering through the creation of the British Mechanical Engineering Confederation (see Parker, 1984). The Offshore Supplies Office tried without success to establish a unified trade association for the offshore supplies industry (Jenkin, 1981, pp. 133–5). However, subtle, behind-the-scenes pressure from government can promote processes of change that have already been started from within an industry. As one experienced association official commented, 'One way in which association rearrangement does take place is via pressure from government departments, who find for example that splintering is at times a handicap to their work.' Moreover, the National Economic Development Office has displayed an interest in rationalising business associations from time to time and materially assisted the formation of new associations in the retail trade in the 1960s and in the clothing industry in the 1980s.

There are three main reasons why government appears to have been reluctant to intervene more systematically in the representative arrangements of business. First, government in Britain operates within a largely pluralist paradigm in which business associations are seen essentially as voluntary organisations outside the system of government. The frequent use of the word 'lobby' is instructive in this respect. Second, government policies have been increasingly directed at firms rather than sectors (see Chapter 3). Third, in so far as government has sought a partnership with organisations representing industry, it has often done so through the medium of research associations or economic development committees. Research associations are seen as less political than representative business associations, whilst economic development committees bring together firms, business associations and unions in one body. They thus offer the potential of more effective and wide-ranging forms of consent than can be offered by business associations.

Although *direct* state intervention has had little influence on the pattern of business associability, the *indirect* consequences of the way in which government is organised can be considerable. Thus, the unintended consequences of government action are of greater importance than the intended consequences. The state does not pursue some organisational grand design in relation to business associations; rather, the actions of government constitute an 'invisible hand' which guides and shapes (but certainly does not determine) the way in which business associations are organised.

One indirect influence of government organisation is the relative degree of functional centralisation or decentralisation in terms of concentration or dispersal of responsibility for a particular industry. As was noted in Chapter 2, each government department tends to act as a focus for a 'policy community' with its own representative associations. For example, in the construction industry, logic of membership factors which encourage associational fragmentation such as size heterogeneity and the contractor – subcontractor divide are reinforced by the variety of government departments dealing with the industry. The Building Employers Confederation looks particularly to the sponsoring ministry for the industry, the Department of the Environment. The Scottish Building Employer's Federation focuses on the Scottish Office, the sponsoring ministry in Scotland. The Federation of Civil Engineering Contractors is oriented towards the Department of Transport and the Department of Energy. Indeed, the absorption of the Department of Transport in the Department of the Environment for a time in the 1970s was resented and resisted by road building interests (see Dudley, 1983, p. 113). Last but not least, the Export Group for the Constructional Industries has a close working relationship with the Department of Trade.

The 'union state' structure of Britain (a middle ground between a unitary state and federalism) fosters distinct associations in Scotland, especially where the Scottish Office is the sponsoring department for the sector. Where Britain as a union state differs from a federal state like Canada is the absence of broadly based *intersectoral* associations at the regional level (see Coleman and Grant, 1985 for a fuller analysis).

As noted earlier, government can structure the market and hence influence the pattern of associative activity. For example, in the pharmaceutical industry, government regulation of the prices of drugs sold to the NHS effectively creates two distinct markets for 'ethical' and 'over the counter' drugs, a divide which is reflected in the existence of two distinct pharmaceutical associations. The creation of a monopoly supplier of milk (the Milk Marketing Board) as a consequence of the statutory milk marketing scheme introduced in 1933 led to a the formation of a new organisation of manufacturers of dairy products. The problems arising from dealing with a statutorily based monopoly supplier have led dairy processors to maintain and develop a highly effective business association throughout the intervening period. (See Chapter 9 for a further discussion.)

Particular government interventions may have the unintended consequence of stimulating the formation of new business associations. In the retail trade, the 1912 Shops Act led to the creation of a new organisation to represent the interests of department stores. The formation of a sector association for the whole retail trade was stimulated by the introduction of the Selective Employment Tax in 1966 (a payroll tax which disadvantaged retailers).

The various factors which have been discussed in this and the preceding section shape the contours of business interest representation, but not the whole landscape; just like the real landscape, it represents the outcome of many individual, usually untraceable decisions taken over a long period of time. However, those decisions take place within a context moulded by economic structure, and a climate influenced by government decisions. Even so, business associations in Britain are voluntary organisations that must attract and retain members, and as well as looking at the overall pattern of associative activity, it is necessary to consider what motivates potential members to join, and to remain in membership.

Olson's analysis of the logic of collective action

For the last twenty years, discussion of the dynamics of interest group activity has been significantly influenced by Mancur Olson Jr's *The Logic of Collective Action* (1965 and 1971). Olson's arguments have been challenged in terms of their assumptions, their internal logic and their compatibility with empirical evidence (see, for example, Marsh, 1976). Nevertheless, Olson's framework of analysis continues to provide a useful starting point for any discussion of the membership of economic interest groups.

Why should this be so? Olson offered an elegant and, in some respects, compelling challenge to an important aspect of the then dominant pluralist orthodoxy, that group formation is relatively easy in a liberal democratic society. Olson pointed out that the collective goods provided by an interest group – any good such that, if any person X_i in a group $X_1, \ldots, X_i \ldots, X_n$ consumes it, cannot feasibly be withheld from the others in that group' (Olson, 1965, p. 21) – would be available to a potential member whether or not membership of the group is actually taken up. Thus a potential member could benefit from the existence of a group without incurring the costs of membership. For example, if a business interest group wins a tax concession from government, that concession will not be confined to its members but will be available to all qualifying businessmen.

How, then, are we to explain the existence of large numbers of economic interest groups in western societies? Olson dealt with this apparent paradox in terms of his by-product theory of interest groups. He argued, 'The large and powerful economic lobbies are in fact the by-products of organisations that obtain their strength and support because they perform some function in addition to lobbying for collective goods' (Olson, 1971, p. 132). In order to organise successfully, economic interest groups, Olson argued, have to provide selective incentives to induce their potential members to join. This could take the form of coercion, but more usually it would be some form of positive inducement such as a service provided by the interest group solely to its members.

It should be noted that this analysis takes no account of differences in the organisation of economic interests from one country to another. For example, membership densities tend to be higher in business interest associations in West Germany than in the

United Kingdom. Such differences in the extent of 'free riding' must be partly a question of national tradition in terms of attitudes towards solidarity of action, or at least something not easily explicable from pure considerations of self interest. The *Unternehmer* tradition of solidarity has clearly been an important influence on the actions of West German employers (see Lawrence, 1980, pp. 94–5; Tylecote, 1981, p. 33). Similarly, Katzenstein (1985, p. 91) observes that 'conditions favour the institutional penetration of the business community in the small European states much more than in the large ones.'

Nevertheless, many of Olson's observations are not invalidated by the persistence of particular national traditions, notably his observations on the particular propensity of businessmen to organise politically. Olson advanced the idea of a privileged group where the amount of the collective good obtained by each member, or at least one member, was such that he would be better off paying the full cost of securing the collective good than if the good were not provided. He also introduced another category of the relatively small group, the 'intermediate' group, where even though no one member obtained a sufficient share of the benefit to encourage him to provide the collective good himself, there were not so many members 'that no one member will notice whether any other member is or is not helping to provide the collective good' (Olson, 1971, p. 50). Olson goes on to argue (p. 143) that the oligopolistic character of much of industry is such that many firms can organise as 'privileged' or 'intermediate groups'. This is an important phenomenon not only in terms of exploring the relative ease or difficulty of business interest organisation, but also in terms of its implications for the democratic process as a whole. Olson argues:

> The small oligopolistic industry seeking a tariff or a tax loophole will sometimes attain its objective even if the vast majority of the population loses as a result. The smaller groups – the privileged and intermediate groups – can often defeat the large groups – the latent groups – which are supposed to prevail in a democracy. (Ibid., pp. 127–8)

This argument is given added significance by Offe and Wiesenthal's contention that there are two 'logics of collective action':

whereas labour power can only be realised through collective organisation, collective organisation is one of a number of alternatives open to employers (see Offe, 1981 and Offe and Wiesenthal, 1985). Moreover, Olson's arguments on this point receive indirect support from work of Salisbury which has focused on the nature of the unit which is being organised. Most business associations organise firms rather than individuals (there are, of course, exceptions to this general rule). Salisbury (1984) argues that, at least in the United States, interest representation tends to be dominated by institutions such as corporations (other examples are churches and local governments). Salisbury argues that 'A central distinction between an institution and an interest group is that institutions have interests that are politically and analytically independent of the interests of particular institutional members' (Salisbury, 1984, pp. 68–9). The leaders of an institution make a judgement about what is in its best interests if it is to survive and flourish. They have to worry less about the short run interests of institutional members. Thus, 'Institutions have greater latitude – more discretionary resources and more autonomous leadership authority – to enter the political arena' (Ibid., p. 68).

It might therefore seem that large corporations as institutions need to pay less attention to the costs and benefits of association membership; if membership is seen as in their long-run interests, they will join. The empirical evidence does, indeed, seem to support this view; an earlier interview study of British businessmen showed that selective incentives were an important determinant of CBI membership only for smaller firms (Grant and Marsh, 1977; Marsh, 1976).

This line of argument has been challenged in a report on a large-scale survey of employers which found that most services provided by employers' associations were utilised to a greater extent by large rather than small establishments (Brown (ed.), 1981, p. 21). However, this study was focused on employers' organisations oriented towards industrial relations where other considerations might apply. More importantly, one should not confuse levels of use of a service with the importance that is attached to that service as a motivation for joining and remaining a member of a business association. Moreover, data from the British contribution to the International Institute of Management study show a very high turnover rate of members in associations made up of small firms, suggesting that short-run, highly calculative assessments of the benefits of membership prevail among such firms. It should be noted, though, that the fact that selective incentives seem to be more important to smaller firms does not mean that all such firms join and remain in business associations. For example, despite its provision of an attractive range of services to members, the Chemical Industries Association has experienced some difficulty in retaining its 'minimum subscription' members (see Chemical Industries Association Annual Report, 1983, p. 7).

An important part of Olson's argument is that business as a whole is more difficult to organise than particular sectors of business. This is because business as a whole is not a small, privileged or intermediate group (Olson, 1971, pp. 145–6). This finding certainly fits in with North American experience, where in both Canada and the United States organisations representing business as a whole, as distinct from sectoral associations or government relations activities by large firms, have been notoriously weak. Indeed, one of the main exceptions to this picture, the Business Roundtable in the United States, is confined to the chief executives of less than 200 leading firms (Useem, 1984, p. 35) and therefore qualifies as at least an intermediate group.

The picture in Britain is rather different in that organisations such as the CBI have managed to organise a large range of businesses. In later work, Olson has portrayed 'encompassing organisations' as an exception to his general strictures about the tendency of special interest organisations to reduce efficiency in the societies in which they operate (Olson, 1982, p. 74). No doubt Olson would regard the CBI as one of those peak associations lacking 'the unity needed to have any great influence on public policy, or even coherent and specific policies' (Ibid., p. 50). It could therefore not be seen as an antidote to the strong organisations and consequent institutional sclerosis which Olson sees as slowing Britain's adaptability.(Ibid., p. 78)

Given that business firms, particularly in Britain, apparently find it relatively easy to organise, perhaps we should not worry too much about why they organise, but rather focus on the consequences of such group activity. After all, if entering the political market is difficult for broadly based interests, but easier for business interests than for others, then a benign or tolerant view of the consequences of group activity is open to challenge. As Olson points out, 'The limited incentive the typical citizen has to monitor public policy also implies that lobbies for special interests can sometimes succeed where matters are detailed or complex but not when they are general or simple, and this increases complexity still further' (Ibid., pp. 69–70).

However, it must not be assumed that organising business interests is a simple matter. All the historical evidence from the British case suggests otherwise (see, for example, Turner (ed.), 1984). The successful organisation of business interests requires a particular kind of talent for organisational design: a combination of enthusiasm, diplomacy, and an ability to assemble an attractive package of incentives to offer at the right moment. Work by Salisbury has emphasised the importance of entrepreneur – organisers in group formation, although Olson sees this as an enrichment of his original theory, with the successful entrepreneur in the large group case being 'an innovator with selective incentives' (Olson, 1971, p. 177) who eases the process of group formation.

Nevertheless, it is clear that even in intermediate or privileged groups, entrepreneurs have played a crucial role in group formation. An important example in the British case was Dudley Docker, the first president of the Federation of British Industries (FBI). Docker founded a number of business associations, but also managed to make 'as successful a use of the merger technique in political association as he had already done in business' (Turner, 1984, p. 37). In designing the organisation of the FBI, Docker tried to learn from foreign experience, especially that of Belgium, but he also consulted Marcus Wallenberg, the founding president of Sweden's Industrial Union (Davenport-Hines, 1984, p. 108). Thus, interest group entrepreneurs do not exist in a vacuum, but trade ideas with one another. They may also, of course, receive outside help, not least from the government, even in Britain. Walker (1983) has shown that in many cases some kind of subsidy, either from other groups of from the government, underwrites some part of the cost of creating and sustaining an organisation. In inter-war Britain, the National Government 'built up the British Iron and Steel Federation as the recognised intermediary between government and the industry', fostering its 'prestige and authority' (Tolliday, 1984, p. 74). Such assistance is not confined to business organisations; indeed, it may be provided more generously elsewhere. Lowe and Goyder (1983, p. 42) note that environmental groups receive significant amounts of assistance from the Department of the Environment or agencies linked to it, with 23 per cent of the groups studied 'heavily dependent on government as their first or second most important source of income'.

One important way in which the debate on how and why business firms organise politically has moved on since Olson published *The Logic of Collective Action* is an emphasis on the distinction between the conditions for group maintenance or survival, as distinct from group formation. Maintaining a group in existence may be easier than forming it in the first place, because members may develop solidaristic and purposive attachments to the group and because the group may carve out (partly as a result of accumulated expertise) some special niche in the provision of particular services to its members. Simple inertia may play a part in group survival, particularly where a business firm pays an annual subscription to an organisation at a cost which is a very small proportion of the firm's turnover. As has been suggested, firms may be less sensitive to such costs than individuals, or at least view them in a different, organisationally conditioned perspective. Of course, organisations do decline and die, and this is something about which we still know relatively little, but on the whole the population of business associations is relatively stable. Only two of the population of organisations studied in Britain in 1980 had disappeared by 1985, and they both underwent a metamorphosis into different forms. The time scale of change is not geological, but it could be termed geomorphological.

Just as it is important to distinguish between the logic of formation and the logic of survival, so it is important to distinguish between the costs and benefits of passive membership and the costs and benefits of active participation. This is an area which has been somewhat neglected by the literature, but the distinction is an important one. The flow of costs and benefits arising from membership may be so low that the costs of deciding whether or not to remain in membership would exceed the net benefits derived either from continuing in membership or leaving. Hence, the issue of whether or not to remain in membership does not appear above a rationality threshold, a theoretical proposition confirmed by some of the empirical evidence (see Grant and Marsh, 1977). In King's study of the Leeds Chamber of Commerce, 23 per cent of those interviewed did not know why their company had joined the chamber (Economic and Social Research Council, 1985, p. 40). Continued membership may be a subject of indifference unless this state of equilibrium is upset by some external disturbance, such as a sharp rise in membership subscriptions or even the arrival of an academic interviewer asking questions about the costs and benefits of membership!

It might be supposed that the recession of the early 1980s would have provided such an equilibrium disturbance, perhaps leading to a freezing out of the smaller associations, allowing the larger units to consolidate. However, whilst many of the more effective associations experienced large cutbacks in staff in cost cutting exercises (for example, a reduction of around 30 per cent in staff establishment at the Chemical Industries Association), many of the smaller associations survived unscathed. In some cases this may be because they have some limited but nevertheless important purpose, such as resisting exhibition promoters who want to encourage the industry to stage more exhibitions, or dealing with a monopoly supplier such as a nationalised industry. The contribution of such an association to government policy-making may be negligible, but the low cost of operation may be more than offset by the provision of an identifiable collective benefit, shared among a small number of participants, which might not otherwise be available.

The costs and benefits of participation

Once a firm sends its senior executives regularly to committee meetings of an association, the costs of membership rise substantially, although the benefits may do so as well. Senior staff away at an association headquarters are not available for the firm's work, and being president of the CBI or of a major sectoral association is almost a full-time job. On the other hand, a firm that actively participates in an association may become aware more quickly of economic and political developments that affect its operations, will be able to make decisions on the basis of a broader understanding of the economic and political context, and may acquire a better appreciation of the strengths and weaknesses of competitors, if only by meeting and observing their senior managers.

To put it more formally, there are certain selective incentives which are available only through participation. The focus here is not on 'solidaristic goods' – taking part in golf matches, attending dinners, etc. – which Olson correctly treats as a special form of selective incentive (Olson, 1971, p. 61). Such incentives are very important in associations of small businessmen; the Federation of Master Builders claims in promotional literature that 'The hallmark of FMB is its friendly, family atmosphere' and states that 'Membership of the Federation opens a door to a new and increased social life for you and your family.' No doubt going on holiday with other builders has its attractions, and business deals may be clinched on the golf course, but solidaristic goods are not generally important in modern business interest associations, although they may help to cement other more rationalistic commonalities of interest.

One can go to the races or hear a talk on antiques (to quote two concrete examples) without belonging to a business association, but there is another form of benefit which is derived through participation and which is relevant to company performance. In successive annual reports, the director-general of the Chemical Industries Association, Martin Trowbridge, has developed a fourfold classification of association activities. His categories of the 'advocacy' or 'representational' functions and of 'bottom line services' conform to the academic labels of 'collective goods' and 'selective goods' respectively. The 'communication' function, dealing with the specialised and mass media and, in the longer term, the education of all the publics with which an association deals, is the focus of the concluding section of this chapter. However, Trowbridge emphasised in the 1984 report, 'Equally important in the portfolio of the Association are the Mutual Aid Activities.' Mutual aid, as described by Trowbridge, involves companies meeting together and discussing problems of mutual concern, in the case of the chemical industry in such areas as safety, health, environmental and other specialised technical and operating matters. These discussions need not lead to any specific representational activity. Rather they are a means of exchanging information between competitors about matters of mutual concern, thus leading to a better understanding of shared problems and the means of solving them. In order to benefit directly from this information exchange, one has to take part in it. Thus the increased costs of participation are offset by an increased flow of benefits.

There is another category of benefits derived from membership which does not require participation in association activities. In his discussion of Olson's work, Moe (1980, p. 117) introduces the idea of purposive incentives for association membership:

> These are various kinds of intangible benefits that accrue to a person by virtue of his support of causes, value systems, principles or ends that he considers to be worthwhile. Unlike solidary incentives, these types need not derive directly from social relationships; the individual may never meet with anyone in the group or even know who the other members are.

As Moe points out, 'a businessman may make contributions to a trade association because he genuinely feels a responsibility to co-operate with others for "the good of the industry"' (Ibid., p. 118). In their evidence to the Devlin Commission on industrial representation, businessmen from large firms, after admitting that they put more into trade associations than they get from them, explained this apparently irrational behaviour in terms of their obligation to the industry or to business in general. This phenomenon is generalised by Useem when he talks of 'the logic of classwide benefits, involving considerations that lead to company decisions beneficial to all large companies, even where there is no discernible, direct gain for the individual firm' (Useem, 1984, p. 5). One does not have to accept Useem's notion of an 'inner circle' of business leaders to agree with his argument that businessmen who take up leadership positions in business associations or act as advisers to government have to transcend the immediate, narrow interests of their own firms.

There are, then, purposeful incentives whether or not one thinks of them as the expression of some classwide interest. Their theoretical importance is that, as Moe points out, Olson's analysis treats collective goods only as collective goods. Hence, he overlooks the fact that selective benefits can be generated in the process of supporting collective goals. The expressive benefits derived from associative activity provide a link between group goals and the individual's own calculus of costs and benefits. Moe (1980, p. 118) concludes, 'Collective goods can actually generate their own selective incentives because of the unique role that purposive incentives can play in connecting the two.'

One should, of course, bear in mind that there is a difference between a company in membership of an association and the individual representatives of that company who participate in the association's activities. They may derive private benefits from participation that lead them to encourage the company to remain active. A claimed 'obligation to the industry' may be a more socially acceptable motive than an admission that association activity provides the individual with a forum and an audience to which he can pontificate on political or quasi political topics, or even a route to recognition in the honours list. Presidents of the CBI usually receive a knighthood; long serving office holders in sectoral associations may receive a CBE or, in subsectoral associations, an OBE. It is easy to be too cynical; many individuals devote a great deal of time and effort to association work in the sincere belief that they are helping their industry and the wider public interest.

In his analysis, Moe (1980, p. 57) draws attention to the importance of the interdependencies in the various incentives provided by economic interest groups (or, more particularly, interest entrepreneurs). Moe comments that 'the entrepreneur's ability to supply selective incentives is often influenced by his ability to achieve political goals, structure political participation, and attract members on political bases' (Ibid.). One could generalise this point and say that what is distinctive about business associations is the particular *mix* of incentives they provide: collective representational goods; services, exhibitions closed to non-members and other selective incentives for membership; solidaristic goods and 'mutual aid'. It would probably be going too far to say that these goods are characterised by an indissoluble jointness of supply in the sense that the supply of beef inevitably involves the supply of hides. There are some groups which provide only collective goods, and others which concentrate almost entirely on selective incentives, so that they start to imitate a non-profit-making firm. However, most business associations provide a carefully balanced mixture of collective, selective and solidaristic goods which appeals to their membership.

Farmers and the agricultural interest

The political organisation of agriculture as a sector has so many special features that it requires separate treatment. These features may be summed up in one word: 'exceptionalism' (see Cox, Lowe and Winter, 1985, p. 131). This 'exceptionalism' takes the form of special privileges, combined with an absence of direct state intervention at the level of the enterprise. Farming has received more government assistance than any other privately owned sector of the economy. In 1977–78, a year in which there was considerable government assistance to manufacturing industry, capital grants to agriculture amounted to 10 per cent of gross investment, compared with less than 1 per cent of investment in fixed assets in private industry (Centre for Agricultural Strategy, 1980, p. 74). Indeed, one agricultural economist has suggested that 'investment in certain types of farm machinery and buildings may have been pushed beyond the limits of economic sense' (Doyle, 1979, p. 270). Certainly, impressive gains in labour productivity have been to a considerable extent achieved through the substitution of capital for labour inputs.

It is also important to consider the way in which this government assistance has been provided. The state has extended beyond the farm gate, but it has done so through the acceptable mechanisms of financial assistance and technical advice provided by the Agricultural Development and Advisory Service. The farmer has considerable autonomy in deciding what use he or she makes of the various forms of assistance available.

Last but not least, farming enjoys a number of exemptions from normal legislative provisions. It is the only industry exempt from paying rates, there are road tax concessions for farm vehicles, and exemption from planning requirements for farm buildings. When controls have been imposed on the industry, it has often been through voluntary arrangements. 'Indeed the place of formal controls has tended to be taken by codes of conduct such as the NFU's Codes of Practice on Straw Burning, Aerial Spraying and Silage Effluent' (Cox, Lowe and Winter, 1985, p. 145).

In order to understand agricultural 'exceptionalism', it is important not just to look at the relationship between the Ministry of Agriculture, Fisheries and Food (MAFF) and the National Farmers' Union (NFU), but at the mutually supportive set of relationships that constitute the agricultural policy community. This is a particularly institutionally dense policy community, with well-defined boundaries which are difficult for outsiders to penetrate. One indicator of this insulation is the existence of a separate ministry for the industry, the only industry to enjoy such a focus within the government machine; indeed, if one takes account of the fact that the Scottish, Welsh and Northern Ireland ministries also have agricultural responsibilities, there are four government departments which can advance the interests of agriculture within government. Another indicator of agriculture's distinctiveness is the existence of a separate system of agricultural education and training.

All this has been achieved by an industry whose voting strength is miniscule by West European standards, although 5 per cent of the Conservative MPs elected in 1983 were farmers (figures derived from Criddle, 1984, p. 237). Part of the explanation is that common interests with farmers are shared by significant portions of manufacturing industry, notably agrochemicals and fertilisers, and the makers of agricultural machinery. The British Agrochemical Association is represented on the NFU Agricultural Publicity Liaison Group, 'a group of various trade associations and other organisations concerned with the communication of the benefits of modern agriculture to consumers and educational establishments' (British Agrochemicals Association Annual Report, 1983–4, p. 7). The fertiliser industry benefited from the introduction of the Land Fertility Scheme in 1937 which involved a subsidy of 25 per cent on the delivered price of basic slag and a 50 per cent subsidy on the delivered price of lime, which was to last, in one form or another, until the mid-1970s. Agriculture's close links with manufacturing industry are symbolised by the NFU's membership of the CBI which it uses to ensure that CBI policies take account of the special needs of farmers.

The fulcrum of the agricultural policy community is the symbiotic relationship between the MAFF and the NFU. Wilson argues (1978, p. 31) that the NFU is 'arguably the best and organisationally strongest of western agricultural interest groups'. In particular, 'The united front presented to the British government by farmers through their Farmers' Union is decidedly unusual' (Ibid., p. 33). With a staff of 840, the NFU is the best resourced business association in Britain. Even if one takes account of the fact that two-thirds of these officials are outside London, and largely concerned with selling insurance and providing other services to members, the NFU's staff still compares with that of the CBI.

The strength of the NFU in large part derives from the effective representational monopoly that it was given by the 1947 Agriculture Act. 'This is the key to the NFU's influence and it is significant that, in the inter-war years, before it achieved this intimate relationship with the ministry – indeed, before the ministry became so closely involved involved in the management of the agricultural sector – the NFU was a relatively weak and marginal interest group' (Lowe, Cox, MacEwen, O'Riordan and Winter, 1986, p. 87). The NFU, and the other principal farmers' organisation, the Country Landowners' Association, must also benefit from the unreceptive attitude of the MAFF towards environmental interest groups (see Cox, Lowe and Winter, 1985, pp. 146–7). The symbiotic relationship between the MAFF and the NFU is exemplified by the exchanges of personnel between them. 'In 1979, Sir Freddy Kearns, second permanent secretary until 1978, became the consultant and policy adviser on European affairs of the [NFU]. In 1981, David Evans, an under secretary, joined the union as its chief economic and policy adviser' (Doig, 1986, p. 41). In May 1984, the MAFF 'appointed as special adviser a farmer prominent in both the NFU and CLA (Lowe *et al.*, 1986, p. 90).

The end of exceptionalism?

The exceptionalism of the agricultural policy community is now under great stress than it has been at any time since the post-war settlement embodied in the 1947 Agriculture Act. The weakening political power of farmers is demonstrated by the imposition of milk quotas in 1984. Many smaller farmers who had been encouraged to expand were placed in jeopardy by this rapid change of policy. The MAFF had 'encouraged small producers, with limited financial reserves, to buy more land and to invest in new buildings, equipment and livestock to expand production on borrowed money' (Lowe *et al.*, 1986, p. 3).

Although more agricultural policy is still nationally determined than generally realised, membership of the EC has considerably changed the relationship between farmers and the state. The tradition of intensive consultation has not ended; indeed, the European farmers' organisation, COPA, is close to the agriculture directorate in the European Commission. The Common Agricultural Policy is, of course, facing increasing budgetary constraints and it was these that led to milk quotas. However, farmers are a larger proportion of voters in other West European countries, and national agricultural ministers are anxious to protect their interests.

The most important consequence of Community membership has been an indirect one: it has led to a greater politicisation of agricultural issues. This was particularly apparent in relation to the arguments over the Green Pound (an exchange rate for settling agricultural prices) during the lifetime of the 1974–79 Labour Government (see Grant, 1981). As long as agricultural issues were relatively depoliticised, they could be largely settled within the agricultural policy community itself. The main exception was the involvement of the Treasury, and, ultimately, the Cabinet, in the annual price negotiations. As a reading of the Crossman diaries shows, government was often being more generous to the farmers than it realised. Once agricultural issues become more politicised, a wider range of actors, not necessarily sympathetic to farmers, becomes involved. Public opinion also becomes a more important factor.

A particular blow was opposition to farming interests from within the Conservative Party. There was growing uneasiness in the 1980s among Conservative backbenchers who were concerned about the absence of a genuine market in agricultural products. This uneasiness was highlighted in 1982 by the publication of a book highly critical of the industry (*Agriculture: The Triumph and the Shame*) by Richard Body, a Conservative MP from an agricultural constituency. His estimate that farmers had been given £40 billion of public supports since 1946 and were still receiving £3.35 billion a year 'came as a revelation to many who were not tuned in to conservationist sources' (Lowe *et al.*, 1986, p. 51).

These criticisms were made against the background of the growing strength of the environmental movement, and an increasing concern by politicians of all parties to see that their policies had at least a green tinge. A national public opinion poll commissioned by the NFU in 1983 revealed 'a growing awareness and hardening of attitudes by the public on animal welfare, environment and healthy food production' (*Farmers' Weekly*, 17 June 1983). However, although these changing attitudes form the background against which public policy is made, one should not exaggerate the influence of the environmental movement. It has certainly made less impact than in West Germany. Unlike the NFU, conservation groups 'are not of central importance to the effective performance of government or the economy, and consequently do not have the same close, symbiotic relationship with senior civil servants. They tend, therefore, to be excluded from the formative stages of policy-making' (Lowe *et al.*, 1986, p.121).

These developments have been matched and reflected by growing disarray within the NFU and the emergence of rival organisations. Within the NFU 'The internal consensus, so essential to a working partnership with the state and achieved relatively easily in the days when mixed farming predominated, is currently in some disarray' (Ibid., p. 91). The potential conflict between livestock and cereal producers has been handled by developing policy through a network of commodity committees and by having deputy presidents responsible for each of two main branches of the industry. In the 1980s, there has been 'a growing rift between arable farmers and intensive livestock producers. Many within the NFU believe it threatens to tear the union apart' (*Farmers' Weekly*, 20 January 1984).

There are a number of reasons why this division of interest among farmers has become deeper, leading 'to the unedifying spectacle of open sniping between the chairmen of the cereals and pigs committees' (Ibid.). First, EC membership has led to a decline in mixed farming and greater specialisation, making it harder for the NFU to reconcile different interests. Second, cereal growers have been the main beneficiaries in Britain of the CAP. Because cereal prices have been maintained at a high level, prices of animal feeds with a cereal base have increased to an extent that has caused difficulties for pig and poultry farmers (although the cereal content in the feed went up less than other ingredients). Third, farmers in the west Britain have blamed East Anglian cereal farmers for giving the industry a bad name with their straw burning practices. Fourth, there has always been a suspicion that the NFU is dominated by arable farmers from areas within easy reach of London, although it has to be said that delegates to the NFU Council from the Midlands, west and north are informally grouped in the so-called 'Bonnington Maffia' (named after the hotel they use rather than the more establishment Farmers' Club).

One of the NFU's greatest strengths, and its credibility with government, has been its internal unity. Its other strength has been the absence of rival organisations (other than the Farmers' Union of Wales). However, the 1980s have seen the formation of a

Tenant Farmers' Association and a Small Farmers' Association, which, although relatively small, blunt the NFU's claim to be the voice of farmers. Tensions have also arisen in the relationship between the NFU and the Country Landowners' Association over how the benefits of an outgoers scheme in the dairy sector should be shared between landowners and tenants. All these difficulties within and between farming organisations are as much a symptom as a cause of a situation in which 'farming interests can now look weak, even in relation to quite modest aims and, on matters of great weight such as the recent imposition of milk quotas, utterly impotent' (Lowe *et al.*, 1986, p. 94). The general lesson to be learnt from an examination of agricultural politics is the weakness of any static analysis of the influence of business interest associations.

Local business associations

Businesses are organised at the local level in chambers of commerce (affiliated to the ABCC) and chambers of trade (affiliated to the National Chamber of Trade). Chambers of commerce are normally found in larger communities; chambers of trade largely tend to represent the retail sector. The two national organisations were discussing the possibility of a merger in 1986. Business persons may also meet informally in other organisations such as the Rotary Club.

Chambers of commerce in continental European countries are often given a privileged status by the state, which includes obligatory membership for firms in the territories that they cover, and the performance of a range of policy functions delegated to them by the state. In West Germany, for example, chambers of commerce have an important role in providing training facilities, monitoring standards of training by employers and setting examinations. In France, chambers are 'empowered to plan, install and manage facilities which are required for the general good of the business community. Such facilities include seaports, river/canal ports, airports, heavy road transport centres, bus stations, warehouses, parking, industrial estates, sports centres, hotels and tourist centres' (Forster, 1983, p. 91).

The professional staff of chambers of commerce in Britain have not been slow to point to the greater status and powers of continental chambers as an argument for the extension of such arrangements to Britain (see, for example, RIPA, 1984). Indeed, the chambers have always had an important role in issuing export documentation to their members. They have also often been able to build up a close collaborative relationship with their local authorities which can extend to sitting on council committees, negotiating over the level of the rates, and vetting planning applications (see Grant, 1983f; King, 1985).

In the 1980s, the range of functions performed by the chambers has tended to widen. A number have sponsored advisory services for small businesses, often funded from public and private sources. Above all, the Thatcher Government gave the chambers formal responsibilities for vetting the implementation of public policy programmes, most importantly the urban aid programme for inner cities. The July 1981 guidelines to local authorities involved in government funded urban aid schemes required detailed consultation with the private sector (normally the local chamber of commerce) as a precondition of programme approval. More recently, local authorities have been required to consult business, usually through the chamber of commerce, when setting the level of the local rate.

However, chambers of commerce are very patchy in the extent to which they cover the country as a whole. Major chambers such as London and Birmingham have been well resourced, have employed a large and professional staff, and have been effective both in their representational activities and in the provision of services to their members. Medium sized chambers have in some cases been highly cost effective, namely, Norwich (see Grant, 1983f). At the other end of the scale is the type of chamber in London which in an appeal for donations of equipment such as a large teapot, cups and saucers, and a calculator noted that "the first floor over a small newsagent's shop is not the best of locations for the Commercial Centre of the Borough's Business Activity" (Stewart, 1984, p. 44).

Stewart's study of chambers of commerce, commissioned by the Thatcher Government, showed that the commitment of many chambers to representational work was limited, and that their input to the public policy-making process was weak. Many chambers seemed unable to adopt the broad perspective that

participation in public policy requires. Even in the larger chambers, an inherent parochialism tended to direct chamber involvement in inner area programmes towards particular projects that
affected members 'rather than upon issues of strategy for the inner
areas or the balance of the programme' (Ibid., p. 47). Stewart
concluded that unless some of the constraints on chambers are
altered, they are likely to continue to play a modest part in public
affairs, and 'any change would require action from central government to increase the formal position and/or resources of Chambers
of Commerce since it is unlikely that the Chamber movement
could sustain greater local activity at present even if it wanted to'
(Ibid., p. 49).

The Italian system of business representation has a strong territorial basis, and in West Germany chambers of commerce form a
significant part of the overall system of business interest associations. However, in Italy there are a number of industrial and
commercial centres (Milan, Turin, etc.); this is also the case in
West Germany (Frankfurt, the Ruhr, Hamburg, etc.) In Britain,
there is a concentration of centres of corporate decision-making in
London. It is therefore not surprising to find that the territorially
based system of business representation is generally less significant
than the sectorally based system.

8 Business and Party Politics

If there are difficulties in the development and expression of business interests through representative associations, then it is possible that other routes may become more important for the defence of business interests. One alternative route that suggests itself is through political parties, especially parties apparently favourable to business interests. This chapter will argue that the weaknesses of business political organisation apparent elsewhere are not compensated for by the defence of business interests through political parties. Indeed, the British Conservative Party was able to develop its own conception of what was good for business under the leadership of Margaret Thatcher. In some respects, the policies developed did coincide with what was wanted by a broad spectrum of business opinion, but in others they were seen by some business persons as having harmful effects, particularly for manufacturing industry. When economic interest and party doctrine diverged, it was often party doctrine that emerged as more influential on the course of events.

The limits of the literature

The relationships between organised (or unorganised) business interests and political parties have been a relatively neglected area of political science research. No doubt this is partly because the study of political parties and the study of interest groups tend to be separate specialisms within political science. (But for an important exception to this general pattern, see Lehmbruch, 1979.) There has also been a tendency to study political parties as 'closed systems': to focus on such topics as factionalism *within* parties; or the roles of party bureaucracies *within* parties; or the ways in which parties select their candidates and leaders. Admittedly, Richard Rose has lifted the debate on to a higher plane with his discussions of the concept of party government (1974) and the issue of whether party alternation actually makes a difference to the content of government policy (Rose, 1980, 1984). Another theme that has attracted considerable attention in the study of British politics has been the notion of adversary politics which is sometimes seen as a distinctive property of the British party system (Finer, 1975; for a more sceptical treatment, see Gamble and Walkland, 1984).

Nevertheless, the relationship between party and interest remains relatively unexplored. One reason is undoubtedly because parties, as vote-seeking organisms, have to transcend particular interests in order to assemble sufficient votes to have a chance of forming a government. There is relatively little mileage in electoral terms in being closely identified with the business interest, especially big business. This is an important consideration for the Conservative Party which is often overlooked by commentators.

In so far as the relationship between political parties and business interests in Britain has been examined, the discussion has tended to focus almost exclusively on donations by business to political parties, above all the Conservative Party. This is a topic which has generated a great deal of heat, many proposals for reform, and relatively little serious analysis. It has also tended to swamp discussion of more important aspects of the relationship betweeen business and political parties. This is not to say that it is without importance and the question of business donations will be discussed in this chapter. However, it is important to remember that only a minority of businesses give money to the Conservative Party or to organisations identified with it; many companies, such as ICI, have a policy of not making political donations.

The general argument that will be advanced in this chapter is that the relationship between business and the political parties is often a difficult and awkward one. Indeed, the Industry and Parliament Trust was formed in 1977 with the specific objective of overcoming misunderstandings between business and elected politicians. The Conservative Party cannot be relied upon to act as the authentic spokesman of business. This is not surprising when one considers that business firms do not have a vote and shareholders are a small percentage of the electorate who are not represented

qua shareholders in the way that trade unionists are represented
qua union members in the Labour Party (and for that matter in the
Conservative Party through the Conservative Trade Unionists).

Somewhat paradoxically, the Labour Party has often appeared
to have a better understanding of the needs and views of manufacturing industry in particular. Moreover, because it is a more
interventionist party, when in government it needs a good working
relationship with industry, but mistrust between the Labour Party
and the business community has tended to deepen in recent years
as the Party has appeared to shift to the left. It should not be
forgotten that the trade unions control some five-sixths of the
votes in the Labour Party conference, and the majority of NEC
places (taking account of their influence on elections to the women's section). Although the unions do not act as a united bloc,
there is no structural equivalent in the Conservative Party for
business compared with the influence the Transport and General
Workers' Union exerts on decision-making in the Labour Party.
The Alliance parties might seem to offer a natural refuge for
business persons alarmed by the excesses of Thatcherism, and
certainly there is reason to believe that many business persons
would prefer the Alliance parties as the main opposition in place
of Labour. However, it will be argued that an Alliance government could, in many ways, be rather uncomfortable for business.

The chapter will focus on four main aspects of the relationship
between business and the political parties. First, there will be a
general discussion of the match (or mismatch) between the outlooks of each of the parties and the interests of business. The
rather vague term 'outlook' is used deliberately since the term
'doctrine' may be too precise for use in this context and because
there is considerable dissension within the main parties about what
the programme of the party should be. Nevertheless, despite these
difficulties, unless one tries to focus on the problem at this general
level, the broad perspective which this problem area requires is
unlikely to be attained. Second, the formation of party policy will
be examined, with particular reference to the emergence of
'Thatcherism'. The argument advanced will be that it was a newly
dominant faction within the Conservative Party that redefined the
interests of business; the supposed leaders of business largely
followed the political lead they were given. Third, the composition
of the political parties will be examined: do business persons play

an active role in them at the local and national level? Lastly, the vexed question of business financing of party activity will be considered.

The difficult relationship between the Conservative Party and business

Most business persons are Conservative supporters, but their support is generally passive rather than active, and they often have considerable reservations about the party's policies. For example, a 1982 Marplan Survey of 500 senior directors in companies with a turnover of over £5 million found that 80 per cent said they would vote for the economic policy of the Conservative Party. Nine per cent preferred the Alliance parties, whilst support for the economic policy of the Labour Party was statistically negligible (*Financial Times*, 13 March 1982). One must not forget that whatever reservations business persons have about the policies of the Conservative Party – and many were seriously worried by the erosion of Britain's industrial base after 1979 – the majority of them have some kind of inclination to support the Conservative Party. This loyalty is often an obstacle to any sustained opposition being mounted within business organisations to Conservative policies. Attempts to mount such a challenge encounter the objection from the more partisan Conservative supporters that business must be loyal to 'our government'.

Conservative Party leaders have often felt badly let down by business. Edward Heath as Prime Minister expressed his frustration at business's failure to invest once, as he saw it, his government had created the economic conditions in which investment could take place. Mrs Thatcher was sceptical about the ability of business to tackle what she saw as labour market rigidities without a clear political lead. Her brand of conviction politics had little time for what were seen as the pleas of vested interests. Mrs Thatcher stated in a television programme in 1984, 'I can give you a check list now of the way in which we have tackled vested interest' (*Weekend World*, 15 January 1984, transcript p. 2/6).

By way of contrast, a leading Conservative moderate has argued, 'A Tory . . . rejects the simple idea that individuals are selfish and good and groups selfish and bad' (Gilmour, 1983, p.

204). Despite their more positive conception of the role of organised interests in a democratic society, the Conservative moderates were displeased by what they saw as the supine posture of business towards the newly ascendent Tory right. Sir Ian Gilmour complained that the CBI 'has become little more than an adjunct of the Conservatives' (Ibid., p. 105). As far as Gilmour was concerned, the CBI was not up to taking the share in governance which he would have been prepared to support in the case of a more effective organisation.

Many Conservative politicians, then, did not have too favourable a view of the legitimacy (on the right) or the effectiveness (among moderate Tories) of the organised representatives of business. Business, for its part, had its worries about the extent to which its needs and problems were understood within the Conservative party. One of the interesting features of Sir Terence Beckett's 'bare knuckles' speech in 1980 was that he articulated business reservations about the Conservative Party that are usually only heard in private. He warned the CBI conference, 'You had better face the brutal fact that the Conservative Party is a rather narrow alliance.' After asking how many of those in Parliament or the Cabinet have actually run a business, he commented: 'They don't all understand you. They think they do, but they don't. They are even suspicious of you, and what is worse they don't take you seriously' (*Financial Times*, 12 November 1980).

These difficulties are not simply the product of poor communication between business and the Conservative Party. They are one manifestation of a more general difficulty that has been stressed throughout this book, that of deciding what represents the best political strategy for business. Useem (1984, p. 57) articulates a widely held viewpoint when he states that 'The overriding and undiminished corporate stress on the growth of profits necessarily dominates the vision of all who enter politics on behalf of the business community.' The creation of conditions in which profits can be protected and maximised must certainly be a central goal of business political activity. However, Useem adds, almost as an afterthought, 'Just how this imperative is translated into specific public policies at a given moment, however, is subject to many interpretations' (Ibid.). This is the central, not a secondary problem. Converting the general goal of profit maximisation into a political strategy is a difficult task, given the range of options available.

Some business persons find themselves ideologically in sympathy with Thatcherism. Moreover, there are some interests that have clearly benefited from actions taken by the Conservatives after 1979: for example, those with an interest in portfolio acquisitions overseas, or those who have purchased, or been involved in the sale of, former state enterprises. Other business persons find themselves less in sympathy with Thatcherism and have been worried by the economic environment that the Government's measures have produced. For instance, as industry's 'industry', the chemical industry has been adversely affected by the shrinking of the manufacturing base of the British economy, and hence of its domestic market. Following the 'bare knuckles' episode, the CBI muted its public criticisms of government policy, whilst continuing to express reservations in private. Nevertheless, the underlying tensions came to the surface from time to time. At the 1985 CBI conference Sir Terence Beckett repeated his plea for lower interest rates and a lower pound against the Deutsche Mark (*Financial Times*, 19 November 1985).

Nevertheless, for all the public disagreements between it and businessmen, the Conservative Party is the nearest thing to a party of business that Britain has. Any doubts that business has about the Conservative party may be quickly resolved by looking at the Labour Party. The policies of the Labour Party are seen by most of them as a major threat to business activity in Britain. When the Conservative Government was elected in 1979, many people in business had convinced themselves that it was the last chance to secure a social market system in Britain; the alternative was often portrayed as a slide into some kind of down market version of East Germany. At the 1979 CBI conference, the organisation's leadership used such phrases as the 'last call for dinner for the market system' and 'drinking in the last chance saloon'. In 1982, Sir Terence Beckett declared that policies advocated by the Labour Party would 'lead to the destruction of business in this country' (*Financial Times*, 1 November 1982). These fears may be exaggerated, but they are real and, to some extent, they help to reconcile doubtful business persons to Thatcherism and perhaps deter them from giving more open encouragement to the Tory moderates.

The Labour Party: a disappointed suitor

Between 1979 and 1985 the Labour Party could be relegated to a broom cupboard of nightmare jokes as far as business was concerned; the chances of it forming a government in the forseeable future seemed slim. However, in 1985, the Labour Party's performance in the opinion polls and the local government elections showed that it was recovering lost ground among the electorate and that it might actually form the next government. Labour spokesmen concerned with economic and industrial matters suddenly found that their diaries were full with invitations for lunch from business enterprises. Business persons had to face the fact that they might once again have to do business with a Labour Government, however much they might not want to.

The Labour Party would like to have an effective working relationship in government with business, especially with manufacturing industry. Its policy aims cannot be achieved by compulsion alone; to be effectively implemented, they require co-operation, or at least acquiescence, from the business community. Under the leadership of Neil Kinnock, the party started to drop or soft pedal policy commitments regarded as particularly worrying by business such as compulsory planning agreements and withdrawal from the EC.

There are historical precedents for business being prepared to work with an incoming Labour Government after a period of Conservative rule perceived to have been economically unsuccessful. Organised business was at least prepared to give the incoming Labour Government in 1964 the benefit of the doubt, and George Brown, as he then was, was able to cajole some quite significant concessions from business interests. However, as is well known, that historic opportunity was squandered and the Labour Government ended up falling out with business, the unions and many of its own supporters. Moreover, it has to be said that any future incoming Labour Government would be perceived less sympathetically by business than was the case in 1964 because the party is seen to have shifted significantly to the left.

The Marplan survey referred to earlier showed that support for Labour among business persons is negligible. Those business persons who are open and committed Labour supporters, such as Nicholas Horsley of Northern Foods, or Robert Maxwell of

Pergamon Press, are so rare as to almost have a curiousity value among ther fellow employers. Nevertheless, the Labour Party has realised at several points in its history that it can benefit from the friendly support of business persons who are supportive of its policies, but who are also prepared to suggest how the party's intentions could best be translated into measures which would have a practical effect at the day to day level of business decision-making. Sceptics who may doubt that it is possible to be an employer and a socialist may be told by business persons who are members of the Labour Party that being a socialist makes you a better employer. One source of support among entrepreneurs for the Labour Party may be among those who started life as immigrants to Britain and found that they were only really welcome in the Labour Party to which they have remained loyal.

The Labour Party has employed a variety of mechanisms to mobilise the advice and support of such business persons as it has among its members. In 1932, the semi-secret XYZ club was formed to bring together Labour sympathisers in the City, economists and a few politicians, with Hugh Gaitskell as secretary. Hugh Dalton linked its activities to party policy-making and 'much of the financial policy in Labour's 1934 document, *For Socialism and Peace*, was a product of XYZ deliberations' (Pimlott, 1985, p. 223). The club was revived in 1944 to discuss a paper prepared for the Labour Party's Financial Committee on post-war employment policy. (see Ibid., p. 395). However, its greatest influence was in the 1930s; although it continued to function after the Second World War, it did so largely 'as a dining club for Gaitskellites' (Ibid., p. 223).

During the 1964–70 Labour Government Harold Wilson made use of *ad hoc* contacts with industrialists he trusted for advice. Similarly, at the Department of Economic Affairs, George Brown sought advice at monthly dinners from a group which had at its core individuals such as Frank (later Lord) Kearton of Courtaulds, George (later Lord) Cole of Unilever and John Berkin of Shell. Brown recalls, 'This unpublicised body of industrial advisers had an enormous influence on the apparatus we set up' (Brown, 1972, p. 94).

The formal committee which was re-established in 1972 with the help of such individuals as the late Lord Wilfrid Brown seems to have been more effective than its predecessors. Care was taken to ensure that members were recruited from individuals with a long record of service to the Labour Party. In opposition, the committee offered practical help on the development of policy. When Labour came into office in 1974, its members continued to provide assistance to busy ministers faced with a complex and pressing range of decisions. Its individual members were also, on an informal basis, able to discuss particular problems or pending decisions on behalf of ministers with civil servants, drawing on their first-hand knowledge of business. Eric Varley, as Industry Secretary and James Callaghan, as Prime Minister, working through the 10 Downing Street Policy Unit, are understood to have made use of the availability of help of this kind.

Labour industrialists are invariably on the moderate wing of the party, and it is therefore not surprising that, when the Labour Party split, some 30 to 40 per cent of the membership of the 1972 committee joined the SDP, where some of them formed a similar organisation (discussed below). This loss of members, and the general crisis within the party, meant that the 1972 committee faded into the background for a while. In 1983, it absorbed the Labour Economic Finance and Taxation Association (LEFTA) which had a membership made up largely of accountants and academics. LEFTA had been more involved in the internal politics of the Labour Party and had undergone something of a decline in effectiveness. The newly merged organisation was named The Labour Finance and Industry Group.

The Labour Finance and Industry Group is not an affiliated organisation, but is registered with the Party under its revised rules. There would be little point in affiliation for a group with some 150 members, of whom some fifty to sixty are active. The Group does not want to be drawn into internal battles within the Party, regarding the conference as a place for the constituencies and the trade unions, although it does hold a reception at the annual conference. About a quarter of the Group's members come from manufacturing industry, including small-scale employers. There are also some senior managers in nationalised industries in membership, as well as accountants, journalists, academics and consultants. The Group does not raise funds for the Party, although some of its individual members provide funds.

The new party leader, Neil Kinnock, was not slow to appreciate the contribution that the Group could make to the work of the

Party, and is understood to have encouraged its activities. One of its roles is to act as a 'think tank', drawing on the knowledge of its members to produce pamphlets on such subjects as industrial co-operatives. However, the Labour Party is not short of pamphlet writers and the Group's distinctive contribution is to provide a broader input into party thinking than could be provided by the trade unions alone. In particular, it is felt that the trade unions tend, for understandable reasons, to ignore the importance of satisfying the consumer with regard to business. Members of the Group have also been able to help with the campaigning work of the Party, contributing to a party political broadcast and more generally to the Jobs and Industry campaign. If Labour returned to office, one might expect that members of the Group would provide advice and assistance as they did in 1974–79, although they probably would not have any formal role. The Labour Party thus has a formal link with sympathetic business persons which does not exist in the Conservative Party , although it could be argued that the Conservative Party is so enmeshed with business interests that it does not need a formal link of any kind.

The Alliance: cuckoo in the nest?

Businessmen who have found the policies and attitudes of the two main parties unpalatable have increasingly found a home in the Alliance parties. It was even reported that a lot of CBI staff 'have joined the Social Democrats from the right wing of the Labour Party and the left wing of the Conservative Party', a development said 'to illustrate the belief in consensus among many people concerned with industry who are tired of the polarisation of the main parties policies' (*Financial Times*, 2 November 1981). Nevertheless, one must be cautious about readily assuming that the Alliance provides a safe refuge for business persons disillusioned with Thatcherism. An Alliance Government would at the very least create a climate of considerable uncertainty, which is the one thing that business does not like, and some of its policies might create new problems for business. The Alliance could well turn out to be a cuckoo in the nest.

However much the Alliance would like to present itself as a united front, there are tensions in the relationship between the two partners which stem from differences in outlook and policy and which might become significant in the unlikely event of an Alliance Government or, the more likely outcome, a government of another party dependent on Alliance support. It is therefore necessary to give separate consideration to the outlooks of the Liberals and the Social Democrats.

The Liberal Party is a heterogeneous and decentralised party about which it is difficult to make sustainable generalisations. One complicating factor is an apparent divergence of outlook on occasions between the Parliamentary Liberal Party and the party in the country. The Parliamentary Party often appears to be less radical in its outlook (or, at any rate, more predictable and consistent), but one should not overemphasise this difference, as there are divisions of outlook within the Parliamentary Party. Although personality factors complicate relations in such a small group, there is a broad difference between those Liberal MPs whose background is in 'community politics' and those (generally in senior leadership positions) who are anxious to convert the Liberal Party from a party of protest to a party of government. Business interests might find themselves at odds with the community politicians in the future, not because they are necessarily anti-business, but because they often have ideas of a populist kind which, if followed through, could adversely affect the environment in which business operates.

In so far as generalisations can be made about the policies of the Liberal Party as a whole, it tends to see itself as the guardian of small business persons, mainly where there is some element of profit sharing or worker co-operation in the running of the enterprise. However, all parties in the 1980s at least purport to be the friend of the small businessman, and there is nothing very distinctive about the Liberal Party in that respect. If there is one interest which, in terms of practical politics, it is especially identified with, it is the rural interest. This is not surprising when one considers that a considerable proportion of the seats that the Liberals actually hold (and many of those they might hope to win) are in the rural areas of Britain. One of the few achievements of the Liberal Party during the Lib–Lab pact of the late 1970s was to block an increase in petrol duty that would have borne heavily on rural areas; they also sought to protect agricultural interests in relation to such matters as the Green Pound (see Grand 1981) and to maintain rural transport services.

The defence of rural interests does not actually harm business, but it does relatively little for manufacturing industry. Moreover, the Liberal Party is probably more committed than any of the other political parties to the defence of the environment. A Labour Government dependent on Liberal support might consider that tougher environmental controls were an acceptable price to pay for such support. A Labour Government with a Liberal Secretary of State for the Environment (or even a Labour environment secretary required to consult with a Liberal spokesman) might lead to a toughening of environmental policy which could prove uncomfortable for some businesses.

It could be argued that it is really the Social Democrats who are the pro-industry wing of the Alliance. There are reasons for believing that the Social Democrats are, at least, likely to be aware of industry's needs. One of the earliest discussion documents brought out by the SDP argued that 'Meeting the needs of industry should be recognised as the top priority in the formulation and implementation of all government policies' (SDP, undated, p. 3). Government, the document argued, should work with the market and not against it. Government should 'play a constructive role in assisting industry to respond to market opportunities because the profitability of industry is now very low' (SDP, undated, p. 2).

Such statements may seem designed to soothe and appeal to employers caught between a Conservative Party that often seems not to care about manufacturing and a Labour Party bent on intervention in industry. Indeed, as will be discussed later in the chapter, the SDP has made considerable efforts to raise funds from business. However, not everything the SDP wants is likely to appeal to business interests. The SDP's emphasis on the importance of competition policy, and in particular on the need for more effective action on the vetting of mergers, is not likely to win favour with companies seeking to expand through acquisition. More generally, the SDP (and many of its large numbers of academic supporters) retains a faith in the extent to which change is possible through institutional action, particularly the reform of existing institutions (or the revival of old ones like the NEDC). Such a belief in institutional reform may not seem to present a threat to business interests. However, whereas institutional reformers in the 1960s were generally centralisers, the 1980s fashion, notably within the Alliance, is for decentralisation. The Labour Government's proposals for devolution were vigorously opposed by business interests, and there is no doubt that many employers are concerned about the way in which their operating environments would be complicated by the creation of any quasi-federal arrangement in the United Kingdom.

Nevertheless, the SDP's outlook is closer to that of business (particularly big business) than the Liberals. However, one does not have to be an electoral expert to forecast that the SDP is likely to continue to be the smaller of the Alliance partners in terms of Parliamentary seats. Its influence on any coalition negotiations in the future is therefore likely to be limited; how limited will depend on the outcome of the relevant election. Business might therefore find itself faced by an Alliance dominated by the Liberals, influencing government policy in a 'green' direction which could pose as many operational problems for business as the more economically oriented interventions envisaged by the Labour Party.

Forming party policy: the case of Thatcherism

The Conservative Party is the party closest to business in Britain, but that does not mean that it is a party *of* business, let alone a party *for* business. Indeed, under the leadership of Margaret Thatcher since 1975, the gap between what business wants and what the Conservative Party does has often seemed wider than at any time in modern history. Nevertheless, as has been argued, business has largely acquiesced in the policies of the Thatcher Government, despite the fact that some of those policies have at times seemed to run contrary to its interests. The explanation that will be advanced here is that business in Britain faced a major economic and political crisis in the 1970s; Mrs Thatcher and her supporters offered a clear, unequivocal set of solutions to that crisis; and, in the absence of any credible alternative, business was largely willing to follow her lead. In other words, a dominant faction in a political party formulated and applied its own solution to the political problems facing business enterprises. A political strategy for business was evolved outside the organisations of business itself.

It is very easy to reify Thatcherism, a trap into which some left-wing commentators fall. After all, what it really amounts to is

little more than three elements: a collection of rather elementary
political principles which are capable of being presented in terms
of a household economy or the operations of a small business –
indeed, the term 'Robertsism' might be more appropriate so as to
refer to the origins of these ideas in Grantham; and unshakeable
conviction that these principles are correct, and a willingness to
implement them with a minimum of deviation, with fervour and
with determination; and a populist instinct for understanding and
expressing the aspirations of a considerable body of ordinary
people. It was the loss of this last element which led Thatcherism
to appear to falter in 1985.

The attachment to certain principles and to populism often
coincide, but they can come into conflict. Indeed, what is often
presented as a coherent and unswerving strategy contains strong
elements of political opportunism within it. It is perhaps worth
recalling that in the 1960s there was some discussion by political
analysts about whether 'Gaullism' amounted to a coherent political doctrine. The question would not seem worth posing in the
1980s, and it may be that twenty years hence, the ink spilt on
analysing the true nature of Thatcherism will have little more than
curiousity value. However, it is worth considering here, if only
because it provides a further illustration of a general theme developed in this book, the relative political weakness of business.

It is worth recalling that the Thatcherite tendency did not
become dominant in the Conservative Party overnight. After all,
throughout the post-war period, it was the 'Tory' or 'one nation',
or in the hydrological terminology of the 1980s, the 'wet' tendency
that predominated in the Conservative Party. This tendency was
not immediately swept aside. The Conservative Party's major 1977
statement on economic strategy, *The Right Approach to the Economy*, reflected a compromise between the Thatcherites and the
more traditional sections of the party. Despite her announced
intention to have a Cabinet with 'only the people who want to go
in the direction which every instinct tells me we have to go' (*The
Observer*, 25 February 1979), Mrs Thatcher was obliged to include
a number of Tory moderates in her team, although most of them
were later removed to the backbenches. It is clear that the Thatcherites had been preparing their ground for some time. A variety of
formal and informal 'think tanks' have played a significant role in
the development of Thatcherite policies, not least the Centre for

Policy Studies, founded in 1974, by Margaret Thatcher and Sir Keith Joseph among others. Mrs Thatcher had to resign as a director in 1975, but she subsequently acknowledged the part that it had played in the development and propagation of a revived 'free society' philosophy (see *Observer* interview, 25 February 1979).

Business was receptive to a new approach. It had seen the effort at tripartite co-operation by the Heath Government collapse in chaos. As Colin Leys (1985, p. 17) argues, a majority of businessmen had come to feel that the survival of capitalism in Britain was at stake:

> Consequently short-term business interests, and even the long-term interests of individuals or firms, had to be sacrificed. Even those who were unconvinced by the Thatcherite project saw no realistic political alternative (this was the feeling to which Mrs Thatcher shrewdly appealed with the TINA slogan – 'There Is No Alternative').

In a posthumously reported interview, the late Sir John Methven, CBI director-general from 1976, described himself as 'a sort of social democrat', but added that 'the situation was now so bad that the shock of Thatcherism might be our last and only chance of survival' (*The Guardian*, 1 May 1980). The CBI had tried to make its own response to what it saw as the crisis faced by business. It produced its own series of policy programmes, starting with *The Road to Recovery* in 1976. However, to some extent these documents simply reflected developments in thinking within the Conservative Party; in other respects, they reflected an uneasy and often rather feeble compromise between 'hard' and 'soft' liners within the CBI. This was apparent in relation to pay determination and incomes policy. In its 1978 document, the CBI stressed the importance of pay moderation, yet also argued that employers must be able to offer sufficient rates of pay to recruit and retain labour, commenting, 'Employers do not want to choose between moderation and freedom; they want both' (CBI, 1978, p. 41).

The CBI continued to produce policy discussion papers, the 1985 paper being particularly interesting for its focus on questions of political reform. However, it is doubtful whether much notice was taken of these documents by businessmen. Leys (1985, p. 19)

notes that 'in 1983 it was still very hard to find any energetic or
informed commitment to the CBI strategy papers among senior
company executives'. This is not surprising when one considers
that only two of the twenty senior businessmen interviewed by
Leys saw 'the definition of national goals and of strategies for
achieving them, as natural concerns of businessmen, and neither
of these had ever sought a major role in forming or leading
business opinion' (Ibid.). If business as a social category is not
prepared to develop its own sense of political direction, or respond
to those who are trying to provide such a sense of direction, it is
not surprising that the task of defining what is in the interests of
business is left to conviction politicians with a sense of mission.

Business persons in politics

Most business persons, especially large employers, are too busy to
pursue a political career, either as party activists or as MPs. For
most of them, becoming an MP would also involve a considerable
financial sacrifice. Nevertheless, many business persons, notably
smaller scale employers and the self-employed, do become involved in the Conservative Party. Provincial small-scale employers
have played a significant role in the constituency parties where one
survey showed that 32 per cent of party chairs were small and
medium proprietors (excluding farmers who accounted for
another 9 per cent) (Pinto-Duschinsky, 1973). Two more recent
pieces of evidence emphasise the particular appeal of the Conservative Party to the small-scale entrepreneur. By departing from
the conventional classifications of social class, Heath, Jowell and
Curtice (1985, p. 20) show that the 'petty bourgeoisie' is the social
category most likely to support the Conservative Party, 71 per cent
voting Conservative in 1983. Similarly, Curtice and Steed (1984, p.
348) show that, although the Liberal Party has long tended to do
better in middle-class seats, in what they call 'business middle-class
seats' which had 'a high proportion of self-made rather than
professionally qualified men', the Alliance improvement on the
1979 Liberal vote was 'clearly and consistently below average'.

However, their importance as voters and activists does not mean
that small-scale entrepreneurs are well represented on the Conservative benches at Westminster. In fact, the ten elections between

1945 and 1974 was the return 'of a mere eleven small businessmen, and of these the majority, seven, sat on the Labour side of the House' (Mellors, 1978, p. 73). There was no lack of businessmen in the House as a whole. The figures provided by Mellors (p. 62) show that 41 per cent of the Conservative MPs elected between 1945 and 1974 were business persons, a figure that rises to 51 per cent if one counts farmers and landowners as being in business. Moreover, 10 per cent of the Labour MPs elected during the period had a business background. Of the Conservatives elected in 1983, 36 per cent had a business background, a figure that rises to 41 per cent when farmers are added in. The Labour percentage of business persons elected held steady at 9 per cent (there was only one Labour farmer). Only one Alliance MP had a business background, but 22 per cent of defeated Liberal candidates and 20 per cent of defeated SDP candidates had business occupations. (Figures from Criddle, 1984, pp. 236–7.)

Given these figures, why were leading business persons so concerned about the lack of understanding between industry and Parliament that in 1977 they formed the Industry and Parliament Trust to bridge the perceived gap and to give MPs direct experience of business operations? First, it depends how one percieves the figures. From one perspective, the fact that less than one-third of the new MPs elected in 1983 had business experience is worrying (CBI, 1985, p. 35) because it means that over two-thirds had no such experience; from another perspective, between a quarter and a third of the intake might seem more than enough. Secondly, it depends what one means by 'business experience'. A few years in the City, or even in an industrial enterprise, before entering Parliament, gives a relatively limited knowledge of the problems of business, and the experience is likely to date and become less relevant over time. Many MPs, of course, acquire non-executive directorships, but such activities are an adjunct to their main work as professional politicians. Indeed, it is increasingly possible to pursue a life-long career as a professional politician. Working as an aide or 'researcher' for an MP or a minister may be a prelude to obtaining a winnable Parliamentary seat. Thirdly, and perhaps most important, one has to ask in what kind of business enterprise the experience was obtained. Although precise figures do not exist, a preponderance of Conservative MPs appear to have acquired any business experience that they have in the City or in some other services sector, such as advertising, property sales or market research, rather than in manufacturing industry.

Indeed, a survey conducted for the Industry and Parliament Trust showed that less than 15 per cent of MPs had had any direct experience of industry. The Industry and Parliament Trust does not confine its operations to manufacturing industry, but, apart from nationalised industries, all but three of its member companies in 1983 were predominantly manufacturing firms (of the other three, one was a clearing bank and two were retailers, of which one had substantial manufacturing operations, and the other maintained very close links with its manufacturing suppliers).

Apart from small-scale employers, it is the manufacturing portion of the business community which is least well represented in the House of Commons. There are, of course, a number of senior business persons in the House of Lords. It is interesting that the 1984–85 House of Lords Select Committee on Overseas Trade, whose report seems to have rattled the Thatcher Government to judge by the robustness of ministerial criticism of its contents, contained a number of experienced business persons, whilst others (peers and commoners) were summoned to give evidence.

Business funding of political parties

In the whole area of relations between business and politics, few issues arouse more political passion than the question of donations by business to party funds. These donations are largely made to the Conservative Party or to organisations close to it, although some funds have gone in recent years to the Alliance parties. Business donations to the Labour Party are negligible.

Given the heat which the issue arouses, it is unfortunate that it is not easy to make a careful analysis of the facts. There are two principal difficulties that stand in the way of this. First, company donations to the Conservative party tend to increase substantially in election years. In the 1979 election year, *Labour Research* figures showed a 63 per cent increase in donations from the previous year; in the 1983 election year, there was an 80 per cent increase. Should one take as the base year for any analysis a non-election year or an election year? Secondly, information on company donations arises from Section 19(1) of the 1967 Companies Act which requires companies to publish in their directors' report donations of more than £200 for a political purpose. What constitutes a political purpose is specified in Section 19(3). However, 'This definition does not appear to be comprehensive enough to catch "conduit" organisations which . . . collect funds from companies and pass them on in whole or in part to the Conservative Party' (Constitutional Reform Centre, 1985, pp. 7–8).

Nevertheless, it is clear that only a minority of businesses give donations to the Conservative Party (or the Alliance). Less than 15 per cent (148) of *The Times 1000* largest companies declared a donation to the Conservative Party in reports published between August 1983 and August 1984. Even if the net is widened to include research centres and propaganda bodies, not all of which are linked to the Conservative Party, the percentage is still under a quarter (223 companies). (Figures derived from Constitutional Reform Centre, 1985, p. 10.)

Which companies give money to the Conservatives?

Pinto-Duschinsky has shown (1985, p. 330) that Conservative Central Office income in real terms in the 1980s was 10 to 20 per cent lower than in the 1950s and 1960s. As far as company donations are concerned, there does seem to have been a trend for the Conservative Party to become increasingly reliant on a smaller number of companies which pay an increasing share of the total amount donated. Labour Party figures suggest that the number of companies donating to the Conservatives declined from 470 in 1979 to 320 in 1983–84 (*The Guardian*, 25 July 1985). The Labour Research Department (not an official Labour Party body) tried to suggest that what was termed a 'dramatic' 19 per cent drop in funding of the Conservative Party by manufacturing companies between 1980 and 1981 'reflects a decline in faith in a government whose policies have devastated the manufacturing base of the economy' (*Labour Research*, August 1982). However, subsequent *Labour Research* figures showed that fifty-two companies who had stopped giving money to the Conservatives between 1979 and 1982 made a donation in the 1983 election year. Pinto-Duschinsky's longer range work (1981, p. 232) shows that 'Over the last thirty years, company contributions have not fully kept up with increases in the cost of living' and 'companies have been less regular and less dependable as political backers.' Moreover, there are indications that some companies may consult their shareholders in future before making political donations. Noting that 'the climate of opinion is undoubtedly changing', the chairman of BET, which gave £10,000 to the Conservatives in 1984, told shareholders at the 1985 annual meeting of the company that they would be consulted in future before any political donations were authorised (*Financial Times*, 6 September 1985).

The long-term trend towards a decline in business financial support for the Conservative Party may be related to gradual changes in the structure of companies operating in Britain. Put simply, there has been an increase in the number of foreign owned companies and a decrease in the number of family dominated companies confined to one industrial sector. One point that is well established in the literature is that British branches of multinational corporations are relatively unlikely to make political donations (Pinto-Duschinsky, 1981, p. 232; Constitutional Reform Centre, p. 18). Such companies may wish to keep a low political profile and to avoid accusations of interference in the domestic affairs of another country.

It is also evident that companies in certain industrial sectors are especially likely to make donations to the Conservative Party. Ross (1983, p. 37) notes that 'Three sectors of the British economy (finance and property companies; food, drink and tobacco firms; construction companies) have steadily been accounting for a larger and larger proportion of Conservative Party donations.' *Labour Research* (1984, p. 205) estimates that 29 per cent of all the donations they covered in 1983 came from banking, insurance, property and investment trust companies. They term this the 'parasite factor': less emotively, it could be said that firms in the financial sector perceive themselves as more likely to benefit from a Conservative Government and to be harmed by a Labour Government. The food, drink and tobacco sector has traditional historical links with the Conservative Party. The construction sector still contains many companies run by the founding family or entrepreneur and is also vulnerable to Labour schemes for nationalisation, greater regulation or the extension of 'direct labour'.

It is also clear that a small number of companies making large donations account for considerable proportion of the total received. Twenty-one donations recorded by *Labour Research* in

1983–84 were of £40 000 or more with a total value of £1 238 191 or 37 per cent of the money recorded. Substantial donors to the Conservative Party, or to organisations donating the greater part of their income to the Conservative Party, have included British and Commonwealth Shipping, an investment company with a wide range of interests; Hanson Trust, a rapidly growing conglomerate; and Allied-Lyons, a food and drink group.

Business funding of the Alliance

When the Social Democrats were formed in 1981, there was widespread speculation that they would attract considerable financial support from industry. Interviews by the *Financial Times* (10 March 1981) with chairmen of major companies showed that 'a considerable number of the chairmen are willing to consider supporting a credible Centre Party'. The reality has been a little more sobering. *Labour Research* estimated that nine companies gave £31 750 to the Alliance in 1983, and the Labour Party's research department came up with a similar figure of £28 700, although Alliance sources suggested that this would rise to £75 000 by the end of 1985 (*Financial Times*, 18 September 1985). Much of the money appeared to come from companies who gave their main donation to the Conservative Party and hedged their bets by giving a secondary donation to the Alliance, although the British School of Motoring was a major donor to the Liberal Party. Companies which have given either to the joint Alliance fund, or to both Alliance parties equally, include Tate and Lyle, and Morgan, Crucible and Pearsons (owners of the *Financial Times*).

It was reported in the summer of 1985 that the SDP had raised £35 000 already from business that year through lunches with Dr David Owen (*The Economist*, 20 July 1985). However, attempts to sell a journal called the *Parliamentary Bulletin* to businessmen at £250 a year as an inconspicuous way of raising money appear to have failed. In the autumn of 1985, the Alliance parties launched a new financial appeal to businessmen, centred around a forty-five minute presentation by senior Alliance figures to boards of directors of companies expressing interest (*Financial Times*, 18 September 1985).

The SDP's equivalent of the Labour Finance and Industry Group, the Industrial Policy Association, has sixty or so businessmen in membership and runs four study groups working on aspects of industrial policy. Unlike its Labour counterpart, it apparently is prepared to contemplate a fund raising role (*The Economist*, 20 July 1985). The chairman of the SDP's financial advisory committee in 1985 was Mr David Sainsbury, finance director of the supermarket company. Sir James Sainsbury, a director of J. Sainsbury and chairman of the textiles group Vanton Viyella, was among the members.

The significance of business donations

It is not easy to assess the significance of the contributions that business makes to party finances because of the difficulty of obtaining reliable figures about party funds at the constituency level. The Constitutional Reform Centre estimated in its report that over 55 to 60 per cent of central Conservative Party funds are provided by companies (Constitutional Reform Centre, 1985, p. 10). However, it should be remembered that the greater part of the Party's funds are raised and spent at the constituency level through individual subscriptions, donations and the various time honoured (and some new) means of fund raising. In 1981–82, the income of Conservative constituency associations totalled £8 million, twice the level of central income (see Pinto-Duschinsky, 1985, pp. 330 and 331). It is difficult to say what proportion of total party income is provided by business donations because relatively little is known about such donations at constituency level. The Houghton Committee (1976 p. 35) found that at constituency level '5 per cent of the Conservative Party's income came from company donations in 1973, rising to 6 per cent in 1974, an election year'. However, in a study of election campaign funds in a marginal constituency, Pinto-Duschinsky found that 23 per cent of the total raised came from company donations. If one was to make an informed guess on the basis of the available evidence, perhaps between a fifth and a quarter of total Conservative Party income comes from business in a non-election year, but this figure could rise to over a third in an election year. The Social Democrats rely much more heavily on subscriptions which provided 63 per cent of their central funds in 1983–84.

The Labour Party is, of course, substantially dependent on institutional finance from the trade unions and 'By 1979 union payments for Labour Party purposes had overtaken company donations to the Conservative Party' (Pinto-Duschinsky, 1985, p. 341). Pinto-Duschinsky estimates that the unions gave £4.4 million to the Labour Party in 1982, of which £2.8 million was paid in affiliation fees to the National Executive Committee. This is not dissimilar to the £2.9 million in donations given to Conservative central funds in 1981–82 (Ibid., p. 330). Although the central income of the Conservatives was more than one and half a half times that of Labour in 1983, Pinto-Duschinsky shows that expenditures per vote by the two main parties were broadly similar in that year: 45 pence for the Conservatives, 44 pence for Labour, but only 33 pence for the Alliance. However, when subsidies in kind (such as free broadcasting) are added in, the relative position of Labour and the Alliance improves: 82 pence per vote for the Conservatives, 85 pence per vote for the Alliance and 100 pence per vote for the Labour Party (Ibid., p. 339).

Even if there is not gross unfairness in the distribution of campaigning finances among the political parties, there is concern about the extent to which the major parties are dependent on institutional funding. A study sponsored by (but not representing a view of) the Hansard Society (1981, p. 45) noted that the growing dependence of the two major parties on institutional funding 'is not only unhealthy in itself, but can lead to a dangerous polarisation of political attitudes, and so distort democratic choice'.

What is often overlooked in the debate about this perceived problem is that British political parties have relatively few individual members in relation to their numbers of votes and charge them relatively little for membership (with the exception of the SDP) compared with, say, West German parties. For example, Labour's individual membership, at 3 per cent of Labour's total vote among the electorate in 1983 'was the lowest proportion of any social democratic party in Western Europe' (Butler and Kavanagh, 1984, p. 46). An insufficient income from individual members leads to a greater dependence on institutional funding. Many commentators have concluded that the only solution is to provide state funding for political parties. However, such funds might further reduce the incentive to parties to attract more individual members. Indeed, the debate on how state funds might be provided distracts attention from the more fundamental question of why it is that British political parties have become less successful at attracting and retaining individual members.

It is often argued that the present funding arrangements tie the political parties too closely to particular interests. The Hansard report argues that the existing financial relationships between the parties and their institutional supporters accentuate social conflict, entrenching class conflict (Hansard Society, 1981, p. 30). However, it should be remembered that there is nothing illegitimate about the expression and organisation of interests in politics; political activity is in large part about articulating and attempting to reconcile divergent interests. It is not surprising that interests should be linked to major political parties. Indeed, they give a solid ballast to parties, a link to the realities of political life which parties might otherwise lack.

Conclusions

This chapter has examined the various ways in which business and political parties relate to one another in Britain, but should not obscure the extent to which the business and political worlds are largely separate ones. Even the Conservative Party's relationship with business is more problematic and tenuous than is often assumed. Although no direct evidence is available, one may speculate with a degree of confidence that business persons spend more time working for business interest associations that they do for political parties. They are naturally preoccupied with the immediate issues affecting their businesses and a trade association can often be more help in those areas than a political party. Political parties are vote-seeking organisms; business persons do not have many votes, particularly large-scale employers; and parties may often be more interested in reassuring groups critical of business such as environmentalists. Business persons cannot ignore political parties, but they cannot rely on them as a principal means of safeguarding their interests.

9 Business Associations and Public Policy

Business interest associations should not only be viewed as 'lobbies', seeking to exert influence on government, customers or suppliers, or as providers of services to their members, important though these functions are. Business associations are capable of contributing, and do so increasingly, to the formulation and implementation of public policy. 'Public policy' is seen as covering a task or activity which government regards as its duty to discharge, or to arrange for its discharge by others within a framework laid down by government.

In Chapter 3, it was pointed out that business can assist in the task of governance in three principal ways: policy design, policy clearance and policy implementation. Some of this assistance is provided by large firms interacting directly with government, but associations have certain advantages as a mechanism for policy implementation, especially in industries where there is a wide spread of firms of different sizes. Even in industries dominated by a few large firms, government may prefer to work through associations to some extent to avoid changes of favouritism.

Although government policies such as aid for high technology projects are often operated by direct contact with firms, without any intermediation by an association (see East 1985), this chapter focuses on the contribution of business associations to policy implementation. The implementation of policies by associations acting as private interest governments, or the provision of associative systems of self-regulation, are more extensive practices than is generally realized. However, as Boddewyn (1985, p. 42) notes, 'the correspondence between the two concepts [of self-regulation and private interest government] is not complete'. For example, codes of practice relating to advertising developed by associations

189

in the pharmaceutical industry, discussed by Sargent later in this chapter, first emerged as attempts to retain public confidence and to prevent legislative action; government involvement came later. This type of self-regulation, at least in its original form, is close to what Boddewyn calls 'pure self-regulation'. The system of self-regulation in the financial services industry discussed later in the chapter is more like 'mandated self-regulation' which occurs when 'An industry is ordered or designated by the government to develop, use and enforce norms' (Ibid., p. 34). As such, it is closer to private interest government which has been defined as 'an attempt to make associative, self-interested collective action contribute to the achievement of public policy objectives' (Streeck and Schmitter, 1985, p. 17).

The privatisation of public policy

The term 'corporatism' could have been used here in relation to delegations of public policy functions to representative organisations, but it is deliberately avoided, except in specific usages, for three reasons. First, despite various attempts at clarification, there is little agreement about what the term 'corporatism' actually means, and it has been used in so many different ways that its deployment here would confuse rather than clarify the discussion. Second, although neo-corporatist writers may have succeeded in stripping the term of its historical associations with fascism, it remains an emotive one even in academic circles and can provoke reactions which frustrate the dispassionate analysis of significant phenomena. Third, and most importantly, corporatism has been generally associated with an interventionist paradigm (see Cawson, 1985, p. 8), in which a state expanding the scope of its activities draws groups representing capital and labour closer to it so as to secure their consent and co-operation in the implementation of policy.

However, as will become apparent from the examples discussed later, the delegation of public policy functions to business interest associations can be associated with a state that is seeking to reduce the scope of its functions, so that public provision is replaced by state sponsored private provision. Such a retreating state may be faced with situations where there are compelling reasons that lead it to assume new responsibilities, but these again may be discharged through self-regulation by business interests. The process as a whole may be characterised as the privatisation of public policy (see Rainbird and Grant, 1985b), with the Thatcher Government in Britain offering a contemporary example.

It must be emphasised that such a process of the privatisation of public policy cannot be adequately conceptualised through the revival of old liberal paradigms of the non-interventionist state. The privatised state does intervene in a wide range of areas of economic activity, even if it does so hesitantly, reluctantly and indirectly. (For a discussion, see Bonnett, 1985.) Such interventions can be said 'to entail a blurring of the line of division, crucial to liberal political theory, between the state and civil society' (Goldthorpe, 1984, p. 324). What is public and what is private is often unclear, and the problems of legitimacy and the 'public interest' which such a situation leads to are often avoided rather than being confronted and resolved. Such an outcome is assisted by the fact that one is talking about a variety of *ad hoc* arrangements operating in particular sectors of the economy with no common underlying rationale except an admission, rarely made explicit, that there are some activities that cannot adequately be performed either by the market or the state.

Because of the particular historical context of this book, many of the examples discussed here relate to a government which regards state failure as more of a problem than market failure. These examples, although refracted through a particular ideological lens, may be seen as pointing to a more general process in western societies which has been characterised by Streeck and Schmitter (1985) in terms of a model of associative order. Associations are seen as providing a distinctive basis for social order, alongside the community, the market and the state. In principle, the notion of 'associative order' is compatible with either an expanding or a retreating state; however, the emphasis in Streeck and Schmitter's discussion is on the links between such arrangements and neo-corporatism. Indeed, they use the term 'corporative–associative order' (Streeck and Schmitter, 1985, p. 17).

Used in a comparative context, and applied to countries such as Austria or Norway, such a linkage may be entirely valid. In the British case, as the examples discussed in this chapter will show, one has a palimpsest which reflects a variety of decisions taken under different historical circumstances. It is therefore difficult to detect any consistent set of enabling conditions. Private organised interests have certainly been used in Britain in the way anticipated by Streeck and Schmitter (Ibid., p. 16) 'to put to public purposes the type of social order that associations can generate and embody'. They have also been used, under the Thatcher Government, in pursuit of what Streeck and Schmitter describe as an alternative strategy: 'The neo-liberal restoration of the *market* aims essentially at the liberation of *individual self-interests* from bureaucratic-regulatory constraints' (Ibid., p. 16). The difficulty with this non-interventionist mode of policy delegation is that there is a tension between a willingness to delegate functions to business associations and a lack of willingness to intervene to ensure that such organisations are capable of discharging their delegated functions properly.

Even if the principles on which the assumption of public policy functions by interest associations have been based are ambiguous or even contradictory, the research on which this book is based suggests that such delegation is extensive. One motivation is that associations may be able to do things that governments might wish to do but, for various reasons, are unable to do on an official basis. A number of examples may be found in the area of foreign trade. Before the United Kingdom recognised the German Democratic Republic (DDR), trade between Britain and the DDR was regulated by agreements between the CBI and the DDR's Chamber of Foreign Trade. (Similar arrangements existed in West Germany; see Streeck, 1983, p. 280.) As sectoral trade agreements have grown as part of a protectionists tendency in the late 1970s and 1980s, so trade associations have acquired an important role in the negotiation of such agreements, acting in effect, if not officially, on behalf of the British Government. Thus, restrictions on the Japanese share of the British car market have been negotiated between the Society of Motor Manufacturers and Traders and its Japanese counterpart. The two fastest growing products in terms of sales in the machine tool industry are computer-controlled lathes and machining centres, and Japanese machine tool manufacturers agreed in talks with the British Machine Tool Trades Association in 1982 to restrain their shipments to the UK, an agreement renewed in 1984.

Of course, many public policy problems are dealt with through regulations enacted and enforced by the state, expecially where EC directives require actions of this kind. However, even EC policies can be implemented with the co-operation of associations. In 1980, the Council of Ministers took a Decision requiring member states to reduce by 30 per cent their consumption of chlorofluorocarbon propellants in aerosols which, it had been hypothesised were adversely affecting the stratospheric ozone layer in the atmosphere. The Department of the Environment asked the British Aerosol Manufacturers' Association (BAMA) to use its 'best endeavours' (a term often used in British official parlance) to achieve the required reduction. The association commented in its annual report, 'In effect, BAMA is acting as an agent of Government without official status although this is preferable in the long run to the possibility of legislative control.' BAMA run explanatory seminars for member and non-member companies and carried out confidential surveys in order to assess progress towards the target reduction of 30 per cent.

In this chapter, four sets of examples of the discharge of public policy functions by business associations are discussed in order to illustrate and amplify the general points made in this introductory section. Two of the cases concern areas where there has been long-standing involvement by business associations in public policy: dairy products and pharmaceuticals. Two of the cases are concerned with efforts by the Thatcher Government to privatise public policy through the involvement of business associations. One of these cases (the provision of industrial training) involves the transfer of functions formerly discharged by statutory bodies (industrial training boards) to employers' associations acting as non-statutory training organisations. The other case concerns the creation of a regulatory framework for the financial services industry based on the concept of self-regulation.

The dairy sector

For more than fifty years, the production and pricing of dairy products in Britain has been regulated by state sponsored and private bodies operating within a general legal framework which seeks to maintain a balance between the interests of the government, the farmer, the dairy processor and the final consumer. In the 1980s, attempts by the Thatcher Government to increase the influence of market forces in this policy arena enhanced the importance of its private governance arrangements. However, during the same period, changes in the industry were placing those arrangements under new strains.

There are a number of complexities in the private interest government arrangements in the dairy sector (e.g., the role of producer retailers and producer processors) which cannot be dealt with in the limited space available here. (For fuller accounts, see Grant, 1985b; Grant, 1985c; Winter, 1984.) This discussion will focus on the relationship between the Milk Marketing Board (MMB) and the Dairy Trade Federation (DTF) representing the independent dairy product manufacturers and retailers, a relationship conducted largely within a body known as the Joint Committee which is discussed further below.

The MMB is, in essence, a state sponsored co-operative to which all farmers producing significant amounts of milk for sale are legally required to belong. The MMB buys all the milk that farmers can produce (although the level of production is governed by EC quotas). It then sells the milk to processors, either for retail sale in liquid form or for transformation into a variety of dairy products. This apparently straightforward division of responsibilities is complicated by the fact that the MMB's commercial arm, Dairy Crest, is itself the largest producer of dairy products: in particular, it dominates the butter and cheddar cheese markets.

Since 1954 there has been an official body established by statutory instrument known as the Joint Committee which is the negotiating forum for the MMB and DTF. The membership of the DTF is conditional in that 'if in the opinion of the Minister that body has ceased to exist or has ceased to represent the views of buyers of milk, such last mentioned members shall be appointed by such other body or bodies as appear to the Minister to represent for the time being the views of the buyers of milk by retail' (Statutory Instrument 1979/249). In other words, a particular organisation is designated by government as the representative of a defined group of businesses.

The Joint Committee negotiates the prices of milk for manufacturing (which vary according to the product being made) and is extensively involved in such matters as training, milk quality and the allocation of milk in the event of a shortage of supply. The Manufacturing Milk Prices Subcommittee of the Joint Committee meets approximately once a month to decide on the prices of milk for manufacturing. Until 1985, the Government fixed the prices at which milk for liquid consumption was sold to the processors, and then on to the consumer. However, the Thatcher Government was ideologically unsympathetic to such intervention in the market and (after some internal arguments) withdrew from the role. Following decontrol of the retail price, the Joint Committee set up a Liquid Milk Prices Committee. This represents a further extension of the role of the Joint Committee, although liquid milk negotiations are likely to be held more sporadically than those for manufacturing prices. More generally, it should be noted that the Joint Committee has been responsible for deciding questions which firms normally regard as matters to be left to their own initiative, the price paid for a basic raw material and the allocation of supplies of that material. The MMB and the DTF have also been involved in negotiations about the rationalisation of the industry's surplus manufacturing capacity. Although final decisions on plant closures were to be left to individual companies, such negotiations are at variance with the assumption that British business associations are incapable of participating in intra-industry adjustment (see Dyson, 1983, pp. 55–6).

The DTF's involvement in a publicly sanctioned negotiating arrangement has had implications for its internal organisation. Not only does it need substantial resources to maintain a large and highly skiled staff, but these resources are provided through a very unusual subscription collection arrangement. The problem of 'free riding' is minimised by the MMB imposing a levy on all first-hand buyers of milk which it then passes on to the DTF. This arrangement is obligatory rather than compulsory, as the relevant clause can always be struck out of the contract, but in practice it ensures that virtually all dairies contribute to the funds of the DTF.

Given that each side has only one vote on the Joint Committee (there is a procedure for arbitration in the event of deadlock), it is clearly important that dairy processors agree among themselves about how that vote should be exercised. The constitution of the DTF therefore requires that decisions shall generally be taken without recourse to voting. Although in practice votes are rare in business associations, the DTF is the only association among those studied that has a constitutional requirement for decision-making by consensus.

The arrangements between the MMB and the DTF represent an intricate and carefully balanced political mechanism operating within a framework established by successive governments. However, in the 1980s, the system was coming under new strains. Surpluses of some products, such as cheddar cheese, led to prolonged arguments over how prices should be determined, given the MMB's wish to protect farmers, and the manufacturers' desire to secure their market. The imposition of quotas led to overcapacity in the industry and arguments about how this should be eliminated. Perhaps the most significant underlying tension was resentment from the independent dairy companies about what they saw as unfair competition from Dairy Crest. A report commissioned by the Ministry of Agriculture (the Touche Ross report) concluded that Dairy Crest had performed less well than an independent company would be expected to and that its strategy had been influenced by the interests of the milk producers which MMB represents. The report cleared the MMB of charges that it had used Dairy Crest directly to assist its negotiating position with independent dairies, but argued that the private companies had been weakened in Joint Committee negotiations over prices by the fact that Dairy Crest had not been represented on their side. Even the most carefully constructed formula for dealing with commercial issues which involves a complex mixture of the public and the private may be disturbed by external factors which are beyond the direct control of the participants.

Business associations and public policy in the pharmaceutical industry (contributed by Jane Sargent)

The Pharmaceutical Price Regulation Scheme

The Pharmaceutical Price Regulation Scheme (PPRS) was first established in 1958 as the Voluntary Price Regulation Scheme (VPRS) with the initial objective of producing a fair and reasonable drugs bill for the National Health Service (NHS). Successive British Governments' dissatisfaction with the ability of the scheme to achieve its principal objective resulted in several revisions of it, and an increasing use by government of supplementary statutory measures to compensate for its perceived weaknesses. What follows is a brief account of the development and partial demise of the PPRS as an example of the involvement of a business association in the development and implementation of public policy on prescription medicine prices.

The PPRS provides the framework within which individual companies supplying medicines to the NHS can negotiate with a government agency the level of profit return on their sales and the range of prices they can charge the NHS for their products. Agreement and implementation of the PPRS are the outcome of separate processes. The scheme is negotiated between the Government (the DHSS and the three regional ministries) and the British prescription medicine industry through their trade association, the Association of the British Pharmaceutical Industry (ABPI). The negotiation process involves the ABPI as a mediator between the Government and the industry, but negotiation of individual companies' returns on their sales to the NHS are conducted without the use of an intermediary. Initially, the ABPI was assigned a role as monitor and provider to government of information essential for the successful administration of the scheme. This role has been eroded over the years, however, as government departments have taken these responsibilities upon themselves.

Introduction and maintenance of the PPRS reflected the belief of successive governments that the prescription medicine industry earned excessively high profits from their sales to the NHS. Government preferred to establish the size of the NHS drug bill by negotiation with the industry because of a reluctance to fix prices, because of a belief that the industry was more likely to accept controls that they had some say in establishing, and because statutory controls were regarded as too rigid and thus incapable of taking into account the circumstances of each company involved. The cost of administration of the scheme by government officials was also a determining factor.

For the industry's part, a willingness to participate in the scheme has reflected a fear that refusal to participate might lead to the introduction of more restrictive, statutory measures. Nevertheless, removal of the word 'voluntary' from the title of the scheme in 1978 reflected the true nature of the industry's participation.

Negotiation of the scheme through the ABPI was the industry's choice initially and reflected their belief that only by acting collectively could they ensure that the controls applied by government were imposed uniformly. The ABPI's role during negotiation of the first and subsequent schemes was to produce a scheme that was satisfactory to both government and industry. During implementation of the early schemes the ABPI supplied government with information about companies' sales, profits and investment and fulfilled an undertaking to prevent pharmaceutical companies from increasing the prices of the medicines they supplied to the NHS. The success of the scheme depended on the ABPI's ability to perform both functions which, in its turn, was dependent upon the ABPI's representativeness of the prescription medicine companies supplying the NHS, its ability to ensure those companies' compliance with the scheme and its ability to provide the information required by the Minister of Health to apply the scheme.

Over the past twenty-five years the ABPI has made several attempts to review its internal procedures and to increase its resources in order to fulfil its role in the price regulation scheme. Neither in 1958, nor subsequently, however, were the ABPI's rules changed to give the association the authority to ensure the compliance of its members with the scheme. Hence the third and subsequent versions of the scheme contained no undertaking by the ABPI on behalf of its members to restrict price increases on the products they supplied to the NHS. The ABPI merely agreed to use its best endeavours when difficulties arose concerning negotiations between government and individual companies. Moreover, despite its attempts to increase foreign and British prescription medicine companies' sense of commitment to the scheme, the Government has resorted to the use of statutory measures from time to time to force the compliance of specific companies. For example, in 1973, the Government permitted companies other than the patent holder, Roche Products Ltd, to provide the NHS with equivalents to Librium and Valium when Roche refused to lower the price of those medicines. (For further details, see Sargent, 1985, pp. 113–14 and p. 120.)

Furthermore, over the past twenty-five years, government has increased its powers to enforce compliance with the scheme and to fix prices without the agreement of the industry or the companies concerned. For example, the National Health Services Act 1977 gave the Minister of Health the power to fix the price of medicines supplied to the NHS by Order if agreement could not be reached with the manufacturers.

Government anxiety about the failure of the scheme to provide a fair and reasonable drugs bill for the NHS has persisted. Thus, in December 1983, without prior consultation with the ABPI, the PPRS introduced in 1978 was modified by the Government to reduce the level of permitted profits from NHS sales and the level of sales promotion expenditure. In addition, the target rate of profits for individual companies was reduced by an average of four percentage points. Regulations enacted in 1985 introduced the 'Limited List' of products doctors could prescribe on the NHS for minor ailments, and some tranquilizers and sedatives, to the cheapest and most effective available. These regulations represented a major departure from the procedure for determining the size of the NHS drugs bill introduced in 1958. This departure reflected the Government's determination to restrict the size of the drugs bill and its belief that, as a monopsonist, it should use any means at its disposal to achieve this end.

The PPRS still has a role to play in determining the price of prescription medicines supplied to the NHS, but the failure of the PPRS to achieve its initial objective without reinforcement by statutory measures reflected the timidity of an industry which was too afraid to permit its collective voice, the ABPI, to participate fully with government on this issue because of a fear that in so doing they might lose their autonomy to set their own prices. Even so, the industry 'voluntarily' agreed to participate in the price regulation scheme because they perceived the arrangement as a safeguard against something worse. Ironically, the prescription medicine industry's timidity has produced the very situation it sought to avoid when agreeing to the first VPRS.

Pharmaceutical advertising

As well as the prescription medicines industry supplying the NHS, the pharmaceutical industry is made up of the non-prescription or proprietary side which supplies medicines direct to the public. The advertising of both prescription and proprietary medicines is controlled by a mix of legislative and self-regulatory measures. The latter embody codes of practice drawn up and enforced by the relevant trade associations in consultation with government bodies: the ABPI in the case of prescription medicines and the Proprietary Association of Great Britain (PAGB) in the case of proprietary medicines.

The systems of control operated by the trade associations are broadly similar but exhibit certain marked differences. Their negotiation, for instance, involves rather different sets of governmental bodies. The PAGB system embodies a procedure for pre-publication vetting of promotional material whilst the ABPI system deals with advertising practices already in operation. Moreover, the codes of advertising practice established by the two associations have a different status in relation to legislative controls. These differences reflect the different natures of prescription medicine and proprietary medicines and the markets they supply (doctors in one case, the general public in the other). The two systems also differ, largely because of the different problems they tackle, in terms of their apparent success as exercises in business association involvement in public policy making and implementation.

All sales promotion activities by prescription medicine companies are covered by the ABPI's code. Companies are issued periodically with guidance notes on its interpretation and since 1984 the ABPI has held seminars for senior executives of relevant companies to increase their awareness of the code's requirements. Proposals for amendments to the code are notified to the DHSS and the British Medical Association (BMA). If a complaint (which could come from a variety of sources) is upheld (following appeal) the company concerned will be requested to discontinue the offending practice, show that the practice has ceased and/or undertake that a similar breach of the code will not be repeated in the future. Any member company which rejects such a decision can be expelled from the ABPI. In practice, this sanction has yet to be used. Indeed, the ABPI claims that 'An outstanding feature has been the success of voluntary compliance with the provisions of the Code and acceptance of the rulings of the Committee' (ABPI, 1984, p. 3).

Governmental appreciation of the code is reflected by the fact that the DHSS encourages non-ABPI members to observe the code and refers complaints against such companies to the ABPI for review, rather than to the courts as the law permits. This is not to suggest that government is wholly satisfied with the code as a control on prescription medicine advertising. A senior DHSS medical officer, Dr Hilary Pickles, was reported as stating that drugs firms break the ABPI code in more than 50 per cent of their advertising to doctors (*The Guardian*, 13 September 1984).

The ABPI code predated, but now supplements, legislative controls on the advertising of prescription medicines, e.g. the code's provisions on misleading advertising are almost identical to the legal requirements of the 1968 Medicines Act. The introduction of legislative controls on advertising of prescription medicines reflected governmental concern that the ABPI did not include in its membership all suppliers of medicines to the NHS and at the fact that compliance with the code was not compulsory. Government also appears to have been dissatisfied with the the ABPI's system of monitoring prescription medicine advertising for in 1974 and 1975 enabling regulations under the 1968 Medicines Act were introduced which required the DHSS to undertake a scrutiny of prescription medicine companies' promotional material — a procedure which the ABPI began to duplicate in 1980.

Thus, the ABPI's code is supplementary to some legislative controls and is regarded as a means of enforcement, in preference to the courts, by the DHSS. The mix of legislative and voluntary controls has until recently appeared to work to the mutual satisfaction of the industry and the Government. The former maintains that 'while it is possible to legislate satisfactorily for testing, manufacture and control of medical products . . . appropriate standards of marketing conduct cannot be defined by the same means. For this reason, members of the Association have concurred in the promulgation of the Code of Practice and submitted to its restraints' (ABPI, 1984, p. 2).

The industry's willingness to undertake the act of self-discipline embodied in the code also reflected their perception that the reputation of the industry and its product would suffer if high standards of advertising practice were not enforced, coupled with a hope that self-regulation would forestall the introduction of more restrictive statutory controls by government. From government's perspective, self-regulation, supplemented where necessary by statutory controls, is believed to permit greater flexibility than statutory controls alone and to have a greater chance of success. However, if government, even a non-interventionist

Government, does not achieve the results it demands from an industry acting 'voluntarily', it will have no hesitation in enforcing compliance by statutory means.

Advertising proprietary medicines

Establishment of the PAGB reflected growing concern by manufacturers of proprietary medicines that the reputation of the industry and its products could only be guaranteed if high standards of advertising practice were maintained. The first edition of the PAGB Code of Standards of Advertising Practice was published in 1936, subsequently being updated periodically to take account of new developments. Compliance with the letter and the spirit of the code became a condition of PAGB membership. This includes both proprietary medicine manufacturers (as full members) and advertising agencies used by full members (as associate members).

The PAGB code differs from the ABPI code in both its scope and its administration. It applies to all forms of promotion of proprietary medicines to the public including labelling and packaging and is operated through a pre-publication vetting procedure. Member companies are required to submit copy for all advertising, labelling and packaging to the PAGB before use. Specialist staff recruited by the PAGB examine the material to ensure that it complies with the code and, if the material is approved, issue a permit which is valid for two years. All material must be resubmitted for examination at regular intervals. The PAGB employs a qualified pharmacist and physician to undertake the examinations and retains specialist legal and medical consultants to advise when required.

Before the mid-1970s there was little legislative control on the advertising of proprietary medicines. The PAGB assisted government to develop various legal measures to regulate the sale and supply of proprietary medicines but took exception in 1974–75 to the DHSS assuming certain powers of pre-publication vetting of medicines advertising, without success. In fact, however, the DHSS has concentrated most of its resources on monitoring prescription medicines advertising as it regards the system operated by the PAGB as satisfactory. (See statement by the Minister of Health, *Hansard*, Col. 199, 6 June 1984.) The PAGB liaises closely with the Advertising Authority and the Advertising Standards Authority to ensure that its code conforms with the British Code of Advertising Practice which the PAGB helped to initiate.

In the PAGB's opinion government should legislate to provide the framework for the manufacture, sale and supply and quality of medicinal products, but self-regulation, assisted by governmental guidelines, is the appropriate means to ensure that high standards of advertising practice are observed. For the Government's part, Sir George Young, speaking as Under Secretary of State for Health, has commented:

> Codes of Practice are . . . much preferred to Regulations because they provide greater flexibility in dealing with the many and varied circumstances to be found in advertising. Furthermore those concerned had a direct hand in drawing up and implementing the arrangements, and are those [sic], I believe, much more prepared to work within the framework and the spirit of the Code. (Wells, 1982, p. 7)

The PAGB code has been widely regarded as a success in a governmental circles. It is an indication of the Government's satisfaction with the arrangement that they have pressed for and succeeded in obtaining permission to implement the 1984 European Community Directive on Misleading Advertising by voluntary measures, which will differ only marginally from those that already exist.

The success of the PAGB code as an example of a business association's involvement in public policy-making and implementation has been due to the willingness of the proprietary medicines industry to accept high standards of control on their promotional activities and to invest in the PAGB the authority and, more important, the resources to ensure compliance with the code. As far as government is concerned, its preference for self-regulatory measures, backed up by legislative measures, to control advertising practices, reflects a belief that they are more flexible than legal controls and more likely to be observed by the industry. In addition, they are seen as less costly in terms of administration by civil servants and the courts.

These examples of business association involvement in the pricing of prescription medicines and pharmaceutical advertising suggest that, although governments may prefer self-regulatory measures to legislative controls in certain circumstances, self-regulation alone is perceived to be inadequate, largely because membership of business associations in Britain is not compulsory. Should companies, through their associations, not be prepared to undertake certain responsibilities 'voluntarily', government will supplement and even replace voluntary measures by legislative controls.

Training policy

In the introduction to this chapter, it was pointed out that policy functions formerly performed by government or by quasi-governmental bodies could be transferred to business interest associations by a retreating state seeking to reduce government responsibilities. Simple abolition may not be an option because there may be a need to supply some form of collective provision of a particular function or, at a minimum, a mechanism whereby subsides can be transferred to firms.

Training policy under the Thatcher Government offers a good example of public policy functions being transferred to business associations. The Thatcher Government retained the body supervising training policy, the Manpower Services Commission (MSC), with its government appointed chairman and its representatives from the CBI, TUC, local authorities and educational interests. Indeed, with the expansion of schemes for the young unemployed, the budget and range of functions of the MSC increased considerably. However, it was seen more as an arm of government policy, and less as a quasi-autonomous tripartite body, than in the past.

At the sectoral level, there was a series of tripartite training boards with representatives from the employers and the unions in the particular industry (nominally appointed by the responsible minister as individuals). Employer attitudes towards these boards were mixed. In some industries they were regarded as a superfluous bureaucratic addition to training work already being done at the level of the firm. In other industries, there was concern that training activity by individual firms would not meet the needs of the industry as a whole. This was notably the case in construction, a skill intensive industry with a highly mobile workforce.

After a process of consultation, the Thatcher Government decided to retain some of the boards, including the construction
board and the single most important board, the Engineering
Industry Training Board. In all, if one counts the Agriculture
Training Board (set up under different legislation) and the recon-
stituted board concerned with offshore supplies, eight boards were
retained. Sixteen boards were dissolved under the 1982 Industrial
Training Act and were replaced by non-statutory training organisations (NSTOs). These were employers' associations, or special
'training councils' set up by employers' associations, or bodies set
up by groups of employers' associations to co-ordinate their training activities. Before a training board could be dissolved, the
Secretary of State for Employment had to be satisfied that an
appropriate non-statutory organisation had been set up by employers in the industry. One incentive for the employers to do this
was that, if they did not, they would have to fund a statutory body
entirely out of their own pockets, government grants for running
costs having been withdrawn. 'Some NSTOs, were clearly established only grudgingly as part of the price of getting rid of the
relevant ITB; they therefore lack the active commitment from
firms which is needed for an NSTO to flourish in the long run'
(Coopers & Lybrand, 1985, p. 13).

In most industries one statutory training board was replaced by
a number of NSTOs. (For a discussion of examples, see Rainbird
and Grant, 1985a.) Although the Government expressed the hope
that there would be opportunities for the trade unions to take part
in the new arrangements, in practice their participation was much
more limited than in the statutory boards. Only some of the
NSTOs made provision for union participation in the work of their
governing body, and then usually on a more limited scale than
under the statutory arrangements; in other cases, unions were
confined to consultative arrangements or excluded altogether.
Even where opportunities to sit on the governing body of a NSTO
were available, the relevant unions, disgruntled by the changes,
were often reluctant to take them up.

The relationship between the NSTOs and the machinery of
government was somewhat tenuous. There was no formal procedure for their designation or for the systematic review of their
activities, nor were they obliged to report to anyone. In practice,
many of them kept in close touch with the MSC so as to influence

the development of training policy and make use of the grants available to NSTOs. These were quite substantial, and provided an important incentive for forming a NSTO. For example, by 1984 the training department of the Chemical Industries Association had obtained grants of nearly £1 million for its member companies.

As well as channelling grants to companies, the NSTOs acted as an information exhange for their members and helped them to keep up to date with developments in training policy. In some cases, they facilitated co-operative self-help efforts by member companies such as the pooling of training facilities in a particular area. In accordance with the traditions of British employers' associations, they were generally reluctant to exert an influence over their member companies. The general philosophy accepted by NSTOs was that training was done most appropriately at the level of the firm, and that their role was to act as a facilitator and perhaps as a catalyst.

This limited conception of their scope of action was very apparent in two important areas. First, most of the NSTOs appeared reluctant to develop codes of conduct for their members. Second, when the funds allocated to them by the MSC for particular training programmes exceeded the amount requested by member firms, they did not discriminate between their member firms on the basis of any conception of merit. The funds were shared out on the basis of some simple empirical formula such as 'first come, first served', or of a sum being made available proportionate to the amount originally requested. Such behaviour is perfectly consistent with the self-image of the associations as member benefit associations rather than agents of public policy. A number of associations stressed in discussions that they saw the provision of training grants and other training aids as an extension of their traditional range of services to members, rather than being part of some major new development in associative activity.

One might therefore ask whether the associations really were discharging public policy functions, or whether they were simply providing government funded selective benefits to their members. In a strategic political sense, there is no doubt that the NSTOs were used by the Government as a smoke-screen to defend itself against charges that it was falling back on a pure market solution. Such a position would be difficult to defend when most training experts agreed that training efforts by firms, even if they met the immediate needs of that firm, would be unlikely to meet the long run needs of the nation as a whole for a supply of highly trained labour. In a deeper sense, the NSTOs were an attempt by the Thatcher Government to cope with the contradiction between its attachment to market ideology, and the fact that the application of such a policy in the area of training would undoubtedly lead to shortages of skilled labour or, perhaps even more important, a deterioration in the rate of acquisition of new skills.

Statutory self-regulation of financial services

As the so-called 'big bang' of 27 October 1986 approached with its abolition of restrictive practices and traditional demarcation lines in the financial sector, there was a widespread recognition that the absence of adequate investor protection could adversely affect the international reputation of London as a financial centre, and hence its ability to attract and retain business. However, the Government was anxious to avoid regulation that would be expensive or hinder the development of new services in response to market opportunities. The Government therefore took the view 'that the regulation of the financial services industry should be no more than the minimum necessary to protect the investor' (Cmnd. 9432, 1985, p. 1). How could these potentially contradictory aims of investor protection and minimum regulation be reconciled?

The answer had been provided in outline for the Government in a report that it had commissioned, the 1984 Gower Report (*Review of Investor Protection*). This envisaged a system of self regulation within a new statutory framework. In adopting the Gower framework, the Government emphasized that self– regulation would be a more effective means of ensuring compliance. Critics of the Government would argue that any concern for effective investor protection was overriden by a sensitivity to the views of the financial sector. Seen from this perspective, the Government's proposals represented an attempt to perpetuate the privileges of the City in a new guise at the expense of effective investor protection.

Although the proposals contained in the Government's Financial Services Bill published in December 1985 were seen as the

most radical overhaul of investor protection for forty years, and
certainly contained an important innovation by making it a crimi-
nal offence to carry on an investment business without authorisa-
tion, it is important to recognise the limitations in the scope of the
measure. The Bill does not cover the Lloyd's insurance market (an
important omission) or the regulation of banks, building societies,
friendly societies and insurance companies. Moreover, the new
Securities and Investment Board (SIB) 'would not have a general
remit to police the City or to prosecute fraud wherever it may
happen. Rather its task would be to prevent the fraudulent being
authorised to do investment business in the first place' (Securities
and Investments Board, 1985, p. 2). Even so, the Board will cover
commodity futures, securities, collective investments, and life
insurance marketing, and it is anticipated that 15 000 investment
businesses are likely to fall within its regulation.

The strengths and limits of the proposed regime

Considerable powers will be delegated to the SIB by the DTI. The
Board will then recognise, and exercise a broad supervision over,
self-regulatory organisations (SROs). A firm may (leaving aside
five special cases) be authorised to do investment by two routes,
either by going direct to the Board or through membership of an
SRO. The SIB hopes that most firms will be authorised and
regulated by SROs, but 'the SIB's procedures, regulations and
rules will be of critical importance in the new system in that they
will set the standards the SROs must match if they are to be, and
remain, recognised. An SRO must demonstrate to the SIB that the
standards required of its members are at least equivalent to the
standards set for directly-authorised firms' (Jacomb, 1985, p. 16).

Although the Financial Services Bill was toughened up in some
respects during its passage through Parliament as a result of
backbench pressure, the effectiveness of the measures it introduces will depend in large part on the way in which relations
develop between the SIB and SROs (of which there could be only
four). It is possible to discern three potential areas of difficulty: the
balance between statutory and self-regulation; the quality of the
SROs; and the concept of the 'lead regulator'.

As far as the first of these is concerned, Mr Brittan, the then
Trade and Industry Secretary, explained that 'Whilst the bill builds

on the tradition of self-regulation it ensures that self-regulation has the teeth and statutory backing it needs to be effective' (*Financial Times*, 20 December 1985). However, it is open to question whether the uneasy balance between self-regulation and statutory regulation in the Bill is the correct one, given the need to meet the potentially contradictory objectives of investor protection and market freedom. In particular, it is open to question whether the powers given to the SIB, including the ability of the Secretary of State to grant powers to prosecute in certain circumstances, sit easily on a body which will be a private company limited by guarantee, rather than the statutory commission favoured by the Opposition.

Second, doubts have been raised about the quality of some of the proposed SROs, and whether they will be able to sort out their internal differences in sufficient time to be ready to operate in January 1987. The deputy chairman of the SIB has recognised that the coverage of SROs is incomplete 'and it is unlikely that any of them will meet the criteria for recognition without at least some changes in their rules and procedures' (Jacomb, 1985, p. 15). Despite the SIB's insistence on equivalence in the regulatory regimes, commercial considerations may lead to divergences in practice. For example, 'it is likely that lower standards will be imposed on the hitherto unregulated market in European securities than on the established London equity market. The fear is that onerous requirements would risk driving the Eurobond market abroad to a more easy-going location' (*Financial Times*, 31 October 1985).

As was noted in Chapter 4, anticipation of the 'big bang' led to the emergence of a number of large conglomerates cutting across traditional boundaries of financial service provision. The SIB's 'lead regulator' policy is intended to reduce the reporting burden on financial conglomerates by transferring responsibility for financial monitoring to the SRO which deals with the largest part of the firm's business. The SIB states that 'Close co-operation between SROs will be an essential part of the system' (Securities and Investments Board, 1985, p. 9). What remains to be seen is whether SROs will work in harmony, sharing relevant information, and agreeing on a clear division of responsibility between the lead regulator for a firm and the other relevant SROs. The broader issue that arises is whether a relatively decentralised system of regulation is suited to a financial sector which is rapidly becoming more concentrated.

The introduction of statutory self-regulation in the financial sector is the most important single experiment in private interest government ever undertaken in Britain. The SIB has produced one of the most comprehensive and carefully thought out blue-prints for a system of private interest government. It is interesting that the controls to be exercised by the SIB over the SROs meet each of the criteria set out in Schmitter's original checklist of the characteristics of societal corporatism (Schmitter, 1979, pp. 20–1). For example, the criterion of controls on leadership selection and interest articulation is covered by the SIB's insistence that SROs must have sufficient financial resources to employ expert staff capable of conducting inspections and initiating disciplinary ac-tions. It is not implied that the SROs are corporatist (the key element of policy concertation is missing), but the degree of intervention in the internal decision-making arrangements of the SROs, if implemented in practice, will go beyond the level of supervision that has hitherto been exercised over private interest governments in Britain.

Whether the system of self regulation of financial services will succeed remains to be seen. In practice, much will depend on whether the financial sector is able to provide active support 'both in terms of providing the necessary resources and of acknowledg-ing the self-restraint which is necessary to make such a system operate effectively' (*Financial Times*, 19 December 1985). The arrangements are vulnerable to a failure to cope with a major scandal, or to a change of government. If they are seen not to work under a sympathetic administration, the privatised approach to public policy will have suffered a setback.

Models of business involvement in public policy implementation

Lehmbruch (1984, pp. 61–2) make a useful distinction between 'corporatist concertation' and 'sectoral corporatism' which can be used as a basis for developing models of business involvement in the implementation of public policy. 'Corporatist concentration', as discussed by Lehmbruch, involves a plurality of organisations, and the co-ordination of their actions with government in relation to the requirements of the national economy. Two particular forms of concertation were observed in this chapter, providing a basis for the subdivision of the category. One is 'commercial' concertation where normal market operations are replaced by state setting of key prices, state sponsorship of organisations, and state provision of a forum for reconciling differences of interest. The arrangements in the dairy sector offer a good example.

The other case might be termed 'allocative' concertation where government sets up a tripartite body to supervise and executive public policy within a defined area, and to provide desired 'goods' or prevent unwanted 'bads'. Examples of the former can be found in the MSC and the statutory training boards, and of the latter in the Health and Safety Commission. Business takes part in such arrangements, if only to counterbalance the influence of the unions. However, these traditional forms of concertation have been eroded under the Thatcher Government with its attachment to the privatisation of public policy.

The other model, which has been increasing in importance in Britan in 1980s, is 'sectoral corporatism', defined by Lehmbruch in terms of a privileged access to government of single, organised interests limited to specific sectors of the economy. The reconciliation of potentially opposed interests is supplanted by advantageous treaties with particular interests. The arrangements made by the Thatcher Government for self-regulation of the financial services sector fit into this definition very well. Businesses are likely to find the limited forms of regulation embodied in the SROs an acceptable alternative to more direct and demanding forms of intervention. However, the very weakness which makes such arrangements acceptable makes them less useful as forms for involving business in the formulation and implementation of public policy. When one privatises public policy, one may end up with something that is neither public nor policy. Indeed, in the case of training policy and the NSTOs, what is on offer is often little more than the public legitimation of market operations.

One final general lesson may be drawn from this chapter. I have found the model of 'associative order', developed by Streeck and Schmitter (1985), a stimulating attempt to encapsulate some important tendencies in modern societies which are often more apparent in countries other than in Britain. Nevertheless, the British example, for all its idiosyncracies, does demonstrate that there are limits to what can be achieved by associative action and that our old friends, the market and the state, continue to provide robust paradigms which shape much political thought and practice. As Willmott reminds us (1985, p. 65), 'in the context of advanced capitalist societies, at least, the market and the state may well continue to be the dominant institutions'.

In contemporary Britain, the market model has been revived, while the model of state action waits in the wings ready to strut and fret its hour on the stage once more. There are many examples of business association involvement in the implementation of public policy in Britain, but they lack an underlying consistency. This reflects the varying periods (from the 1930s to the 1980s) at which they have been established, the *ad hoc* character of their formation, and above all, the absence of any legitimising philosophy of private interest government.

10 The Organisation of Business Interests for European Community Representation

Jane Sargent

This chapter considers how business interests are organised for representation in the European Community (EC) and the channels of representation they use when seeking to influence EC decisions. It is important to consider the EC dimension of business representation because the Community's decisions directly affect the day-to-day activities of British business. Moreover, there has been considerable speculation about the impact of Community membership on British business interests.

This chapter seeks to establish the impact of EC membership on representatives of British business interests in order to establish how such groups are organised for EC representation. It does so by examining the impact of EC membership on the internal decision-making structures, resources and relations between five business organisations; the channels of representation these groups opened up in order to influence EC decisions; and the priorities they attached to these channels of representation during Britain's first decade of EC membership. The five groups discussed are the Association of British Chambers of Commerce (ABCC); the Association of Independent Business (AIB), originally the Society of Independent Manufacturers and later the Smaller Businesses Association; the British Bankers' Association (BBA); the Confederation of British Industry (CBI) and the Retail Consortium (RC). Together these groups represent both large and small

213

firms in all sectors of the economy: manufacturing, distribution and commerce, including the financial services industry. Moreover, the groups themselves represent a range of different types of business organisation: all-industry peak associations (CBI and ABCC), sector specific trade associations (BBA and RC) and specialist interests (AIB). In order to set the findings in their proper perspective, as one aspect of British companies' representations in the EC, consideration is also given to the relationship between the EC related representational activities of the five groups and those of their respective members.

It will be shown below that during Britain's first decade of EC membership the organisation of business interests for representation in the EC was in a constant state of transition. This suggests the existence of a learning process which in its turn was reflected by changes in the ways in which business organisations were organised internally for EC representation the channels of representation, they opened in order to influence EC decisions and the priorities they attached to these channels.

Internal arrangements for EC representation

To establish the internal arrangements the five business organisations in question established for representation in the EC, it will be useful to examine the impact of EC membership on their internal structures for policy-making and representation on EC related matters, the resources they devoted to representation in the EC and the relations that developed between the groups for the purpose of EC representation.

Internal structures

Each of the groups decided to deal with EC related matters as domestic as opposed to foreign policy. Thus, each of their respective departments and committees was required to deal with relevant EC related matters. Some of the groups, however, appointed bodies to co-ordinate the EC related work of their various departments and committees. The ABCC, for instance, required its International Department and corresponding committee to undertake this function and in 1981 the ABCC set up a 'support group', consisting of the secretaries of ABCC regional chambers, to facilitate the exchange of information and views between the Association's members and its chief representative on EC related matters, the head of the International Department. Lacking a departamental structure, the AIB required its European and International Committee to undertake the co-ordination role. The Retail Consortium's two main policy committees shared this responsibility which involved co-ordinating the EC representations of the Consortium's UK operations (which liaised with the British Government, Parliament and the press) and, from 1979 onwards, the European office which dealt with representations through European interest groups and direct to EC bodies. Only the CBI set up a permanent office in Brussels, but the responsibilities of this office changed several times during Britain's first decade of EC membership as the London-based CBI staff and committees became more familiar with the operation of the Community and assumed full responsibility for those EC related matters which fell within their respective areas of responsibility. Initially, the CBI's European Co-ordination Department had responsibility for co-ordinating the EC related activities of the CBI's London and Brussels offices as the two operated under different CBI directorates. By 1979, however, the European Support Department, which replaced the Co-ordination Department's successor, the European Policy Department, existed to co-ordinate the work of the Brussels office and ensure that the EC related activities of the CBI's London-based departments and committees supported the work of the Brussels office.

A number of the groups were worried about the cost of EC representation, but, in practice, this was not as great a problem as had been feared. (See Table 10.1 for details of the resources available to the groups.) One of the main reasons the groups were able to cope with the cost of EC representation was that each of them depended very heavily upon the assistance of voluntary workers who acted both as the groups' official representatives and on behalf of the groups in unattributed ways on the basis of briefings received from the groups. This was the basis of the 'Linkman Scheme' set up by the CBI in 1980 under which individual business persons, who were willing to do so, established links with their local MEPs and, on behalf of the CBI but not in its name, explained to MEPs how particular EC related matters

Table 10.1 Details of five business organisations' resources for representation in the EC (1982)

	ABCC	AIB	BBA	CBI	RC
Total income	£308 606	£66 497	£829 439	£8 308 499	£100 00 for representation at EC level 1982–84 and annual income of £239 215
Cost of affiliation to European interest group(s)	£14 592	£200	£54 823	approx. £140 000	£10 713
Secretariat	12 full-time and 1 part-time	2 full-time and 1 part-time	20	350	10
No. of officials with full-time responsibility for EC representations	2	0	20	8	2
Regional network	12 Regional Chambers	11 Regional Councils		13 Regional Councils	
Membership	86 Chambers representing approx. 50 000 companies	approx. 30 000 companies through direct and associate members	107 full and 237 assoc. banks	approx. 15 000 companies and over 200 trade/employer associations	7 member organisations representing approx. 85% of retail companies

affected their respective companies in the MEPs' constituencies.

The importance the groups attached to voluntary assistance from their member organisations and/or companies was due partly to financial restrictions which limited the number of paid representatives the groups could employ for EC work. Partly too, however, it was due to British business persons' traditional preference for self-representation as opposed to representation by professional interest organisation officials. Thus, voluntary workers were required, primarily, to represent the groups at meetings of their respective European interest groups; at meetings with members and officials of EC bodies, both on behalf of the groups and in the name of their European interest groups; and at meetings and in correspondence with meetings and officials of the British Government, Parliament and the press on behalf of the groups.

In practice, the extent to which the groups relied upon voluntary workers differed. The AIB relied exclusively upon voluntary workers to undertake its EC representations between 1972 and 1982 whilst the Retail Consortium placed greater emphasis upon representations undertaken by its paid officials, whom voluntary workers were asked to assist from time to time. Similarly, the ABCC's voluntary workers assisted its paid staff with EC representations although the ABCC had hoped that the reverse would be the case. Few of the groups received the amount of assistance they required from voluntary workers. This was due primarily to widespread indifference, and opposition, to Community membership during the decade following accession. In addition, as the decade marked a period of economic recession in Britain, many businessmen, who would otherwise have participated voluntarily in the groups' representations in the EC, lacked the time and/ or money to do so. These constraints also meant that some of the groups lacked the back-up they traditionally received from their members in connection with non-EC related matters, namely a willingness on the part of the members to assume responsibility for undertaking representations on matters of specific interest to them but not of general interest to the groups' memberships. Only the BBA received this type of back-up from its membership on the scale required by the group, largely because its members were anxious that the Community should not destroy the essence of the British banking system. The other groups' members did not perceive the Community's decisions to have such a potentially damaging impact upon British manufacturing, distribution or commerce. Thus, the CBI, for instance, expended considerable resources on a general education programme designed to encourage its members to make representations on their own behalf on EC related matters of specific interest to them, especially at European level, and educated its members in the art of lobbying in the EC (CBI, 1981). The importance the CBI attached to the back-up it lacked is reflected in the following statement: 'The CBI cannot take the place of a company or trade association in lobbying the EC on individual or sectoral issues . . . But it can advise and support them by drawing on its hard-won experience and that of others to show what works best' (CBI Annual Report, 1981, p. 20).

As mentioned in Chapter 5, many large firms have their own public affairs representative in Brussels. Such persons are usually involved in the work of the relevant Brussels based European level business federations. American companies are also involved in the work of the EC Committee of the American Chamber of Commerce. Apart from liaising between their company and such organisations, such representatives can supplement the work of the European level federations, drawing their attention to potentially threatening issues, preparing briefing papers, and undertaking lobbying efforts which may be beneficial to the industry as a whole as well as their own company. European level associations usually have limited resources in relation to the tasks they have to tackle, and the government relations specialists of firms can provide additional coverage at, say, the European Parliament. Of course, they will always have to pay attention to the commercial priorities of their own companies. Public affairs representatives who 'go native' and become obsessed with the minutiae of Brussels life are of little value to their own companies, or indeed to the industries with which their company is concerned.

Relations between business organisations

Considerable bilateral liaison concerning EC representations was developed between the CBI and each of the four other business organisations between 1972 and 1982, but no links were established between these four groups. Although the ABCC did not act as the Devlin Commission suggested and 'fuse' with the CBI, accession to the EC inspired closer liaison between the two organisations. Regular meetings between the ABCC's director and the CBI's director-general were established in 1975 which covered EC issues; the head of the ABCC's International Department was invited to attend meetings of the CBI's Europe Committee as an observer and this official established informal links with members of the CBI's European Support Department and its predecessor. These contacts were facilitated by this official's status as a former CBI employee. Links were also developed between certain CBI and ABCC regional organisations in connection with EC related matters. CBI East Midlands, for instance, developed 'regular contact with the chamber of commerce in this region and discuss[ed] EC problems with them, usually at staff level, from time to time'. (Personal communication from regional director, 23 March 1984).

No formalised links were established between the AIB and the CBI but the former relied heavily upon unofficial links with the CBI to defend and promote its members' interests on EC related matters. These links involved the AIB relying upon representatives of AIB member companies which were also affiliated to the CBI providing the AIB with information from the CBI about EC issues of interest to the AIB's membership and feeding back opinions on these issues to the CBI, primarily through its Smaller Firms Council. As the AIB's views on EC issues corresponded to the opinions adopted by the CBI in the majority of cases, this contact with the CBI provided the AIB with a valuable means to avoid unnecessary duplication on EC representations.

The BBA was the only one of the four groups in question to affiliate to the CBI. The Retail Consortium decided against affiliation but in 1979 links were established between the Consortium's European Office and officials of the CBI's European Support Department. In addition, the Consortium's European interest groups, the Committee of Commercial Organisations of the EC (COCCEE) and its successor the European Confederation for Retailing (CECD), liaised with the CBI's European interest group, UNICE, on social and employment issues under the auspices of the Employers' Liaison Committee, a body set up by UNICE to facilitate liaison of this kind between a number of

European interest groups representing employers' interests. The Committee also maintained working relations with a number of non-members, for instance, the BBA's European interest group, the European Banking Federation (BFEC).

Liaison with the CBI reflected a high degree of membership overlap between this organisation and each of the other four (although, as mentioned previously, links between the CBI and the BBA were formalised with the latter's affiliation to the former). The main object of liaison between the CBI and the other organisations was to facilitate co-ordinated representations on EC related matters whenever possible and to avoid unnecessary duplication. Thus, a division of labour, a separation of EC related roles, emerged whereby the organisations rarely acted on the same EC related matters and, when they did so, they attempted not to undermine each other's representations, if possible. Thus, the BBA supported the CBI's policy on the Second Supplies Directive in 1977 and four of the five groups put forward complementary, rather than competitive, views on an EC proposal on product liability.

The CBI maintained links with the other groups on the basis of the belief that 'The more broadly-based the lobbying can be, the more effect it will have. The first object is therefore always to find out how widely one's view is shared' (CBI, 1981, p. 19.) The other groups shared this view but their object in determining when the CBI shared their views was to establish when EC representations of their own were not necessary. In other words, they sought, through liaison with the CBI, to reserve the resources they allocated to EC representations to issues of vital interest to their respective memberships concerning which their members' views differed from the policies adopted by the CBI, whether in principle or in detail, or when reinforcement of the CBI's policy was justified. Duplication of the CBI's EC representations was not regarded as unnecessary under all circumstances. Each of the organisations believed that the British Government and Parliament and EC bodies responded to the quantity as well as to the quality of submissions and, as a result, were more likely to respond favourably to a view expressed by representatives of each of the main parties affected by a proposal than to a view put forward by only one organisation, regardless of whether or not it represented all the main interests concerned.

This does not mean that the groups never put forward conflict-ing views on EC issues. Differences of opinion arose between the groups and their members sometimes on matters of principle and at others concerning the details of EC proposals. The AIB may have been an exception, however, as the AIB's EC representa-tions were undertaken by the few members who were interested in this dimension of the organisation's activities.

Liaison between the groups (and between the groups and their respective members) did not amount to the degree of co-ordination advocated by the Devlin Commission and the Inter-Bank Research Organisation. In fact, it may have been the case that the types of links developed between the CBI and the four other business organisations (and between these organisations and their members) removed any necessity for the more formalised links advocated by the Devlin Commission and the IBRO.

To summarise this section on the internal arrangements the groups established for EC representation, it appears that these differed considerably. The financial and manpower resources the groups devoted to EC representations varied widely, although each of the groups dealt with EC issues as domestic policy. The nature of the links established between the groups for EC rep-resentational purposes also varied. Were these differences re-flected in the channels of representation the groups established in order to influence EC decisions and the priorities they attached to these channels?

Channels of representation

Table 10.2 indicates that by 1982 each of the groups was 'thinking European'. As the Hansard Society noted, the groups were:

> Taking whatever opportunity exists for working together with groups in other member states . . . maintaining direct contacts with the Commission, . . . using the Economic and Social Com-mittee and the European Parliament as a means of information and publicity, and generally . . . extending their pressure group role beyond UK Government to the Community level. (Han-sard Society, 1977, p. 146.)

Table 10.2 *The channels of individual and collective representation opened by five business organisations (1972–82)*[1,2]

	Association of British Chambers of Commerce Indiv.	Coll.	Association of Independent Businesses Indiv.	Coll.	British Bankers' Association Indiv.	Coll.	Confederation of British Industry Indiv.	Coll.	Retail Consortium Indiv.	Coll.
National bodies										
Other member states administrations										
· Ministers	x							x		x
· Government officials/embassies		x					x	x		
· Permanent delegation to EC							x	x		
British administration										
· Ministers	x		x				x	x	x	
· Central government officials	x		x		x		x	x	x	
· Local government officials	x				x		x	x		
· Permanent delegation to EC	x		x		x		x	x		
· Government advisory committees	x				x		x	x		
· (Bank of England)					x					
British legislature										
· Westminster parliamentarians	x		x		x		x		x	
· Westminster parliamentary committees	x				x		x		x	
· (Parliamentary consultancy)									x	
Other national interest groups										
· British	x		x		x		x	x	x	
· Non-British (sister federations)				x			x	x		
National media										
· British	x		x				x	x	x	
· Non-British			x				x	x		

Transnational interest groups
. European
. International

EC bodies

European Council

Council of Ministers
. Members
. Advisory committees

Commission
. President
. Other commissioners
. Officials
. Advisory committees

European Parliament
. Members
. Members' assistants
. Committees
. Political groups
. Secretariat

Economic and Social Committee
. Members
. Secretariat

[1] Individual channels of representation to those channels opened independent of a group's sister federations.

[2] Collective channels of representation refer to those channels obtained through a group's European interest group.

In addition to developing channels of representation to national
bodies, European interest groups and direct to EC bodies, the CBI
and the ABCC added an international dimension to their EC
representations by means of channels of representation to international interest groups. The CBI attempted to influence the
Community's proposals on the rights of employees of multinational undertakings, between 1972 and 1982, through the International Organisation of Employers and the Business and Industry
Advisory Committee to the OECD. In addition, the ABCC sometimes attempted to influence EC customs related matters through
representations to the International Chambers of Commerce. Use
of these channels of representation reflected the groups' perceptions of the interrelationship between certain EC policies and
those of various other supranational organisations such as the
United Nations and OECD. Hitherto, evidence has only come to
light of certain British trade unions making occasional use of their
international interest groups to influence EC decisions (Butt
Philip, 1985, p. 74.)

Each of the groups obtained numerous points of access to
various national and EC bodies, but these were not identical in any
two cases. Only the Retail Consortium, for instance, employed the
services of a UK parliamentary consultancy which it sometimes
used in order to influence the Westminster Parliament's views on
EC proposals, such as a draft directive on doorstep selling in 1981.
Moreover, the CBI and the Retail Consortium regarded their links
with the UK Permanent Delegation in Brussels as a useful channel
of representation, even though officials of the delegation maintained, in interviews with the writer, that they were simply the
British Government's 'ambassadors' to EC bodies and thus had no
powers to influence government policy or to promote the views of
specialist interests to the Community. Conversely, political parties
were not an important channel of representation to the groups,
whereas links with other British interest groups and the media
were regarded as valuable channels of representation by a number
of the groups.

Each of the groups opened a range of direct and indirect
channels of representation and the priorities they attached to these
are examined below. As regards development of the groups'
channels of representation, the evidence suggests that some were
more developed than others both on accession and at the end of

Britain's first decade of EC membership and that some developed at a faster rate than others during that period. However, each of the groups sets of channels of representation was in a constant state of transition during that time. By the time Britain joined the EC, the CBI, the BBA and the ABCC had long-established contacts with the appropriate European interest groups, the CBI had developed close contacts with the EC Commission, and both the CBI and the ABCC had used their traditional channels of representation to the British Government to express views on the principle of accession. By mid-1975, when Britain held a referendum on the question of continued membership of the EC, the Retail Consortium and the AIB had begun to develop channels of representation to influence EC decisions. The AIB had established direct contacts with the Commission and members of the UK Permanent Delegation to Brussels in 1973, but by 1975 it no longer used these channels and only made occasional representations to its European interest group. The Retail Consortium had also joined the appropriate European interest group by this time. The BBA, however, had established extensive contacts with EC bodies at European level but left its constituent members and the Bank of England to make representations on EC related matters to the British Government and Parliament. Both the ABCC and the CBI developed further their channels of representation at national, European and international levels during Britain's first few years of EC membership.

From 1975 onwards each of the groups continued to develop its channels of representation although some did so less than others either, as in the case of the CBI, because its channels were well developed by 1975, or, in the case of the AIB, because of a lack of resources for EC representations and/or a lack of interest in the Community's activities among its membership. Nevertheless, it appears that, by the end of Britain's first decade of EC membership, the groups would continue to develop their channels of representation further, albeit not at the same pace during Britain's second and subsequent decades of membership.

Development of each of the groups' channels of representation reflected a relationship of mutual dependency between the groups and the targets of their EC representations. The groups sought access to bodies involved in EC policy-making and implementation, in an attempt to maximise their influence on EC decisions, whilst the targets of their representations sought assistance from the groups in order to fulfil the targets' functions. The assistance the targets generally required of the groups was technical expertise, detailed information on the practical implications of EC proposals for the groups' memberships and, occasionally, assistance with implementing EC decisions. In August 1980, for instance, the Retail Consortium organised for the author of the Commission's proposals for a draft directive on returnable beverage containers, a visit to several British retail outlets in order to underline the practical problems associated with the proposals. From 1974 onwards the CBI and the BBA regularly provided labour cost statistics to the Commission. In 1977–78 the CBI assisted British Government officials to draw up a code of conduct for companies with employer interests in South Africa to facilitate implementation of a voluntary agreement among the Community's member states' governments.

It should be noted that there was considerable variability in the receptiveness of directorates-general within the Commission to representations from industry. For example, the environmental directorate has often been seen as unfavourably disposed to arguments advanced by business. By way of contrast, DG 3, the internal market and industrial affairs directorate, sometimes acted as a spokesman for industrial interests within the Commission, imitating in some respects the functions of a sponsoring division in the British system (see Chapter 3). However, even DG 3 could not be relied upon to be *industriefreundlich*. Changes of official have been said to lead to changes of outlook, and, even if an official is sympathetic to the industry he or she covers, there are limits to what can be achieved by one senior official trying to cover a large European industry. One tactic that is used by European industry groups to influence directorates-general that do not favour their case is to work through the *cabinets* of other Commissioners to encourage them to get their Commissioner to take the matter up when it is discussed by the Commission.

Few of the groups' choice of channels of representation was based simply on financial considerations. The main exceptions to this rule were the channels of representation to European interest groups and the Retail Consortium's UK parliamentary consultants. This explains why the considerable differences in the size of the groups' financial resources are not accurately reflected in the number and range of channels of representation the groups established in order to influence EC decisions. The size of the groups' financial resources influenced in part the priorities the groups attached to these channels of representations.

Priorities in the use of channels of representation

Each of the groups used its channels of representation selectively and on a policy-by-policy basis. At such times they selected between different channels of representation rather than between different sets of channels, for instance, channels of representation to national bodies, European interest groups and direct to EC bodies. This selection process produced numerous strategies of representation – combinations of channels chosen for particular reasons – none of which was used significantly more frequently than any of the others. Hence, a simple policy study approach to illustrate the priorities the groups attached to their channels of representation would not be representative. Similarly, little can be gained from comparing the strategies of representation the groups developed with ideal–typical strategies such as those suggested by William Averyt (1977). This is because Britain was a late entrant to the Community and because the Community lacks a legislative timetable. Thus, few, if any, of the EC related matters that interested the five groups in question passed through all the appropriate legislative stages during the period of the study – Britain's first decade of EC membership. Ideal–typical strategies are based on the assumption that groups have the opportunity to influence EC decisions at each and every legislative stage.

Nevertheless, certain generalisations can be drawn from evidence of the representations the groups made on EC related matters between 1972 and 1982. In particular, generalisations can be made about the preferences they appear to have attached to their channels of representation to national bodies, European interest groups and direct to EC bodies; the priorities they attached to what may be termed their 'individual' and 'collective' channels of representation; and the priorities they attached to their direct and indirect channels of representation.

The groups did not consciously choose between their national and European levels of representation when selecting the means to use in order to influence specific EC related matters. Nevertheless, it is possible to draw some general conclusions about the priorities the groups attached to their channels of representation to national bodies, European interest groups and direct to EC bodies. (Details of the particular channels used by each group are provided in Table 10.2.)

It appears that the majority of the groups generally placed equal emphasis on their channels of representation to national bodies (primarily government officials), and to their European interest groups, although during the first five years of Britain's membership of the Community the BBA and the Retail Consortium attached greater importance to channels of representation to European interest groups and, in the BBA's case, channels of representation direct to EC bodies, than to channels of representation to national bodies. From 1979 onwards, however, both the BBA and the Retail Consortium began to increase the importance they attached to their channels of representation to national bodies, while the Retail Consortium placed increasing emphasis on channels of representation direct to EC bodies rather than through intermediaries.

The CBI placed equal emphasis as a rule on its channels of representation to national bodies, its European interest group and direct to EC bodies from accession onwards. The AIB, by contrast, generally attached greater importance to its channels of representation to national bodies (the CBI) than to channels of representation to its European interest group or direct to EC bodies. The ABCC regarded channels of representation to national bodies and European interest groups as alternatives, each to be supplemented, as occasion demanded, with channels of representation direct to EC bodies, namely the Commission.

The size of the groups' financial and manpower resources determined in large part the general preferences they attached to their channels of representation to national bodies, European interest groups and direct to EC bodies. It is notable that, although the groups did not consciously select between these different sets of channels of representation when determining which channels to use in connection with any EC related matter, they clearly attached high priority to channels which could be operationalised at national level, in the United Kingdom. These included not only all channels of representation to national bodies, but also channels of representation to the European Parliament through its British members and to the Economic and Social Committee, through British members of the Committee. Channels of representation to the Commission through British Government officials were preferred whenever possible to direct channels of representation to the Commission. However, because the Commission was perceived to attach greater weight to views shared by the groups' counterparts in other European Community states, the groups were prepared to attach high priority to the relatively costly channel of representation to European interest groups.

Individual and collective channels of representation

The groups' individual channels of representation are those they opened independently from their fellow members of their respective European interest groups, or 'sister federations' whilst their collective channels of representation are those which they opened and used in conjunction with their sister federations in the name of the appropriate European interest groups.

Under a number of conditions, the groups were found to have avoided or bypassed representations through European interest groups. As mentioned previously, the Retail Consortium developed direct links with EC bodies in 1979 following the demise of its European interest group, but these channels of representation were not abandoned with the establishment of a viable alternative to this European interest group (on the Retail Consortium's initiative). Similarly, when an EC related matter had implications for only the British members of a European interest group, the British groups were not able to make use of their collective channels of representation. The ABCC, for instance, found itself in this position in 1975 and again in 1977 concerning the question of whether or not the British practice of charging for certificates of origin contravened EC rules.

During the implementation of EC laws by means of UK enabling legislation, the groups also placed greater priority on their individual channels of representation. Hence, during implementation of the fourth directive on Company Law the CBI and the BBA, in the latter's case to gain exemption for banks, restricted themselves to using individual channels of representation to national bodies, namely British Government officials and Parliament.

The groups also gave preference to their individual channels of representation when they did not agree with the policies adopted by their European interest groups. Thus, in 1979 and 1980 the Retail Consortium made individual representations to British Government officials and the EC Commission to express objections to a draft directive on energy labelling which its sister federations agreed to in principle.

Sidjanski (1972), observing the reactions of non-British interest groups to EC membership, suggested that national interest groups would utilise collective channels of representation to express a general policy statement on an EC related matter but use their individual channels of representation to object to the details of proposals. He also suggested that national interest groups would sometimes use their individual channels of representation to support the views of their European interest groups. As regards the latter observation, some of the five British business organisations in question were found to have acted in this way. In 1981, for instance, the CBI stressed to the appropriate subcommittee of the House of Lords EC's 'Scrutiny' Committee that its views on the Commission's procedures were shared by its European interest group.

It has been suggested (Lindberg, 1963) that national interest groups would give greater priority to individual channels of representation to national government in connection with proposals for negative policy harmonisation but that the development of proposals for positive policy harmonisation would encourage such groups to place greater emphasis on their collective channels of representation. It appears that whatever the nature of the proposals of interest to the groups if they affected the groups' vital interests, especially negatively, the groups would endeavour to gain the support of their sister federations and utilise their collective (and individual) channels of representation. In connection with issues of lesser importance to the groups the support of their sister federations was not regarded as so essential. Thus, in connection with a proposal to harmonise the member states' banking systems, the BBA, which sought to defend the unique flexible system of British banking, succeeded in persuading its sister federations to oppose the Commission's proposals and to adopt alternative proposals drafted by the BBA and presented to the Commission by the BBA's European interest group (Sargent,

1982). The importance of collective channels of representation under such circumstances reflected the groups' perception that the EC Commission attached more importance to views shared by representatives of similar interests throughout the European Community than to the views of specialist national organisations.

Occasionally, the groups used their collective channels of representation to add weight to their individual representations to national bodies. In 1981, for example, the CBI's European interest group submitted evidence to the House of Lords' EC 'Scrutiny' Committee on the Community's Competition Policy and elaborated on the CBI's view on this issue. Under such circumstances the groups' collective and individual channels of representation were mutually reinforcing. Only occasionally did the groups regard their collective and individual channels of representation as alternatives rather than as complementary channels of representation. Accordingly, collective channels of representation were not developed at the expense of traditional individual channels of representation to national bodies and did not preclude the development of channels of representation direct to EC bodies.

Individual (national and European level) and collective channels of representation were developed primarily to supplement and complement each other and to compensate for each other's limitations. This last point is evident in the priorities the groups attached to their individual and collective channels of representation according to the targets of their representation on EC related matters.

As a rule, when seeking to influence the EC Commission, priority was given to collective channels of representation. This also applied to approaches to the secretariats and committees of the European Parliament and when making representations to EC committees consisting of representatives of European interest groups, such as the Tripartite Social and Economic Conference. Conversely, when seeking to influence the views of national bodies on EC related matters British members of the European Parliament and British members of the Economic and Social Committee, the groups generally gave priority to their individual channels of representation.

The groups generally preferred to use a mixture of collective and individual channels of representation to complement and supplement each other when seeking to influence EC decisions. It should be emphasised, however, that interviews with representatives of the five business organisations indicated that the groups attached more importance to their European interest groups as channels of representation to their respective sister federations than as channels of representation to EC or national bodies to which the groups could and did establish individual channels of representation. The value of European interest groups as channels of representation to the groups' sister federations was twofold. First, to establish the degree of support they could expect from their counterparts in other EC member states for their views on EC related matters, specifically those of vital interest to the British groups. Secondly, to encourage their sister federations to support their British counterparts' views, not only through collective representations but also through their own individual representations to EC bodies and to their respective national governments. The British groups perceived that the balance of decision-making power in the Community was invested in the member states' governments as members of the Council of Ministers. Thus, although the groups' individual and collective channels of representation were designed to be mutually reinforcing and complementary as and when appropriate, they were used as replacements for each other whenever necessary.

The groups attached no fixed priorities to their direct and indirect channels of representation, and they rarely made use of all channels at their disposal during any particular legislative stage, to any particular target, or in connection with any single EC related matter. The more important an EC issue to the groups, the greater the number of direct and indirect channels of representation they were likely to use and the greater priority they were likely to attach to direct channels to such bodies as the EC Commission and British members of the Council of Ministers. The object of opening numerous direct and indirect channels of representation was to maximise the number of channels from which they could select on a policy-by-policy basis.

Executive and parliamentary channels of representation

There are two aspects to the question of the priorities the groups attached to their parliamentary and executive channels of representation: (a) the preferences they attached to parliamentary as compared to executive channels of representation and (b) the relative importance to the groups of channels of representation to the Community's two executive bodies – the Council of Ministers and the EC Commission. As regards the latter, Annette Morgan (1981, p. 103) has indicated that British interest organisations shifted their attention from the Commission to the Council of Ministers, through channels of representation to the British Government, as the Commission's legislative powers were eroded by the Council of Ministers. It appears, however, that the priorities the five business organisations in question attached to channels of representation to the two arms of the Community's executive differed according to the type of Community decision involved. Thus, the primary target of their EC representations was the Council of Ministers in the case of Council laws and the Commission in connection with Commission laws, although the Commission was also an important target for representations concerning Council laws at certain stages in their legislative process, in particular the drafting, formal consultation and implementation stages. At these stages the Commission was perceived to have greater influence over EC policies than the Council of Ministers which had the ultimate decision-taking powers.

Moreover, there is little evidence to suggest that the importance the groups attached to their channels of representation to the Council of Ministers increased at the expense of their links with the Commission in connection with Council laws during Britain's first decade of EC membership.

Morgan has suggested that the importance British interest organisations attached to contacts with the European Parliament would increase after the introduction of direct elections (Ibid., p. 104). In addition, the Hansard Society suggested that the Westminster Parliament's importance as a channel of representation would always be restricted by the limited role invested in it during the Community's legislative processes by the treaties establishing the EC (Hansard Society, 1977, ch. 2). It appears, however, that the importance the CBI attached to its channels of representation to the Westminster and European Parliament for EC representations increased during Britain's first decade of EC membership. As regards the former, this followed establishment in 1974 of 'scrutiny' committees by the House of Lords and the House of Commons to examine the implications of EC legislative proposals for British interests.

Extension of the European Parliament's powers in the

mid-1970s and introduction of direct elections to the European Parliament in 1979 encouraged the CBI to increase the importance it attached to representations to the Parliament. Links with the European Parliament were valued as a means to influence both the Commission, which was the only EC body to have the power to amend proposals for EC laws, and the Council of Ministers as the decision-making body. Links with the Westminster Parliament were regarded as a useful channel of representation to British members of the Council of Ministers. Throughout Britain's first decade of EC membership, however, the CBI attached greater importance to its executive channels of representation to British members of the Council of Ministers and to the Commission than to its legislative channels of representation to these executive bodies.

Numerous factors helped to determine the priorities the groups attached to their respective channels of representation. Many of these were changeable and thus the priorities the groups attached to their channels of representation varied from one matter to another, with the result that the strategies of representation they developed during Britain's first decade of EC membership to influence EC decisions were highly varied and rarely repeated.

Industry sector and product groups at EC level

The discussion so far has concentrated on sector unspecific associations or on sectoral associations in the financial and distributive sectors. However, EC membership has also had a considerable impact on the activities of industrial sector and product associations. Indeed, EC membership has increased the importance of such associations to large firms. Even a firm with a sophisticated government relations operation in Brussels cannot cover all its product interests and needs European level and national associations for formal representations and negotiations at the British and European levels on such matters as trade policy or proposed environmental directives.

It should be emphasised that the impact of membership of the EC differs considerably from one sector to another. Of the four sectors studied in the IIM project, the greatest impact was in chemicals, followed closely by food processing, with less impact in machine tools and very little in construction. Outside these sectors, one can think of others such as steel which have been considerably affected by EC membership.

The impact of EC membership on the chemical industry was emphasised by the Chemical Industries Association in its 1984 activities report:

> The activities of the UK chemical industry are largely dependent on controls many of which now arise from the EC or from conventions entered into by the UK Government based on the activities of OECD and other international groups. In this respect the importance of the Conseil Européen des Fédérations de l'Industrie Chimique (CEFIC) to the chemical industry of Europe cannot be overstated. We are increasingly working in an environment where directives and regulations designed and enacted in the Community have a profound influence on the daily life of our industry, our member companies and all our employees in one way or another.

CEFIC has over fifty sector groups, a staff of over forty and has been served by presidents drawn from the leading European chemical companies (from 1984 to 1986 Sir John Harvey-Jones of ICI). Admittedly, CEFIC is one of the better resourced European level groups, reflecting the international character of the chemical industry. However, even product level groups, although they often operate on a shoestring, are the focus of considerable activity by their members. The activities of the national member organisations are often dominated by European Community questions. This is true of many product level organisations in the food processing industry. Research by de Vroom (1985) shows that, apart from metal products, machinery and equipment, the food, beverages and tobacco industry has the largest number of European-level associations (sixty-five) of any two digit (industry) sector. For example, there is a European Mustard Association (CIMCEE) which has been involved in discussions with the Commission about a range of volumes for mustard.

Conclusions

It has been shown above that each of the five groups studied in detail established three sets of channels of representation: to

national bodies, to European interest groups and direct to EC
bodies. In addition, some introduced an international dimension
with channels of representation to international interest groups.
These organisations, namely the CBI and the ABCC, also included in their national channels of representation a regional
dimension.

Common to all the groups were channels of representation to
British Government officials, European interest groups and direct
to the EC Commission, although the priorities they attached to
these and others of their channels of representation varied. At
least in the early years of EC membership the Retail Consortium
and the BBA focused primarily on their European level channels
of representation whilst the AIB maintained a preference for its
informal links with the CBI. The CBI, by contrast, concentrated
equally throughout Britain's first decade of EC membership on its
three main sets of channels of representation. The ABCC, however, attached different priorities to these sets according to the
type of EC related matter than it dealt with. In fact, the priorities
each of the groups attached to its channels of representation varied
from EC related matter to EC related matter.

Moreover, during the decade 1972–82 their experiences and
events encouraged the groups to modify the general preferences
they attached to their channels of representation. To recap, the
AIB altered its opinion of the Economic and Social Committee as
a channel of representation once it fully understood this EC body's
role, and the introduction of direct elections to the European
Parliament encouraged most of the groups to attach more importance to channels of representation to this body than they had done
prior to June 1979. The experience of participating in European
interest groups encouraged them to attach more importance to
their European interest groups as channels of representation to
their respective sister federations than as channels of representation to EC bodies.

The requirement to influence EC decisions had a major impact
on the groups themselves in terms of their decision-making structures, their resources, their relations with each other and their
relations with their respective members. The internal organisations the groups established for representation in the EC certainly reflected the lessons of experience. This was reflected in the
changes the groups made to the internal structures in which they

invested responsibility for co-ordinating their respective EC related activities; the resources they allocated to EC representation, in particular their increasing concern at the inadequacy of the back-up and support they receive from their member organisations and/or companies; and the types of links which were developed between the groups between 1972 and 1982, which at no time approached the formalised structures advocated by the Devlin Commission or the Inter-Bank Research Organisation.

The size of the groups' financial resources had less impact upon the channels of representation they opened in order to influence EC decisions than might have been expected. This was because the vast majority of the groups' channels of representation were based upon an exchange relationship between the groups and the targets of their representations, whereby the groups were granted access to EC bodies and national bodies in exchange for certain services, rather than on the basis of their financial resources. The exception to this rule, as stated previously, was the groups' channels of representation to European interest groups and the Retail Consortium's parliamentary consultancy. Conversely, the limited size of the groups' manpower resources, especially their unpaid manpower resources or voluntary workers greatly affected the groups' representations on EC related matters and resulted in the groups placing considerable emphasis upon channels of representation that could be operationalised at national level.

The learning process evident from the modifications the groups made to their internal arrangements for EC representation, the channels of representation they opened in order to influence EC decisions and the priorities they attached to these channels of representation between 1972 and 1982 indicates that the ways in which the groups were organised for EC representation would continue to be modified during Britain's second and subsequent decades of EC membership. It seemed unlikely at the outset of the second decade that the learning process would result in a specific type of organisation common to all business organisations or that it would culminate at all in a fixed format. Changeable factors such as shifts in the balance of decision-making power in the Communities; alterations to the groups' understanding of the Community's political system; changes in general environmental factors such as the state of the economy in Britain and other EC member states; changes in the scope of EC policy proposals; changes in the groups themselves in terms of their memberships, relations with their members and resources; and changes in the political parties in power in the UK and other EC member states would all require modifications to the ways in which the groups were organised for EC representation.

Contrary to the expectations of some commentators that group activity might facilitate the integration process, a central problem has been the weakness of many of the European level federations, arising from a lack of commitment by the national federations, particularly in terms of providing the necessary resources. Reference has been made in this chapter to the fact that, for a time, there was no European level organisation for retailers. The European level organisation for the food processing industry (CIAA) was for over twenty years simply a committee of UNICE, only becoming an independent organisation in 1982. Even UNICE itself, despite CBI involvement in reorganisation efforts, has been a source of disappointment to British industrialists. There is little evidence to suggest that during future decades of EC membership British interest groups would place greater emphasis on channels of representation to their respective European interest groups, at the expense of their channels of representation to the British Government, even if the Commission was successful in drawing up proposals for positive policy harmonisation. Thus, the indications for further integration in Western Europe, if left to British business organisations, were less optimistic at the end of Britain's first decade of EC membership than at the beginning.

In fact, British business organisations can be expected to continue to maintain and use a mixture of national level and European level channels of representation, embodying channels of representation to national bodies, European interest groups and direct to EC bodies (and, in some cases, channels of representation to international interest groups), from which they will select those which appear to them to be the most appropriate, on a policy-by-policy basis.

11   Conclusions

The central theme of this book has been that the economic power
of business in Britain is not matched by a capacity for developing a
coherent political viewpoint and articulating it to government.
This inhibits the development of any concertative relationship
between business and government, and leaves the way open for
political solutions in which the interests of business are defined by
politicians (on the right and left) who place a higher value on the
ideological purity of their policies than on their effectiveness in
tackling such problems as relative economic decline. This is not to
be interpreted as a covert plea for the Alliance parties; indeed, a
lack of links to particular interests can be a weakness as well as
strength. In particular, it may encourage a naive optimism about
some of the harsher realities of economic life. The message in this
book is, then, mainly addressed to moderate Tories and mainstream Labour supporters who wish to work with organised interests, rather than seeking to undermine them. As was noted in
Chapter 8, moderate Tories see interests as an acceptable constituent of a harmonious policy, whereas the Thatcherite view is that
vested interests are an unhealthy aspect of society which need to
be weakened and restrained. Similarly, the Labour Party under
Kinnock, Hattersley and Smith does not seek to eliminate private
enterprise any more than Wilson or Callaghan did. Hence, in
order to successfully implement its policies successfully, it requires
a measure of cooperation and goodwill from business.

This observation recalls the point made in Chapter 2 that there
is an underlying capitalist logic to western capitalist systems which
limits the range of options open to politicians. Capital is able to
enjoy power for much of the time without overtly exercising it,
because western societies evaluate the success of governments in
terms of criteria as profitability, growth, etc. Such goals both
reflect the central importance of capital accumulation in such

societies, and also require the cooperation of business if they are to be attained.

Business is capable, through the economic power it is able to exert in product markets, labour markets, etc., of exerting a considerable influence over people's everyday lives. Workers and consumers have some countervailing power, but national governments and even intergovernmental institutions have difficulty in influencing the operations of the emerging global capital market. Politicians must pay attention to the requirements of business, if they wish to gain re-election as the result of being able to claim that they have managed the economy successfully.

One conclusion that could be drawn is that capitalism can only be challenged through revolutionary action that substitutes a new underlying logic, that of socialism. However, as sophisticated analysts such as Heilbroner (1986) admit, socialism has a real problem with freedom. Under capitalism, it is possible to live an existence independent of politicians and administrators; socialism has in practice demanded subservience to political authority. One might add that state socialist countries have had a problem with economic efficiency, hence the experiments in increasing enterprise autonomy and making greater use of the price mechanism. Indeed, while this book was being written, I received an enquiry from one such country about how business associations might be set up or revitalised.

For those who prefer an authentic rather than a surrogate market economy, is it possible to construct a political bargain with capital which channels its energies without curbing them? The political process offers the possibility of regulating business activity so that certain kinds of actions (e.g. racial and sexual discrimination) can be prohibited. It also offers the possibility of a constructive dialogue between business and government about the broader economic and social goals of a society. One of the conditions of such a dialogue is an ability on the part of business interests to express a collective viewpoint, other than at a lowest common denominator level. In some smaller European countries, such as Austria and Sweden, business organisations do seem to have developed a capability to engage in a dialogue with the unions and with government. That is not to say that the conditions for such a relationship exist in Britain. Unfortunately, an observation which Clement Attlee made in 1930 remains applicable today:

'The individualism of the British industrialist, which in the past has been largely responsible for his success, and his conservatism, have made him slower than his foreign rivals to recognise the need for collective action' (Harris, 1982, p. 570). Because business has often been incapable of deciding what it really wants, politicians have often made up their own minds about what is good for business, often with unhappy results.

'Business', then, rarely acts as an entity. Although there has been speculation that the CBI has become a Confederation of British Business in all but name (see Keegan, 1977), in reality it falls short of that aspiration. Its coverage of smaller businesses is patchy and financial institutions are largely members for 'liaison' and goodwill purposes; they have other channels through which they can defend their interests. Business interests are not united politically, although there is a tendency in the literature to over-state the differences between finance and industry, so that they are portrayed as being separated by a chasm of misunderstanding when the reality is more like an ill-defined and much bridged ditch.

That is not to say that financial interests have not had certain advantages in relation to those of manufacturing industry. Governments have largely left the City to its own devices; regula-tion and economic interventions have been concentrated on the manufacturing sector. The emergence of large financial conglom-erates, and the internationalisation of the financial sector, may further alter the balance of power between the financial and manufacturing sectors, even if this development is accompanied by a merger boom, and a trend towards greater concentration, in manufacturing. It is also widely maintained that the industrial sector suffers from the supposed fact that Britain is the only industrial country with an anti-industrial culture. Although there is something in this argument, particularly when a contrast is made with the long-standing emphasis on technological excellence in West Germany, it does not fit with the finding that one of the characteristics of the British industrial economy is the divergence in the performance of leading and laggard firms (see Jones, 1981, p. 147). If the prevailing culture has such a depressing and universal impact as is sometimes claimed, why do some firms manage to do very well indeed by international standards?

Probably a greater divergence than that between the financial sector and manufacturing industry is the different operating

environments of international companies and those whose operations are confined to the domestic market. One must make a
distinction here between British based transnationals and foreign
transnationals operating in the UK. Although the former may now
undertake the greater part of their activities outside the UK, they
usually still have their corporate headquarters in London and have
well-established working relationships with the British Government. A director of a major American multinational operating in
Britain commented in interview, 'No doubt that one or two of the
very biggest British companies [in industry concerned] have an
unusual amount of political pull, don't know how it's done.' This
respondent admitted that his company had tended to keep a low
political profile in the UK, and such behaviour has been characteristic of other foreign owned companies operating in Britain,
although obviously there are variations in the management style of
different companies in this respect. Even so, for reasons of political prudence, and, in the case of some American companies, a fear
of anti-trust law, foreign owned transnationals have tended to limit
their involvement in British business associations. There are also
indications that British companies have sometimes not treated
them as full members of an industry's 'policy community'. One
must not, of course, exaggerate these differences; foreign investment is officially welcomed in the UK and, over time, foreign
companies tend to become integrated in domestic policy networks.
Nevertheless, they are not generally political 'insiders' in the sense
that some of the long-established British based multinationals are.

Apart from their political status, British based international
companies simply have more options in terms of the opening up of
new markets, the balancing of differences in production costs and
the management of financial paper. As writers such as Longstreth
have argued, such companies have a natural identity of interest
with the financial sector. A major international company such as
ICI is operating in a completely different political environment
from, say, a company serving a specialised and localised market in
the catering industry. The two may be playing the same game, but
they are playing it in a very different league. Smaller scale business
persons have the strength of numbers, so that they have some
electoral significance, and they benefit from the generally shared
perception that the encouragement of the small entrepreneur is
economically and socially desirable (indeed, many large compa-

nies are involved in programmes to provide advice to emerging small businesses). However, smaller businesses lack the economic importance and political access and sophistication of the larger company.

It must be stressed that it is not being implied that the actions of international companies are necessarily against the national interest. The export of capital (and, it is argued, jobs) overseas is a politically sensitive issue, but an academic study of the subject came to the conclusion 'that if overseas investment had not taken place, some extra investment in the UK would probably have occurred, but it is doubtful whether the effect would have been substantial.' Moreover, 'the absence of overseas investment would have adversely affected the invisible balance of payments' (Shepherd, Silberston and Strange, 1985, p. 155). The real issue may not be whether the actions of British transnationals are against the national interest, but whether they are sufficiently large and efficient to compete effectively with their global rivals. It has been noted that in comparison with those from other countries, British multinationals 'seem to be heavily skewed towards relatively low-technology industries like tobacco, building materials, paper, textiles, alcohol or hotels' (Stopford and Turner, 1985, p. 13). Stopford and Turner argue (1985, p. 16) that, apart from the oil giants, too many of the remaining leading British multinationals are small by international standards in their industries'. The general picture is one 'of companies which just fail to dominate the industries in which they operate' (Ibid., p. 123).

The question of what is the correct domestic policy to adopt towards transnationals lies beyond the scope of this book. What is clear is that there are important divergences of interest between different types of business. However, one must be wary of relying on over rigid categorisations of such differences. As was emphasised in Chapter 5, much depends on the corporate political philosophy of the individual enterprise and, indeed, on the preferences of dominant members of its board. The lesson that has been drawn at a number of points in this book is that common business interests are difficult to identify and, even when they have been identified, it may not be easy to devise a political strategy to pursue them.

It could, of course, be argued that the collective interests of business are identified and pursued through a network of informal contacts arising from the system of non-executive directorships. One should not underrate such contacts as a means of facilitating (or frustrating) company mergers, or of exchanging 'inside dopester' information about economic, financial and political trends. Useem (1984, p. 194) argues that networks of intercorporate ownership and directorship linkages in an increasingly concentrated economy 'define a segment of the business community whose strategic location and internal organization propel it into a political leadership role on behalf of the entire corporate community'. The 'multiple directors' guide major business associations, act as gatekeepers for the formal and informal consultative circles linking government and business, but above all 'the transcorporate network becomes a quasi-autonomous actor in its own right'. (Ibid., p. 195). Having a network of informal contacts does not, of itself, equip business with the ability to develop an effective political position, and the exercise of political influence in a modern polity requires a more sophisticated and sustained effort than a quiet word in the right ear, important though such contacts may be. Firms in Britain have made increasingly effective use of their own government relations divisions, and no doubt contacts on the corporate network sometimes help them in the pursuit of their immediate goals, but it is in effective, collective action which can assist the pursuit of longer run public policy goals that British business has been most defective.

This deficiency is of particular significance given the propensity of wage and salary rises in the British economy to increase above the level justified by improvements in productivity or, indeed, the rate of inflation. From 1974 to 1984 wage costs in the UK rose 260 per cent compared to 70 per cent in West Germany and 110 per cent in the USA. Relative productivity fell over the same period with the result that unit labour costs rose more rapidly than in all countries except Italy (figures from House of Lords, 1985, p. 31). In a review of the operations of the British labour market since 1979, the OECD suggests that the failure of wages to adjust to lower inflation and to soaring unemployment is at the core of Britain's economic problems. The survey contrasts the downward pressure on wages resulting from higher unemployment in other developed countries with the much weaker impact seen in Britain where earnings have continued to rise strongly. The evidence suggests that the rate of change in the unemployment level in

Britain may be as important as the actual jobless total in moderating pay, so that much of the wage restraining effect of unemployment would disappear if it stabilised at a high level (see OECD, 1986). This suggests that there is a need for improvements in bargaining arrangements, including mechanisms for taking account of broader economic policy considerations. However, such innovations are made difficult to achieve by the decentralised and fragmented organisation of British employers just as much as by the factor which usually receives more attention, the decentralisation and fragmentation of the trade union movement.

Given that business has found it difficult to make a collective response to such central problems as the matter of income restraint, the state has found itself, often reluctantly and by default, trying to play a leading role in developing and applying solutions. Government in Britain is, of course, ill-fitted to discharge such a role, both in terms of the absence of a dirigiste tradition and the appropriate machinery for the development and application of policy (see, for example, Wilks 1984). The type of state-led adjustment that has emerged in Britain is rather different from that envisaged by Zysman (1983) in his major comparative study of government–industry relations. Zysman outlines three models of industrial adjustment: a state-led model, a company-led model and a tripartite negotiated model.

Zysman discusses Japanese and French variants of his state-led model of industrial adjustment, but a common feature is that:

> State-led strategies of adjustment require state structures that permit bureaucrats partial autonomy from parliament and from interest groups that attempt to influence them. They also require that bureaucrats have both the legal discretion to discriminate between firms when implementing policy and the administration and financial instruments to exert their will. (Zysman, 1983, p. 300)

In other words, the state-led model seems to assume a non-partisan bureaucracy commited either to implementing goals which are generally shared, or which it is able to impose on the polity because no other grouping in the society is sufficiently strong or sure of what it wants to challenge the bureaucracy's sense of purpose. In fact, state-led adjustment could involve a dominant political party using the bureaucracy's skills to implement a strategy to which it is committed.

What has happened in Britain under the Thatcher Government is partisan (i.e. party political) state-led adjustment in what are seen by government as the interests of business. It must be stressed that the Thatcher Government's approach is different from the company-led model, although its ultimate aim could be said to create conditions in which company-led adjustment is possible. In the company-led model, 'the basic choices are made by individual firms without outside interference (Ibid., p. 92). What is most significant is that 'Above all, the government does not have a long-run view of the development of government and industry' (Ibid., p. 92). Although the Thatcher Government has not had an industrial strategy in the sense of a vision of what the economy should be like in the future (other than that it will be more service oriented), it has tried to shift the economy from a mixed to a market form. Certain obstacles are seen to stand in the way of this process, such as rigidities in the labour market supposedly caused by the activities of trade unions, and the Government has engaged in quite detailed intervention to remove these barriers to the changes it favours.

Unlike company-led adjustment where the task of change is left in the hands of companies operating in an approximation of a market economy, partisan state-led adjustment involves interventions by government in order to create the conditions in which, ultimately, such company-led adjustment can occur. State intervention is necessary because companies lack the political will and capacity, and the managerial determination, to see adjustment through on their own. Conditions must be created in which free enterprise can flourish, but business cannot do this by itself, partly because of what is seen as spinelessness, partly because the obstacles are so great that they can only be tackled through the determined use of state power. Most importantly, state power must be used to curtail the power of organised labour. In short, the problem of the unions' vetoing power identified by Zysman and other writers is tackled by inflicting what is intended to be lasting political defeat on the trade unions.

There are three main problems with this strategy. First, the costs of conflict may exceed those of co-operation: the effort to reshape the polity and society may rend its very fabric so that the task of government becomes permanently more difficult. Second, government's political definition of what is in the interests of capital may differ from the business community's own definition of its interests: hence at crucial points in the implementation of the strategy, the state may find that it lacks the support of business, or may even find itself openly criticised by leading employers or business organisations. Third, and perhaps most vital, even if business is released from its bonds British private enterprise may not prove equal to the task it faces. A company-led industrial strategy has really only worked in the United States, and even there it has faced problems in those parts of the country whose industrial structure most resemble that of Britain, leading to economic interventions at the state government level. There is enough evidence of the failures of British management in marketing and workplace organisation to suggest that it might have difficulty in flourishing in a truly free market.

If one rules out state-led and company-led forms of adjustment, then one is left with a tripartite negotiated solution. However, as should be clear from the earlier chapters, that is not really an option in Britain. Hesitant attempts at tripartism have failed because neither employers' nor workers' organisations are sufficiently cohesive and disciplined to sustain them for any length of time. State action could, of course, be taken to change the nature of the organisations, but this would meet severe resistance in a country with a liberal, individualistic culture. In any case, the available evidence suggests that tripartite arrangements work best where they develop organically from below, rather than being imposed from above, and where they are based on a satisfactory working relationship between capital and labour which is then facilitated by the state (see, for example, Marin 1985). It is therefore not surprising that Zysman (1983, p. 229) concludes that Britain has failed politically in the sense that 'No solution could be imposed, and none was negotiated'. The nature of this failure, and the character of relations between business and government, can best be understood in a more elaborated comparative context. In the following section, relations between business and government in the western world's leading industrial powers (the G–7 countries that participate in world economic summits) are briefly reviewed.

248   *Business and Politics in Britain*

Business and politics: a comparative overview

In the United States, the business–politics relationship is, perhaps
surprisingly, a difficult one. Although there have been some
changes of emphasis under the Reagan administration, businesses
are heavily regulated, both in the area of anti-trust and environmental regulations, not to mention affirmative action programmes.
The anti-trust laws in particular 'reflect an historic American
concern with excessive economic power, both private and public'
(Connor, Rogers, Marion and Mueller, 1985, p. 351). In the
environmental area, administrators have been less sympathetic to
the problems of business than in Britain, and less inclined to find
co-operative solutions (see Vogel, 1986). In 1983 (the latest available figures), US manufacturing establishments with more than
nineteen employees spent $2.0 billion in capital and $9.9 billion in
operating costs on pollution abatement (United States Department of Commerce, 1986, p. 11–7). Despite assumptions that
might be made about the United States as a land in which free
enterprise can flourish without hindrance, the business–politics
relationship is often adversarial, a tendency reinforced by the
importance of lawyers and law suits in the relationship.

The Canadian case is an interesting one because it offers unique
mix of a British tradition of politics and administration and a more
American orientation to enterprise, although there is more public
ownership in Canada than in the States. Some sectors of business
in Canada have been able to 'colonise' parts of the administration
to their advantage, whilst in areas such as the dairy industry
corporatist type relationships have developed (in Quebec, there
have even been forms of state corporatism – see Coleman, 1985).
However, sectors such as the extractive industries have come
under heavy environmental and other regulation inducing pressures, although some extractive industries (such as forestry) are
more regulated than others such as mining and petroleum and
natural gas production. The non-programmatic character of the
two main Canadian political parties has led them to emphasise
vote seeking as a predominant goal, and does not dispose them to
take particular account of business interests, other than perhaps
those of small business. Moreover, power is more devolved to the
constituent federal units in Canada than in the United States, thus
increasing the complexity of the political environment faced by

business. Like their American counterparts, Canadian business persons are represented by a number of organisations at the national level, rather than having a principal spokesman with companies and associations as members like the CBI.

Japan presents a contrast to the American and Canadian cases. Large firms in Japan have been prepared to tolerate a considerable amount of guidance from the Ministry of International Trade and Industry (MITI) and the Ministry of Finance, although it should be stressed that they have not always done as they have been told, and have been less willing to go along with government wishes in recent years. Indeed, accounts of the Japanese experience have probably placed too much emphasis on the role of MITI, and not enough on the importance of the low cost of capital, facilitated by the need of individual Japanese citizens to save to provide for their retirement. Financial liberalisation is bringing about important changes in this sphere in Japan, and the cost of capital is likely to rise. Nevertheless, although conventional accounts of Japan may have suffered from misperceptions, and although there have been some important recent changes, there is a sense in which the notion of 'Japan Inc.' makes sense. One must not also forget the domination of the post-war political scene by one political party, with intra-party factions offering scope for the defence of particular interests on the political stage. Good relations between business and government have been inadvertently facilitated by Japanese cultural traditions, especially that of 'descent from heaven'. In order to prevent an equal becoming a superior, the whole of the rest of a year's intake to a ministry will retire when one of their number attains the rank of the equivalent of permanent secretary. With the assistance of the ministry, the most able take jobs in business and finance, thus facilitating business–government contacts (see Hills, 1983, pp. 68–9).

France has a long-standing *étatiste* tradition. Its effective functioning has been facilitated by circulation of élites between government and business, the development of bureaucratic autonomy and economic expertise during the Fourth Republic, and the relative success of the political institutions of the Fifth Republic. France has had its problems of economic management, not least in the early years of the Mitterrand administration, and there has been a tendency for British analysts to overstate the successes, importance and durability of the French system of indicative planning. Nevertheless, whatever one thinks of the use of nuclear power for electricity generation, it is interesting to contrast the way with which the French Government carried out a civil nuclear power programme with the delays, uncertainties and confusions that have occurred in Britain. As Zysman (1983, p. 132) comments, 'Twice the French state has shifted the base of the economy, once from coal to oil and once from oil toward nuclear power. It did so by imposing on the society choices made inside government.' The prospect of Britain becoming a net importer of electricity from France underlines differences in the success of the two countries in tackling key problems. More generally, the French economy has undergone a substantial process of modernisation in the post-war period.

West Germany has been portrayed as being characterised by close links at the élite level between civil servants, ministers, trade union leaders, bankers, industrialists and economic experts, links which are utilised to pursue a common objective of maximising German economic prosperity. There has perhaps been an exaggeration of the importance of 'concerted action' in West Germany long after its disappearance in a formal tripartite sense. Moreover, the importance and value of links between house banks and firms has often been overstated (see Grant, Paterson and Whitston, 1985). Nevertheless, by British standards West Germany has a coherent and centralised system of trade associations and trade unions. Above all, 'The secret of West Germany's industrial policy lies in its invisibility; there exists a division of labour between the public and the private sector understood and appreciated by almost everyone' (Katzenstein, 1985, p. 68). What this means is that, despite government claims that West Germany does not have an industrial policy, there has been substantial intervention to reorganise and support particular sectors such as coal and aerospace, an effort supported by the 'private' industrial policy pursued by institutions such as the banks. There has also been substantial support for research and development, both from the state in the form of grants and tax incentives and through collective self-help programmes by certain industries such as that found in chemicals.

Italy is, as always, difficult to characterise. One of the most distinctive features of its business élite has been the continuing importance of organisation on territorial lines, particularly those associations based in Milan and Turin. Many firms affiliate to

Confindustria only through territorial associations, rather than through their industry associations as well. (see Treu and Martinelli, 1984, p. 271). As far as the organisation of the economy is concerned, one of the most significant features has been the presence of giant state holding companies with interests throughout the economy, often used as instruments of political patronage. In the 1980s, there has been a greater emphasis on efficiency and the attainment of economic goals in the management of these companies, as well as the first steps towards a measure of privatisation. Much of Italy's economic strength may lie in its smaller manufacturing firms, whose flexible specialisation, emphasis on quality and design, ability to adjust to changing patterns of demand, and, it has to be said, existence for much of the time in the black economy, offsets the inefficiencies apparent elsewhere (see Piore and Sabel, 1983). Indeed, Italy's strength and weakness has been the lack of a proper state apparatus. This has made it difficult for government to grapple effectively with the country's problems, and, indeed, to raise taxes properly, but has also created conditions in which flexible specialisation has been able to flourish.

How would one characterise Britain? Is it a variant of the American adversarial pattern, albeit it with more effective collective organisation of business as a whole, rather than the co-operative patterns of West Germany, or the state-led patterns of France or Japan? It is certainly the case that business persons and politicians in the UK often seem to exist in different worlds, with communication difficult and often leading to misunderstanding. To use Vogel's (1978) terminology, businessmen do not see the state as 'their state', as would arguably be the case in West Germany and Japan. The British pattern is not a simple reflection of the American one of the relying on market solutions to the majority of problems. In many respects, Britain is an intermediate position between America and West Germany: its businesses use government relations divisions to handle their political relationships, not on an American scale, but in contrast to the absence of a similar development in West Germany; their representative organisations are better developed than those of the United States, but are less coherent and effective than those found in West Germany. Business attitudes towards the state in Britain are contradictory rather than simply adversarial, a point well made by an experienced businessman, Sir Kenneth Corfield, who states that the relationship between government and industry 'is typified by industry's suspicion of "intervention" on the one hand, and a curiously paradoxical recognition that government has a responsibility towards industry on the other' (Corfield, 1985, p. 92).

Dualism versus corporatism

These differences in national styles in government–business relations, and the nature of the Thatcher experiment discussed earlier, can be pursued further in a discussion of the distinction between corporatism and dualism. Following Katzenstein (1985, p. 32), democratic corporatism may be seen as having three distinguishing traits: an ideology of social partnership; a relatively centralised and concentrated system of interest groups; and the co-ordination of conflicting objectives through continuous political bargaining. Attempts to develop corporatist arrangements have often, in practice, been an attempt to contain the increased power of organised labour by co-opting it into the development, and, more importantly, the implementation of public policy (see, for example, Goldthorpe, 1984, p. 328). Organised employers have become involved in such arrangements, from the state's perspective, to increase their inclusiveness and legitimacy, and from the employers' perspective, to defend their interests against those of the unions.

Efforts in this direction in Britain have been sporadic, hesitant and ineffective. Moreover, even though we should heed Schmitter's (1982, p. 266) warning not to take every breakdown in corporatist arrangements as a sign of their demise, the difficulties faced by such patterns of bargaining seem to be increasing, not least in such bulwarks of the corporatist heartland as Austria. Goldthorpe suggests that there is another alternative to the limitations of pluralism other than corporatism: what he terms 'dualism'. Rather than building on, and institutionalising, pluralism, as with corporatism, this involves limiting the beneficiaries of pluralist provisions (see Goldthorpe, 1984, p. 335). Under dualism, government abandons the attempt to maintain any particular pattern of economic activity, repudiates political bargaining with the unions and attempts to enlarge the freedom of action of employers. It should be stressed that these are not 'either or' paradigms; Goldthorpe (1984, p. 336) points out that corporatist and dualist tendencies can coexist within the same society. What is significant about dualism in the context of this study is that, whereas under corporatism, employers are reluctantly drawn into bargaining because it is preferable to standing aside, in the case of dualism, 'it is employers and their managements who are of central importance' (Goldthorpe, 1984, p. 336). As was noted in Chapter 8, the Thatcher Government has delegated existing or potential public policy functions to employer or employer based organisations. In certain key areas of public policy, tripartite bargaining, or government regulation, is replaced by employer self-regulation.

Although the concept of dualism is thus a fruitful one, it has its limitations. Like corporatism, it focuses on the politics of production. The politics of production (represented in such issues as wages policy, union rights, industrial democracy, etc.) dominated West European politics for much of the post-war period. However, in the 1980s, what may be termed 'the politics of collective consumption' has assumed a new importance. Issues such as food additives, acid rain and animal rights have assumed a new importance. In West Germany, by and large, the political imperative of the 1980s has not been how to co-opt the trade unions, but how to accommodate the Greens. Indeed, legislation relating to benefits paid to those laid off as a result of a labour dispute proposed by the CDU/FPD Government has been seen as a threat to the stability of industrial relations. Corporatist bargaining systems like Austria have found it difficult to incorporate ecological issues which lie outside the bargaining arrangements based on production oriented interests. The issue of nuclear power in Austria was defused, if not resolved, by a referendum, but the limits of corporatist bargaining were graphically underlined by Austria's use of the police to break up a demonstration against a proposed hydroelectric plant. Issues of this kind redefine the scope of the political agenda and present new challenges to business.

The political future for business in Britain

What does the political future hold for business in Britain? Much will, of course, depend on national economic performance, and despite improvements in some indicators in the mid-1980s, there are grounds for pessimism about the long-run possibilities (see, for example, House of Lords, 1985; Institute for Employment Research, 1985). However, the concern of this book is with the role of business in the political process. What would a third term of the Thatcher administration mean for business? Thatcherites would claim that one result would be an enterprise culture, although I am sceptical about the extent to which government interventions can actually change a culture. Perhaps the outcome would be more like an 'acquisition culture'. The strong stock exchange in Britain already encourages a predisposition to solving the problems of companies through a process of take-over, leading to the creation of broadly based conglomerates which tend to judge performance in terms of the satisfaction of short-run financial objectives. Industrial conglomerates could be matched by a series of financial conglomerates, skilled at dealing in financial paper, but with little incentive to take a long-run view of the needs of industry.

In the long run, application of Thatcherite remedies would lead to a further decline in those industries most opposed to such policies, and expansion in those service sectors most well disposed to them. Hence, the effectiveness of any political resistance by industry to Thatcherite policies would tend to decline over time, a tendency that would be reinforced by the further privatisation of the nationalised industries. What remained of traditional manufacturing industry might be more homogeneous in its views, but also more supine in its posture, and less capable of defending itself politically if it wanted to. However, business as a whole would not be living in some *laissez-faire* Victorian paradise. It would still be taxed by government, it would still be influenced by government as a major customer, and it would still be regulated by government and, increasingly, the EC. In such a situation, sectoral associations and government relations divisions would become even more important than at present in defending very particularistic business interests. As a result, sectors of industry and commerce with effective associations, and firms with well-run government relations divisions would be able to protect their interests reasonably well; the sectors (probably a majority) with less effective associations, and smaller firms, would tend to lose out.

If Labour won a general election outright in the late 1980s, there would not be a simple reversion to the 1970s. The unions are weaker, the manufacturing economy is weaker, and a Labour

Government would need industrial co-operation more than ever before. Despite some rhetorical flourishes, and some symbolic policy initiatives which might have an irritant value, behind the scenes Labour's relations with business would be remarkably pragmatic. The CBI would find itself back in a more prominent position again, moderating government policy in private whilst attacking it in public.

The real clash would come over Labour's declared intention to limit overseas investment. Some business persons can see a pragmatic case for a National Investment Bank to provide long-run finance for riskier projects: indeed, such a concept, but with minority state participation unlike the Labour model, has been advanced by an NEDC committee. However, limiting industrial investment overseas would strike at the fundamental interests of many large companies; a domestically oriented political party would be brought into conflict with an increasingly international-ised business community. In practice, much would depend on how the policy was implemented and whether it required merely sym-bolic concessions or real changes.

The most uncertain outcome of a future election is the most likely one, a Labour government dependent on Alliance support. At first sight, this might seem to offer a recipe for an even more pragmatic form of Labourism than that which would occur under a Kinnock–Hattersley government with a working majority. How-ever, as I argued in Chapter 8, I am less certain. The Labour Party is a party which recognises the central importance of production, especially manufacturing production. They are a party of the politics of production, even allowing for the 'patchwork quilt' alliances of various minority groups which make up many local Labour parties. The Alliance, particularly the Liberal Party, is much more identified with the politics of collective consumption. The emphasis of Liberal supporters on such issues as protecting the environment, increasing the rights of consumers, etc. is in many respects more threatening to long-run business interests than the more traditional production oriented concerns of trade union-ists. Indeed, employers and trade unions often work together in a production coalition in relation to such issues as overcapacity, foreign competition, energy prices, etc. Employers are less accus-tomed to dealing with, say, public criticism of food additives. Although they are now starting to respond to challenges on such questions, they still run the risk of being portrayed as acting against the public interest, mainly by politicians looking for issues on which they can gain favourable publicity, but which do not require large public expenditure commitments.

Whatever the outcome of the next election, and whatever the balance is between the politics of production and the politics of collective consumption by the turn of the century, I am not optimistic about the likelihood of British business developing more coherent and effective representational structures. The rather weak and *ad hoc* pressures for reform are unlikely to overcome the inertia arising from individualistic employer attitudes and historical organisational loyalties. Given that the economy is likely to become more concentrated, the government relations divisions of large firms will probably help to increase the political sophistication of businessmen; perhaps in time they may be allowed to exert some influence on the business associations to which their firms belong. Organisations like the Industry and Parliament Trust can help to educate politicians in the priorities of business, but also business persons in the ways of politicians. Defects in the collective political organisation of business in Britain make it more difficult to devise and implement practical solutions to the country's economic problems, whilst the pressures of relative economic decline make it more difficult to focus on the need for structural reform. The long-run consequence may be that business will find itself operating in a less favourable economic, social and political environment.

Guide to Further Reading

Chapter 1

Dyson's (1983) essay is a good introduction to different conceptions of the firm and business associations and their roles in society and politics in Britain compared with other countries. Tylecote (1981) offers an emphatic analysis of the importance of the absence of employer solidarity in Britain compared with its strength in West Germany. Leys (1985) is a key article which tackles a number of important issues which arise in any analysis of business and politics in Britain.

Chapter 2

Truman (1951) offers a classic pluralist analysis of the role of business in society, whilst Lindblom (1977) offers an important account of the view that business is a privileged interest. An analysis of business which is more oriented to the British case is to be found in Coates, David (1984). Heilbroner (1986) provides a more general analysis of the underlying logic of capitalist societies.

Chapter 3

Englefield (ed.) (1985) contains a number of interesting essays by civil servants, business persons from the private and public sectors and politicians on relations between government and business. Curwen (1986) provides a comprehensive, up-to-date text on the nationalised industries. Peacock (1984) is a useful introduction to the regulatory role of government.

Chapter 4

For a straightforward introduction to financial institutions and markets, see Taylor (1984). Michael Moran is the leading expert on the politics of the financial sector in Britain, and all his work is worth reading, especially Moran (1983), Moran (1984b), and the series of working papers on current developments he issues free of charge from the Department of Government, University of Manchester, Manchester M13 9PL. Ingham (1984) has written one of the conceptually richest and most original books about the economic and political role of the financial sector. Longstreth's (1979) essay remains an important departure from conventional analyses of the City–industry divide.

Chapter 5

The political activities of individual firms are unfortunately something of a neglected subject. Englefield (ed.) (1985) contains some relevant material. Edwardes (1983) offers the observations of an industrialist involved in an enterprise with a high political profile. Reader (1975) offers insights into the political activities of one of Britain's most publicly oriented private firms (ICI). Doig (1986) and Jordan (1985) are useful starting points for understanding the controversies surrounding the activities of political consultants.

Chapter 6

For an illuminating history of the CBI's predecessor, see Blank (1973). Material on the development of the CBI is to be found in Grant and Marsh (1977). Richardson (1982 is an interesting case study which throws light on the limitations of the CBI as an organisation. Windmuller and Gladstone (1985) allows one to place the CBI in a comparative international context.

Chapter 7

Turner (ed.) (1984) contains some valuable historical insights into the development of business associability in Britain. Fuller information on the activities of business associations in Britain, compared with those in West Germany, can be found in W. Grant, *Why Employer Organisation Matters* (free of charge from the Department of Politics, University of Warwick, Coventry CV4 7AL). There is a very rich literature on agricultural interests; particularly recommended is the well written and informed account to be found in Lowe, Cox, MacEwen, O'Riordan and Winter (1986). For chambers of commerce, see King (1985).

Chapter 8

The literature on business and political parties is not well developed. Ross (1983) has some interesting, if polemically presented, information on the Conservative Party and business. The Hansard Society's (1981) study is a sensible analysis of the funding of political parties.

Chapter 9

Streeck and Schmitter (1985) offer a theoretical overview of the potential role of business associations in public policy implementation. On the dairy sector, see Grant (1985b, 1985c) for further analysis; on the pharmaceutical industry, see Sargent (1985); on employers and training policy, Rainbird and Grant (1985a, 1985b); on investor protection, Moran (1986a). Lehmbruch (1984) offers a means of linking the developments discussed in this chapter to the literature on corporatism.

Chapter 10

For a more general analysis of interest organisation at the EC level, see Butt Philip (1985). Sargent (1982) provides a case study of the European activities of a particular business group. Grant, Paterson and Whitston (forthcoming) will contain a considerable amount of material on the political activities of business in relation to the EC.

Chapter 11

Stopford and Turner (1985) provide a readable and wide-ranging analysis of the impact of both home based and foreign multinationals on the UK. Shepherd, Silberston and Strange (1985) offer a careful analysis of the consequences of the overseas orientation of much of British business. Zysman (1983) offers an interesting comparative perspective on government–industry relations, and Wilks (1984) provides a cogent analysis of the inadequacies of the relationship in Britain. Goldthorpe's (1984) essay poses some fundamental questions about the future direction to be taken by western industrial societies.

Bibliography

ABPI (1984) *Code of Practice for the Pharmaceutical Industry (6th edn) together with the Constitution and Procedure for the Code of Practice Committee* (London: Association of the British Pharmaceutical Industry).

Almond, G. (1983) 'Corporatism, Pluralism and Professional Memory', *World Politics*, 35, pp. 245–60.

Artis, M. and S. Ostry (1986) *International Economic Policy Co-ordination*, Chatham House Papers 30 (London: Routledge & Kegan Paul).

Averyt, W. (1977) *Agro Politics in the European Community: Interest Groups and the Common Agricultural Policy* (New York: Praeger).

Barnett, J. (1982) *Inside the Treasury* (London: Andre Deutsch).

Batstone, E., A. Ferner and M. Terry (1983) *Unions on the Board* (Oxford: Basil Blackwell).

—— A. Ferner and M. Terry (1984) *Consent and Efficiency: Labour Relations and Management Strategy in the State Enterprise* (Oxford: Basil Blackwell).

Beer, S. (1982) *Britain Against Itself* (London: Faber & Faber).

Blank, S. (1973) *Industry and Government in Britain: The Federation of British Industries in Politics* (Farnborough: Saxon House).

—— (1978) 'Britain: the Politics of Foreign Economic Policy, the Domestic Economy, and the Problem of Pluralistic Stagnation', in P. Katzenstein (ed.), *Between Power and Plenty* (Madison: University of Wisconsin Press).

Boddewyn, J. J. (1985) 'Advertising Self-Regulation: Organization Structures in Belgium, Canada, France and the United Kingdom', in W. Streeck and P. Schmitter (eds), *Private Interest Government: Beyond Market and State* (London: Sage).

Bonnett, K. (1985) 'Corporatism and Thatcherism: Is There Life After Death?', in A. Cawson (ed.), *Organized Interests and the State: Studies in Meso-Corporatism.* (London: Sage).

British Agrochemicals Association (1984) *Annual Report and Handbook 1983–4* (London: British Agrochemicals Association).

Brittan, S. (1975) 'The Economic Contradictions of Democracy', *British Journal of Political Science*, 5, pp. 129–59.

Brown, G. (1972) *In My Way* (Harmondsworth: Pelican).

Brown, W. A. (1980) 'The Structure of Pay Bargaining in Britain', in F. Blackaby (ed.), *The Future of Pay Bargaining* (London: Heinemann).

—— (1981) 'Comments', in F. Cairncross (ed.), *Changing Perceptions of Economic Policy* (London: Methuen).

Burns, P. (1984) 'State Contracts: How to Crack the Market', *The Director*, May 1984, pp. 38–40.

Butler, D. and D. Kavanagh (1984) *The British General Election of 1983* (London: Macmillan).

Butt Philip, A. (1985) 'Pressure Groups in the European Community', (London: University Association of Contemporary European Studies, Occasional Paper No. 2).

Cabinet Office (1978) *Industrial Innovation* (London: HMSO).

Causer, G. (1978) 'Private Capital and the State in Western Europe', in S. Giner and M. S. Archer (eds) *Contemporary Europe: Social Structures and Cultural Patterns* (London: Routledge & Kegan Paul).

Cawson, A. (1982) *Corporatism and Welfare* (London: Heinemann).

Cawson, A. (1985) 'Introduction', in A. Cawson (ed.) *Organised Interests and the State* (London: Sage).

CBI (1978) *The Road to Recovery* (London: Confederation of British Industry).

—— (1981) *Getting the Business View Across in the European Community* (London: Confederation of British Industry).

—— (1985) *Change to Succeed* (London: Confederation of British Industry).

Centre for Agricultural Strategy (1980) *The Efficiency of British Agriculture* (Reading: Centre for Agricultural Strategy).

Centre for Policy Studies (1984) 'Which Direction? Board Appointments in Nationalised Industries' (London: Centre for Policy Studies).

Chester, D. (1975) *The Nationalisation of British Industry 1945–51* (London: HMSO).

Cmnd 9432 (1985) *Financial Services in the United Kingdom: A New Framework for Investor Protection* (London: HMSO).

Cmnd 9571 (1985) *Lifting the Burden* (London: HMSO).

Coates, David (1984) *The Context of British Politics* (London: Hutchinson).

Coates, Dudley (1984) 'Food Law: Brussels, Whitehall and Town Hall', in D. Lewis and H. Wallace (eds), *Policies into Practice* (London: Heinemann).

Coleman, W. D. (1985) 'State Corporatism as a Sectoral Phenomenon: The Case of the Quebec Construction Industry', in A. Cawson (ed.), *Organised Interests and the State: Studies in Meso-Corporatism* (London: Sage).

—— and W. Grant (1985) 'Regional Differentiation of Business Interest Associations: A Comparison of Canada and the United Kingdom', *Canadian Journal of Political Science*, 18, pp. 3–29.

Connor, J. M., R. T. Rogers, B. W. Marion and W. F. Muller (1985) *The Food Manufacturing Industries* (Lexington: D.C. Heath).

Constitutional Reform Centre (1985) 'Company Donations to Political Parties: A Suggested Code of Practice' (London: Constitutional Reform Centre).

Coopers & Lybrand Associates (1985) *A Challenge to Complacency: Changing Attitudes to Training* (Sheffield: Manpower Services Commission).

Corfield, Sir K. (1985) 'An Industrialist's View – the Private Sector', in

D. Englefield (ed.), *Today's Civil Service* (Harlow: Longman).

Cowling, K. (1982) 'Monopolies and Mergers Policy: A New Perspective', in D. Currie and M. Sawyer (eds), *Socialist Economic Review 1982* (London: Merlin Press).

Cox, G., P. Lowe and M. Winter (1985) 'Changing Directions in Agricultural Policy: Corporatist Arrangements in Production and Conservation Policies', *Sociologia Ruralis*, 25, pp. 130–54.

Criddle, B. (1984) 'Candidates', in D. Butler and D. Kavanagh (principal authors), *The British General Election of 1983* (London: Macmillan).

Curtice, J. and M. Steed (1984) 'An Analysis of the Voting', in D. Butler and D. Kavanagh (principal authors), *The British General Election of 1983* (London: Macmillan).

Curwen, P. (1986) *Public Enterprise* (Brighton: Wheatsheaf).

Daly, A., D.M.W.N. Hitchens and K. Wagner (1985) 'Productivity, Machinery and Skills in a Sample of British and German Manufacturing Plants', *National Institute Economic Review*, February 1985, pp. 48–61.

Davenport-Hines, R.P.T. (1984) *Dudley Docker: The Life and Times of a Trade Warrior* (London: Cambridge University Press).

Department of Trade and Industry (1985) *Burdens on Business* (London: HMSO).

Devlin Report (1972) *Report of the Commission of Inquiry into Industrial and Commercial Representation* (London: Association of British Chambers of Commerce/Confederation of British Industry).

Doig, A. (1986) 'Access to Parliament and the Rise of the Professional Lobbyist', *Public Money*, March 1986, pp. 39–43.

Doran, A. (1984) *Craft Enterprises in Britain and Germany: A Sectoral Study* (London: Anglo-German Foundation).

Doyle, C. (1979) 'A Comparative Study of Agricultural Productivity in the UK and Europe', *Journal of Agricultural Economics*, 30, pp. 261–70.

Dudley, G. (1983) 'The Road Lobby: a Declining Force?', in D. Marsh (ed.), *Pressure Politics* (London: Junction Books).

Dunleavy, P. (1982) 'Quasi-Governmental Sector Professionalism: Some Implications for Public Policy-Making in Britain', in A. Barker (ed.), *Quangos in Britain* (London: Macmillan).

Dyson, K. (1983) 'Cultural, Ideological and Structural Context', in K. Dyson and S. Wilks (eds), *Industrial Crisis* (Oxford: Martin Robertson).

East, N. (1985) 'Face-to-Face: A Case Study', in D. Englefield (ed.), *Today's Civil Service* (Harlow: Longman).

Economic and Social Research Council (1985), 'Why Do Firms Join Chambers of Commerce?', Newsletter No. 55, June 1985.

Edwardes, M. (1983) *Back From the Brink* (London: Collins).

England, G. (1985) 'An Industrialist's View – the Public Sector', in D. Englefield (ed.), *Today's Civil Service* (Harlow: Longman).

Englefield, D. (ed.) (1985) *Today's Civil Service* (Harlow: Longman).

Esser, J., W. Fach and K. Dyson, '"Social Market" and Modernisation Policy: West Germany', in K. Dyson and S. Wilks (eds), *Industrial Crisis* (Oxford: Martin Robertson).

Fidler, J. (1981) *The British Business Elite* (London: Routledge & Kegan Paul).

Finer, S. E. (ed.) (1974) *Adversary Politics and Electoral Reform* (London: Antony Wigram).

Forster, N. (1983) 'Chambers of Commerce: A Comparative Study of Their Role in the UK and in Other EEC Countries' (London: Industrial Aids Limited).

Foster, C. (1971) *Politics, Finance and the Role of Economics* (London: Allen & Unwin).

Gamble, A. M. and S. A. Walkland (1984) *The British Party System and Economic Policy 1945–83* (Oxford: Oxford University Press).

Gilmour, Sir I. (1983) *Britain Can Work* (Oxford: Martin Robertson).

Glasgow University Media Group (1976) *Bad News* (London: Routledge & Kegan Paul).

_____ (1980) *More Bad News* (London: Routledge & Kegan Paul).

_____ (1982) *Really Bad News* (London: Writers and Readers Publishing Co-operative Society).

Goldthorpe, J. H. (1984) 'The End of Convergence: Corporatist and Dualist Tendencies in Modern Societies', in J. H. Goldthorpe (ed.), *Order and Conflict in Contemporary Capitalism*, (Oxford: Oxford University Press).

Gospel, H. (1972) *Employers' Associations and Industrial Relations* (London: HMSO).

Grant, W. (1981) 'The Politics of the Green Pound', *Journal of Common Market Studies*, 19, pp. 313–29.

_____ (1982a) 'British Industrial Policy: The Problem and its Perception', *Parliamentary Affairs*, 25, 1982, pp. 282–96.

_____ (1982b) *The Political Economy of Industrial Policy* (London: Butterworths).

_____ (1983a) 'The Organisation of Business Interests in the UK Chemical Industry' (Berlin: International Institute of Management labour market policy discussion paper).

_____ (1983b) 'The Organisation of Business Interests in the UK Construction Industry' (Berlin: International Institute of Management labour market policy discussion paper).

_____ (1983c) 'The Organisation of Business Interests in the UK Food Processing Industry' (Berlin: International Institute of Management labour market policy discussion paper).

_____ (1983d) 'The Organisation of Business Interests in the UK Machine Tools Industry' (Berlin: International Institute of Management labour market policy discussion paper).

_____ (1983e) 'The National Farmers' Union: The Classic Case of Incorporation?', in D. Marsh (ed.), *Pressure Politics* (London: Junction Books).

_____ (1983f) 'Chambers of Commerce in the UK System of Business Interest Representation', University of Warwick, Department of Politics, Working Paper No. 32.

_____ (1984) 'Large Firms and Public Policy in Britain', *Journal of Public Policy*, 4, pp. 1–17.

―― (1985a), 'The Politics of Industrial Subsidies', paper submitted to the ECPR Joint Sessions, Barcelona.

―― (1985b) 'Corporatism and the Public–Private Distinction', in J-E Lane (ed.), *State and Market: the Politics of the Public and the Private* (London: Sage).

―― (1985c), 'Private Organisations as Agents of Public Policy: The Case of Milk Marketing in Britain', in W. Streeck and P.C. Schmitter (eds), *Private Interest Government: Beyond Market and State* (London: Sage).

―― (ed.) (1985) *The Political Economy of Corporatism* (London: Macmillan)

―― (ed.) (forthcoming) *Business Interests, Organisational Development and Private Interest Government: An International Comparative Study of the Food Processing Industry* (Berlin: de Gruyter).

―― and D. Marsh (1974) 'The Representation of Retail Interests in Britain', *Political Studies*, 22, pp. 168–77

―― and D. Marsh (1977) *The CBI* (London: Hodder & Stoughton).

―― and S. K. Nath (1984) *The Politics of Economic Policymaking* (Oxford: Basil Blackwell).

―― W. E. Paterson and C. Whitston (1985) 'Government – Industry Relations in the Chemical Industry: An Anglo-German Comparison', paper presented at the ESRC Conference on Government – Industry Relations in the Major OECD Countries, Cambridge.

―― W. E. Paterson and C. Whitston (forthcoming) *International Industry, National Governments and the EEC: The Chemical Industry in Britain and West Germany* (provisional title).

―― and W. Streeck (1985) 'Large Firms and the Representation of Business Interests in the UK and West German Construction Industry', in A. Cawson (ed.), *Organised Interests and the State: Studies in Meso-Corporatism* (London: Sage).

Group of Thirty (1985) 'The Foreign Exchange Market in the 1980s, the Views of Market Participants.' (New York: Group of Thirty).

Hague, D., W.J.M. Mackenzie and A. Barker (1975) *Public Policy and Private Interests: The Institutions of Compromise.* (London: Macmillan).

Hansard Society (1977) *The British People: Their Voice in Europe* (Farnborough: Saxon House).

―― (1981) 'Paying for Politics: The Report of the Commission Upon the Financing of Political Parties' (London: Hansard Society for Parliamentary Government).

Harris, K. (1982) *Attlee* (London: Weidenfeld & Nicolson).

Harvey-Jones, J. (1985) 'Memorandum submitted by Mr Harvey-Jones', House of Lords, Report from the Select Committee on Overseas Trade, Vol.2. (London: HMSO).

Heath, A., R. Jowell and J. Curtice (1985) *How Britain Votes* (Oxford: Pergamon).

Heilbroner, R. L. (1986) *The Nature and Logic of Capitalism* (New York: Norton).

Hills, J. (1983) 'The Industrial Policy of Japan', *Journal of Public Policy*, 3, pp. 63–80.

Holmes, M. (1982) *Political Pressure and Economic Policy* (London: Butterworths).

Houghton, Lord (Chairman) (1976) *Report on the Committee on Financial Aid to Political Parties* (London: HMSO).

House of Commons (1985) *1st Report from the Select Committee on Members' Interests, 1984–85* (London: HMSO).

House of Lords (1985) *Report from the Select Committee on Overseas Trade 1984–85, Vol. 1, Report* (London: HMSO).

Ilersic, A. and P. Liddle (1960) *The Parliament of Commerce: The Story of the Association of British Chambers of Commerce* (London: Newman Neane).

Imberg, D. and J. Northcott (1981) *Industrial Policy and Investment Decisions* (London: Policy Studies Institute).

Industry and Trade Committee (1980) *House of Commons Industry and Trade Committee, Session 1979–80, Department of Industry* (London: HMSO).

Ingham, G. (1984) *Capitalism Divided? The City and Industry in British Social Development* (London: Macmillan).

Institute for Employment Research (1985) *Review of the Economy and Employment, Volume 1* (Coventry: University of Warwick Institute for Employment Research).

Jacomb, Sir M. (1985) 'The Role of the Securities and Investments Board', *The Treasurer*, 7, 11, pp. 15–18.

Jenkin, M. (1981) *British Industry and the North Sea* (London: Macmillan).

Jones, D. T. (1981) 'Catching up with our Competitors: The Role of Industrial Policy', in C. Carter (ed.), *Industrial Policy and Innovation*, (London: Heinemann).

Jordan, G. (1985) 'Parliament Under Pressure', *Political Quarterly*, 56, pp. 174–82.

—— and Richardson, J. (1982) 'The British Policy Style or the Logic of Negotiation', in J. Richardson and G. Jordan (eds), *Policy Styles in Western Europe* (London: Allen & Unwin).

Katzenstein, P. J. (1984) *Corporatism and Change: Austria, Switzerland and the Politics of Industry* (Ithaca: Cornell University Press).

—— (1985) *Small States in World Markets* (Ithaca: Cornell University Press).

Kay, J. A. and Z. A. Silberston (1984) 'The New Industrial Policy – Privatisation and Competition', *Midland Bank Review*, Spring, pp. 8–16.

Keegan, V. (1977) 'Devlin by Default', *The Guardian*, 23 September 1977.

Kellner, P. and Lord Crowther-Hunt (1980) *The Civil Servants* (London: Macdonald).

King, R. (1985) 'Corporatism and the Local Economy', in W. Grant (ed.), *The Political Economy of Corporatism*, (London: Macmillan).

Kipping, Sir N. (1972) *Summing Up* (London: Hutchinson).

Lawrence, P. (1980) *Managers and Management in West Germany* (London: Croom Helm).

Lehmbruch, G. (1979) 'Liberal Corporatism and Party Government', in P. Schmitter and G. Lehmbruch (eds), *Trends Towards Corporatist Intermediation* London: Sage).

—— (1984) 'Concertation and the Structure of Corporatist Networks', in J. H. Goldthorpe (ed.), *Order and Conflict in Contemporary Capitalism* (Oxford: Oxford University Press).

Lewis, N. and P. Wiles (1984) 'The Post-Corporatist State', *Journal of Law and Society*, 11, pp. 65–90.

Leys, C. (1985) 'Thatcherism and British Manufacturing: A Question of Hegemony', *New Left Review*, no. 151, pp. 5–25.

Lindberg, L. (1963) *The Political Dynamics of European Economic Integration* (Stanford: Stanford University Press).

Lindblom, C. (1977) *Politics and Markets* (New York: Basic Books).

Litvak, I. A. (1981) 'Government Intervention and Corporate Government Relations', *Business Quarterly*, Autumn, pp. 47–54.

Lively, J. (1978) 'Pluralism and Consensus', in P. Birnbaum, J. Lively and G. Parry (eds), *Democracy, Consensus and Social Contract* (London: Sage).

Longstreth, F. (1979) 'The City, Industry and the State', in C. Crouch (ed.), *State and Economy in Contemporary Capitalism*, (London: Croom Helm).

Lowe, P., G. Cox. M. MacEwen, T. O'Riordan and M. Winter (1986) *Countryside Conflicts: The Politics of Farming, Forestry and Conservation* (Aldershot: Gower).

—— and J. Goyder (1983) *Environmental Groups in Politics* (London: Allen & Unwin).

McIntosh Report (1976) *A Study of UK Nationalised Industries* (London: National Economic Development Office.

MAFF (1984) Ministry of Agriculture, Fisheries and Food, 'Review of Food Legislation: Consultative Document' (typescript).

Marin, B. (1985) 'Austria – the Paradigm Case of Liberal Corporatism?', in W. Grant (ed.), *The Political Economy of Corporatism* (London: Macmillan).

Marsh, D. (1976) 'On Joining Interest Groups: An Empirical Consideration of the Work of Mancur Olson', *British Journal of Political Science*, 6, pp. 257–71.

—— (1983) 'Interest Group Activity and Structural Power: Lindblom's *Politics and Markets*', *West European Politics*, 6, pp. 3–13.

—— and G. Locksley (1983) 'Capital in Britain: Its Structural Power and Influence over Policy', *West European Politics*, 6, pp. 36–60.

May, T. (1984) 'The Businessman's Burden', *Politics*, No. 4, pp. 34–8.

Mellors, C. (1978) *The British MP* (Farnborough: Saxon House).

Middlemas, K. (1979) *Politics in Industrial Society* (London: André Deutsch).

Middlemas, K. (1983) *Industry, Unions and Government: Twenty-One Years of the NEDC* (London: Macmillan).

Moe, T. M. (1980) *The Organisation of Interests* (Chicago: University of Chicago Press).

Moran, M. (1983) 'Power, Policy and the City of London', in R. King (ed.), *Capital and Politics* (London: Routledge & Kegan Paul).
____ (1984a) 'Politics, Banks and Markets: An Anglo-American Comparison', *Political Studies*, 32, pp. 173–89.
____ (1984b) *The Politics of Banking* (London: Macmillan).
____ (1986a) 'Corporatism Resurrected: Economic Interests and Institutional Change in the City of London', No. 3 in a series of working papers available from the author at the Department of Government, University of Manchester.
____ (1986b) 'Investor Protection and the Culture of Capitalism', No. 2 in the author's series of working papers.
Morgan, A. (1981) 'Pressure Groups and Harmonisation' in Carol Cosgrove Twitchett (ed.), *Harmonisation in the EEC* (London: Macmillan).
Mueller, A. (1985) 'A Civil Servant's View', in D. Englefield (ed.), *Today's Civil Sevice*, (Harlow: Longman).
Nettl, J. P. (1965) 'Consensus or Elite Domination: The Case of Business', *Political Studies*, 8, pp. 22–44.
OECD (1983) *Positive Adjustment Policies: Managing Structural Change* (Paris: Organisation for Economic Co-operation and Development).
____ (1986) *OECD Economic Surveys 1985–86: United Kingdom* (Paris: Organisation for Economic Cooperation and Development).
Offe, C. (1981) 'The Attribution of Public Status to Interest Groups: Observations on the West German Case', in S. Berger (ed.), *Organising Interests in Western Europe* (London: Cambridge University Press).
____ (1985) *Disorganised Capitalism* (Cambridge: Polity Press).
____ and Wiesenthal, H. (1985) 'Two Logics of Collective Action', in C. Offe (principal author), *Disorganised Capitalism* (Cambridge: Polity Press).
Olson, M. (1965) *The Logic of Collective Action* (Cambridge, Mass.: Harvard University Press).
____ (1971) *The Logic of Collective Action* (2nd edn) (Cambridge, Mass: Harvard University Press).
____ (1982) *The Rise and Decline of Nations* (New Haven: Yale University Press).
Parker, S. (1984) 'Corporatism and Business Interest Associations: The Relationship Between the Confederation of British Industry and Its Member Associations with Special Reference to the BRIMEC Experiment', M.A. thesis, University of Warwick.
Peacock, A. (1984) *The Regulation Game* (Oxford: Basil Blackwell).
Pimlott, B. (1985) *Hugh Dalton* (London: Cape).
Pinto-Duschinsky, M. (1973) 'Stratification and Power in the British Conservative Party', *American Behavioural Scientist*, 17, pp. 285–92.
Pinto-Duschinsky, M. (1981) *British Political Finance 1830–1980* (Washington: American Enterprise Institute).
Pinto-Duschinsky, M. (1985) 'British Political Funding 1979–83', *Parliamentary Affairs*, 38, 328–47.
Piore, M. J. and C. F. Sabel (1983) 'Italian Small Business Development: Lessons for US Industrial Policy', in J. Zysman and L. Tyson (eds),

American Industry in International Competition (Ithaca: Cornell University Press).

Pryke, R. (1981) *The Nationalised Industries* (Oxford: Martin Robertson).

Rainbird, H. and W. Grant (1985a) *Employers' Associations and Training Policy* (Coventry: University of Warwick Institute for Employment Research).

—— and W. Grant (1985b) 'Non-Statutory Training Organisations and the Privatisation of Public Policy', *Public Administration*, 63, pp. 91–5.

Reader, W. J. (1975) *Imperial Chemical Industries: A History*, Vol. 2 (London: Oxford University Press).

Rhodes, R. A. W. (1986) *The National World of Local Government* (London: Allen & Unwin).

Richardson, J. (1982) 'Tripartism and the New Technology', *Policy and Politics*, 10, pp. 343–61.

—— and G. Jordan (1979) *Governing Under Pressure* (Oxford: Martin Robertson).

RIPA (1984) 'Local Public/Private Co-operation: The Way Forward', report of a speech by J Warburton, director of Birmingham Chamber of Industry and Commerce, *RIPA Report*, Winter 1984, pp. 12–14.

Rose, R. (1974) *The Problem of Party Government* (London: Macmillan).

—— (1980) *Do Parties Make a Difference?* (2nd edn 1984) (London: Macmillan).

Ross, J. (1983) *Thatcher and Friends: The Anatomy of the Tory Party* (London: Pluto Press).

Salisbury, R. H. (1984) 'Interest Representation: The Dominance of Institutions', *American Political Science Review*, 78, pp. 64–76.

Sargent, J. (1982) 'The British Bankers' Association and the EC', *Journal of Common Market Studies*, pp. 269–85.

—— (1983a) 'The Organisation of Business Interests in the UK Pharmaceutical Industry' (Berlin: International Institute of Management labour market policy discussion paper).

—— (1983b) 'The Politics of the Pharmaceutical Price Regulation Scheme' (Berlin: International Institute of Management labour market policy discussion paper).

—— (1985) 'The Politics of the Pharmaceutical Price Regulation Scheme', in W. Streeck and P.C. Schmitter (eds), *Private Interest Government: Beyond Market and State* (London: Sage).

Scase, R. and R. Goffee (1980) *The Real World of the Small Business Owner* (London: Croom Helm).

Schmitter, P. C. (1979) 'Still the Century of Corporatism?', in P. C. Schmitter and G. Lehmbruch (eds), *Trends Towards Corporatist Intermediation* (London: Sage).

—— (1982) 'Reflections on Where the Theory of Neo-Corporatism Has Gone and Where the Praxis of Neo-Corporatism May Be Going', in G. Lehmbruch and P. C. Schmitter (eds) *Patterns of Corporatist Policy-Making* (London: Sage).

—— and W. Streeck (1981) 'The Organisation of Business Interests: A

Research Design to Study the Associative Action of Business in the Advanced Industrial Societies of Western Europe' (Berlin: International Institute of Management labour market policy discussion paper).

SDP (undated) 'Towards Full Employment: A Common-Sense Approach to Economic Policy', SDP Green Paper No. 1 (London: SDP).

Securities and Investments Board (1985) 'Regulation of Investment Business: The New Framework' (London: Securities and Investments Board/Marketing of Investments Board Organising Committee).

Select Committee on Nationalised Industries (1970) *First Report from the Select Committee on Nationalised Industries 1969–70, Bank of England* (London: HMSO).

—— (1977) *Second Special Report from the Select Committee on Nationalised Industries, 1976–77, Comments by Nationalised Industries on the National Economic Development Office Report.* (London: HMSO).

—— (1979) *Sub-Committee E, Minutes of Evidence taken before the Committee on 7 March 1979* (London: HMSO).

Shepherd, D., A. Silberston and R. Strange (1985) *British Manufacturing Investment Overseas* (London: Methuen).

Sidjanksi, D. (1972) 'Pressure Groups and the European Economic Community', in M. Hodges (ed.) *European Integration* (Harmondsworth: Penguin).

Slatter, R. (1983) 'Managing the Socio-Political Environment in Post–Industrial Society', M.Phil thesis, Oxford Centre for Management Studies.

Stewart, M. (1984) 'Talking to Local Business: The Involvement of Chambers of Commerce in Local Affairs', Working Paper No. 38, School for Advanced Urban Studies, University of Bristol.

Stocker, T. (1983) 'Pressures on Policy Formation', in J. Burns, J. McInerney and A. Swinbank (eds), *The Food Industry: Economics and Politics* (London: Heinemann).

Stopford, J. M. and L. Turner (1985) *Britain and the Multinationals* (Chichester: John Wiley).

Streeck, W. (1983) 'Beyond Pluralism and Corporatism: German Business Associations and the State', *Journal of Public Policy*, 3, pp. 265–84.

—— (1984) *Industrial Relations in West Germany* (London: Heinemann).

—— and P. C. Schmitter (1985) 'Community, Market, State – and Associations? The Prospective Contribution of Interest Governance to Social Order', in W. Streeck and P. C. Schmitter (eds), *Private Interest Government: Beyond Market and State* (London: Sage).

Strinati, D. (1982) *Capitalism, the State and Industrial Relations* (London: Croom Helm).

Taylor, T. W. (1985) *The Financing of Industry and Commerce* (London: Heinemann)

Tivey, L. (1979) 'Structure and Politics in the Nationalised Industries', *Parliamentary Affairs*, 22, pp. 159–75.

—— (1982) 'Nationalised Industries as Organised Interests', *Public Administration*, 60, pp. 42–55.

Tolliday, S. (1984) 'Tariffs and Steel, 1916–1934: The Politics of Industrial

Decline', in J. Turner (ed.) *Businessmen and Politics* (London: Heinemann).

Treu, T. and A. Martinelli, (1985) 'Employers Associations in Italy', in J. P. Windmuller and A. Gladstone (eds) *Employers Associations and Industrial Relations* (Oxford: Clarendon Press).

Truman, D. (1951) *The Governmental Process* (New York: Knopf).

Turner, J. (1984) 'The Politics of Business', in J. Turner (ed.), *Businessmen and Politics* (London: Heinemann).

_____ (ed.) (1984) *Businessmen and Politics* (London: Heinemann).

Tylecote, A. (1981) *The Causes of the Present Inflation* (London: Macmillan).

US Department of Commerce (1986) *1986 US Industrial Outlook* (Washington, DC: Department of Commerce of the United States of America).

Useem, M. (1984) *The Inner Circle: Large Corporations and the Rise of Business Political Activity in the US and UK* (New York: Oxford University Press).

_____ and A. McCormack (1981) 'The Dominant Segment of the British Business Elite', *Sociology*, 15, pp. 381–406.

Utton, M. (1982) *The Political Economy of Big Business* (Oxford: Martin Robertson).

Vogel, D. (1978) 'Why Businessmen Distrust Their State: The Political Consciousness of American Corporate Executives', *British Journal of Political Science*, 8, pp. 45–78.

_____ (1986) *National Styles of Regulation; Environmental Policy in GB and the US* (Ithaca: Cornell University Press).

de Vroom, B. (1985) 'The Rise of a New "State" and the Development of Interest Associations: The Case of Business Interest Associations on EC Level', Sociological Institute, University of Leiden, typescript.

van Waarden, F. (forthcoming) 'Sector Structure, Interests and Associative Action in the Food Processing Industry', in W. Grant (ed.), *Business Interests, Organisational Development and Private Interest Government: An International Comparative Study of the Food Processing Industry* (Berlin: de Gruyter).

Walker, J. (1983) 'The Origins and Maintenance of Interest Groups in America', *American Political Science Review*, 77, pp. 390–406.

Watkinson, Viscount (1976) *Blueprint for Survival* (London: Allen & Unwin).

Wells, J. P. (1982) 'Advertising of Medicines to the Public', unpublished paper delivered by J. P. Wells FPS at the BRIA Symposium on Labelling Data Sheets and Advertising, Pharmaceutical Society of Great Britain, October 1982.

Westergaard, J. and H. Resler (1976) *Class in a Capitalist Society* (Harmondsworth: Pelican).

Wigham, E. (1973) *The Power to Manage* (London: Macmillan).

Wilks, S. (1984) *Industrial Policy and the Motor Industry* (Manchester: Manchester University Press).

Williams, J. (1983) 'GEC – an Outstanding Success?', in K. Williams and

D. Thomas, *Why are the British Bad at Manufacturing?* (London: Routledge & Kegan Paul).

Williams, P. (1982) *Hugh Gaitskell* (London: Oxford University Press).

Williams, S. (1980) 'The Decision Makers', in Royal Institute of Public Administration (ed.), *Policy and Practice: the Experience of Government* (London: Royal Institute of Public Administration).

Willmott, H. C. (1985) 'Setting Accounting Standards in the UK: The Emergence of Private Accounting Bodies and Their Role in the Regulation of Public Accounting Practice,' in W. Streeck and P. C. Schmitter (eds), *Private Interest Government: Beyond Market and State* (London: Sage).

Wilson, G. (1978) 'Farmers' Organisations in Advanced Societies', in H. Newby (ed.), *International Perspectives in Rural Sociology* (Chichester: Wiley).

Windmuller, J. P. and A. Gladstone (eds) (1985), *Employers Associations and Industrial Relations* (Oxford: Clarendon Press).

Winter, M. (1984) 'Corporatism and Agriculture in the UK: The Case of the Milk Marketing Board', *Sociologia Ruralis*, 24, pp. 106–19.

Wormell, J. (1985) *The Gilt-Edged Market* (London: Allen & Unwin).

Young, H. and A. Sloman (1984) *But, Chancellor* (London: BBC).

Zysman, J. (1983) *Governments, Markets and Growth* (Ithaca: Cornell University Press).

Index